The Cowboy Humor of Alfred Henry Lewis

by
Alfred Henry Lewis

Illustrations by
FREDERICK REMINGTON

Edited by
Richard D. Myers

THE LINCOLN-HERNDON PRESS INC.
818 South Dirksen Parkway
Springfield, Illinois 62703

D1522548

The Cowboy Humor of Alfred Henry Lewis

First Edition

Manufactured in the United States Of America.

For information write to:

The Lincoln-Herndon Press, Inc.
818 South Dirksen Parkway.
Springfield, Illinois 62703

Library of Congress Cataloguing in Publication Data.
Library of Congress Catalog Card Number: 87-081540
ISBN 0-942936-12-4

Table of Contents

Introduction

Alfred Henry Lewis (1857-1914) was, early in life, a lawyer who rose to be City Prosecuting Attorney of Columbus, Ohio, where he was born. His father, a carpenter, moved west and A. H. Lewis moved with him to spend several years as a wandering cowboy and saddle-bum in Kansas where he drove cattle to Dodge City, then wandered the Texas panhandle and worked his way to Nevada and onto southeastern Arizona. Somewhere in his travels, he piloted a six-mule team. His cowboy days ended with a stint on the Kansas City Star after which he moved up in the Hearst newspaper chain until he was chief of the Washington office. Later, he moved to New York, the center of the newspaper and publishing world.

But the claim to fame of A. H. Lewis, an immortality of a good sort, rests on the tales he wrote about his years on the western ranges. His fiction, tales of Wolfville (Tombstone), Arizona hold some of the funniest, wisest and most perceptive writing on the subject of western, frontier cowboy life. Best of all is his superb humor, his use of cowboy lingo, that picturesque, poetically funny and wonderfully precise language the cowboy used. These stories give Americans a solid sense of how it was, back then, when the west was untamed wilderness . . . and dangerous for a careless man.

The cowboy life is seen through the eyes of The Old Cattleman, a prototype of Lewis himself, and the stories remind us of the moral standards of those times. He presents the deep integrity, the sense of justice (often precipitate!) and fair play, a reverence for womankind and, as well, a distaste for those different from the majority as, in the case of Wolfville . . . Indians, Mexicans, Chinese. The bigotry is not admirable but is typical, and Lewis records it faithfully. Thus, we see a frontier town and its cowboy citizens, see it in all its humor, enterprise and character . . . see it warts and all, plain and without cosmetics.

The language is ungrammatical, joyous, brilliantly inventive and descriptive . . . a language suitable to those times. Somehow, it works, is great fun, even poetic. Not easy to read, at first, if the reader but stays with it a short, short time, the reading becomes fun, a joy and with it comes heightened understanding of those adventurous times, those dangerous yet fruitful times when the west was won. All told, the Wolfville tales presented here are a lovely, rib-tickling cache of Americana and history . . . to be read today and forever as a vital part of the Miracle that is America.

Lewis wrote seven books about the town of Wolfville and its rival, Red Dog. As his biographer, Prof. Abe C. Ravitz says: "With unassuming dignity and noble simplicity, Lewis brought to the early twentieth century reader a close-up vision of the Western ethos. In the Wolfville stories he examined that segment of the American dream that was unfolding across the plains."

And finally, to properly introduce his book, it is fitting that Alfred Henry Lewis himself tell us about the Great American Cowboy, that "legendary figure hovering over the landscape as did Captain John Smith and Daniel Boone."

Some Cowboy Facts

There are certain truths of a botanical character that are not generally known. Each year the trees in their occupation creep further west. There are regions in Missouri—not bottom lands—which sixty years ago were bald and bare of trees. Today they are heavy with timber. Westward, beyond the trees, lie the prairies, and beyond the prairies, the plains; the first are green with long grasses, the latter bare, brown and with a crisp, scorched, sparse vesture of vegetation scarce worth the name. As the trees march slowly westward in conquest of the prairies, so also do the prairies, in their verdant turn, become aggressors and push westward upon the plains. These last stretches, extending to the base of that bluff and sudden bulwark, the Rocky Mountains, can go no further. The Rockies hold the plains at bay and break, as it were, the teeth of the desert. As a result of this warfare of vegetations, the plains are to first disappear in favour of the prairies; and the prairies to give way before the trees. These mutations all wait on rain; and as the rain belt goes ever and ever westward, a strip of plains each year surrenders its aridity, and the prairies and then the trees press on and take new ground.

These facts should contain some virtue of interest; the more since with the changes chronicled, come also changes in the character of both the inhabitants and the employments of these regions. With a civilised people extending themselves over new lands, cattle form ever the advance guard.

Then come the farms. This is the procession of a civilised, peaceful invasion; thus is the column marshalled. First, the pastoral; next, the agricultural; third and last, the manufacturing; —and per consequence, the big cities, where the treasure chests of a race are kept. Blood and bone and muscle and heart are to the front; and the money that steadies and stays and protects and repays them and their efforts, to the rear.

Forty years ago about all that took place west of the Mississippi of a money-making character was born of cattle. The cattle were worked in huge herds and, like the buffalo supplanted by them, roamed in unnumbered thousands. In a pre-railroad period, cattle were killed for their hides and tallow, and smart Yankee coasters went constantly to such ports as Galveston for these cargoes. The beef was left to the coyotes.

Cattle find a natural theatre of existence on the plains. There, likewise, flourishes the pastoral man. But cattle herding, confined to the plains, gives way before the westward creep of agriculture. Each year beholds more western acres broken by the plough; each year witnesses a diminution of the cattle ranges and cattle herding. This need ring no bell of alarm concerning a future barren of a beef supply. More cattle are the product of the farm regions than of the ranges. That ground, once range and now farm, raises more cattle now than then. Texas is a great cattle State. Ohio, Indiana, Illinois, Iowa, and Missouri are first States of agriculture. The area of Texas is about even with the collected area of the other five. Yet one finds double the number of cattle in Ohio, Indiana, Illinois, Iowa, and Missouri than in Texas, to say nothing of tenfold the sheep and hogs. No one may be calm; one is not to fall a prey to any hunger of beef.

While the farms in their westward pushing do not diminish the cattle, they reduce the cattleman and pinch off much that is romantic and picturesque. Between the farm and the wire fence, the cowboy, as once he flourished, has been modified, subdued, and made partially to disappear. In the good old days of the Jones and Plummer trail there were no wire fences; and the sullen farmer had not yet arrived. Your cowboy at that time was a person of thrill and consequence. He wore a broad-brimmed Stetson hat, and all about it a rattlesnake skin by way of band, retaining head and rattles. This was to be potent against headaches—a malady, by the way, which swept down no cowboy save in hours emergent of a spree. In such case the snake cure didn't cure. The hat was retained in defiance of winds, by a leathern cord caught about the back of the head, not under the chin. This cord was beautiful with a garniture of three or four perforated poker chips, (red, yellow, and blue.)

There are sundry angles of costume where the dandyism of a cowboy of spirit and conceit may acquit itself; these are hatband, spurs, saddle, and leggins. I've seen hatbands made of braided gold and silver filigree; they were from Santa Fe, and always in the form of a rattlesnake, with rubies or emeralds or diamonds for eyes. Such gauds would cost from four hundred to two thousand dollars. Also, I've encountered a saddle which depleted its proud owner a round twenty-five hundred dollars. It was of finest Spanish leather, stamped and spattered with gold bosses. There was gold-capping on the saddle horn, and again on the circle of the cantle. It was a dream of a saddle, made at Paso del Norte; and the owner had it cinched upon a bronco dear at twenty dollars. One couldn't have sold the pony for a stack of white chips in any faro game of that neighbourhood (Las Vegas) and they were all crooked games at that.

Your cowboy dandy frequently wears wrought steel spurs, inlaid with silver and gold; price, anything you please. If he flourish a true Brummel of the plains his leggins will be fronted from instep to belt with the thick pelt, hair outside, of a Newfoundland dog. These "chapps," are meant to protect the cowboy from rain and cold, as well as plum bushes, wire fences and other obstacles inimical, and against which he may lunge while riding headlong in the dark. The hair of the Newfoundland, thick and long and laid the right way, defies the rains; and your cowboy loathes water.

Save in those four cardinals of vanity enumerated, your cowboy wears nothing from weakness; the rest of his outfit is legitimate. The long sharp heels of his boots are there to dig into the ground and hold fast to his mother earth while roping on foot. His gay pony when "roped" of a frosty morning would skate him all across and about the plains if it were not for these heels. The buckskin gloves tied in one of the saddle strings are used when roping, and to keep the half-inch manila lariat—or mayhap it's horsehair or rawhide pleated—from burning his hands. The red silken sash one was wont aforetime to see knotted about his waist, was used to hogtie and hold down the big cattle when roped and thrown. The sash—strong, soft and close—could be tied more tightly, quickly, surely than anything besides. In these days, with wire pastures and branding pens and the fine certainty of modern round-ups and a consequent paucity of mavericks, big cattle are seldom roped; wherefor the sash has been much cast aside.

The saddle-bags or "war-bags,"—also covered of dogskin to match the leggins, and worn behind, not forward of the rider—are the cowboy's official wardrobe wherein he carries his second suit of underclothes, and his other shirt. His handkerchief, red cotton, is loosely knotted about the cowboy's neck, knot to the rear. He wipes the sweat from his brow therewith on those hot Texas days when in a branding pen he "flanks" calves or feeds the fires or handles the irons or stands off the horned indignation of the cows, resentful because of burned and bawling offspring.

It would take two hundred thousand words to tell in half fashion the story of the cowboy. His religion of fatalism, his courage, his rides at full swing in midnight darkness to head and turn and hold a herd stampeded, when a slip on the storm-soaked grass by his unshod pony, or a misplaced prairie-dog hole, means a tumble, and a tumble means that a hundred and fifty thousand dollars worth of cattle, with hoofs like chopping knives, will run over him and make him look and feel and become as dead as a cancelled postage stamp; his troubles, his joys, his soberness in camp, his drunkenness in town, and his feuds and occasional "gun plays" are not to be disposed of in a preface. One cannot in such cramped space so much as hit the high places in a cowboy career.

At work on the range and about his camp—for, bar accidents, wherever you find a cowboy you will find a camp—the cowboy is a youth of sober quiet dignity. There is a deal of deep politeness and nothing of epithet, insult or horseplay where everybody wears a gun.

There are no folk inquisitive on the ranges. No one asks your name. If driven by stress of conversation to something akin to it the cowboy will say: "What may I call you, sir?" And he's as careful to add the "sir," as he is to expect it in return. You are at liberty to select what name you prefer. Where you hail from? where going? why? are queries never put. To look at the brand on your pony—you, a stranger—is a dangerous vulgarity to which no gentleman of the Panhandle or any other region of pure southwestern politeness would stoop. And if you wish to arouse an instant combination of hate, suspicion and contempt in the bosom of a cowboy you have but to stretch forth your artless Eastern hand and ask: "Let me look at your gun."

Cowboys on the range or in the town are excessively clannish. They never desert each other, but stay and fight and die and storm a jail and shoot a sheriff if needs press, to rescue a comrade made captive in their company. Also they care for each other when sick or injured, and set one another's bones when broken in the falls and tumbles of their craft. On the range the cowboy is quiet, just and peaceable. There are neither women nor cards nor rum about the cow camps. The ranches and the boys themselves banish the two latter; and the first won't come. Women, cards and whiskey, the three war causes of the West, are confined to the towns.

Those occasions when cattle are shipped and the beefherds, per consequence, driven to the shipping point become the only times when the cowboy sees the town. In such hours he blooms and lives fully up to his opportunity. He has travelled perhaps two hundred miles and has been twenty days on the trail, for cattle may only be driven about ten miles a day; he has been up day and night and slept half the time in the saddle; he has made himself hoarse singing "Sun Bass" and "The Dying Ranger" to keep the cattle quiet and stave off stampedes; he has ridden ten ponies to shadows in his twenty days of driving, wherefore, and naturally, your cowboy feels like relaxing.

There would be as many as ten men with each beef-herd; and the herd would include about five thousand head. There would be six "riders," divided into three watches to stand night guard over the herd and drive it through the day; there would be two "hoss hustlers," to hold the eighty or ninety ponies, turn and turn about, and carry them along with the herd; there would be the cook, with four mules and the chuck wagon; and lastly there would be the herd-boss, a cow expert he, and at the head of the business.

Once the herd is off his hands and his mind at the end of the drive, the cowboy unbuckles and reposes himself from his labours. He becomes deeply and famously drunk. Hungering for the excitement of play he collides amiably with faro and monte and what other deadfalls are rife of the place. Never does he win; for the games aren't arranged that way. But he enjoys himself; and his losses do not prey on him.

Sated with faro bank and monte—they can't be called games of chance, the only games of chance occurring when cowboys engage with each other at billiards or pool—sated, I say, with faro and Mexican monte, and exuberant of rum, which last has regular quick renewal, our cowboy will stagger to his pony, swing into the saddle, and with gladsome whoops and an occasional outburst from his six shooter directed toward the heavens, charge up and down the street. This last amusement appeals mightily to cowboys too drunk to walk. For, be it known, a gentleman may ride long after he may not walk.

If a theatre be in action and mayhap a troop of "Red Stocking Blondes," elevating the drama therein, the cowboy is sure to attend. Also he will arrive with his lariat wound about his body under his coat; and his place will be the front row. At some engaging crisis, such as the "March of the Amazons," having first privily unwound and organised his lariat to that end, he will arise and "rope" an Amazon. This will produce bad language from the manager of the show, and compel the lady to sit upon the stage to the detriment of her wardrobe if no worse, and all to keep from being pulled across the footlights. Yet the exercise gives the cowboy deepest pleasure. Having thus distinguished the lady of his admiration, later he will meet her and escort her to the local dancehall. There, mingling with their frank companions, the two will drink, and loosen the boards of the floor with the strenuous dances of our frontier till daylight does appear.

For the matter of a week, or perchance two—it depends on how fast his money melts—in these fashions will our gentleman of cows engage his hours and expand himself. He will make a deal of noise, drink a deal of whiskey, acquire a deal of what he terms "action"; but he harms nobody, and, in a town toughened to his racket and which needs and gets his money, disturbs nobody.

"Let him whoop it up; he's paying for it, ain't he?" will be the prompt local retort to any inquiry as to why he is thus permitted to disport.

So long as the cowboy observes the etiquette of the town, he will not be molested or "called down" by marshal or sheriff or citizen. There are four things your cowboy must not do. He must not insult a woman; he must not shoot his pistol in a store or bar-room; he must not ride his pony into those places of resort; and as a last proposal he must not ride his pony on the sidewalks. Shooting or riding into bar-rooms is reckoned as dangerous; riding on the sidewalk comes more under the head of insult, and is popularly regarded as a taunting defiance of the town marshal. On such occasions the marshal never fails to respond, and the cowboy is called upon to surrender. If he complies, which to the credit of his horse-sense he commonly does, he is led into brief captivity to be made loose when cooled. Does he resist arrest, there is an explosive rattle of six shooters, a mad scattering of the careful citizenry out of lines of fire, and a cowboy or marshal is added to the host beyond. At the close of the festival, if the marshal still lives he is congratulated; if the cowboy survives he is lynched; if both fall, they are buried with the honours of frontier war; while whatever the event, the communal ripple is but slight and only of the moment, following which the currents of Western existence sweep easily and calmly onward as before.

Alfred Henry Lewis

1

The Stinging Lizard.

"THAR'S no sorter doubt to it," said the Old Cattleman after a long pause devoted to meditation, and finally to the refilling of his cob pipe, "thar ain't the slightest room for cavil but them ceremonies over Jack King, deceased, is the most satisfactory pageant Wolfville ever promotes."

It was at this point I proved my cunning by saying nothing. I was pleased to hear the old man talk, and rightly theorized that the better method of invoking his reminiscences just at this time was to say never a word.

"However," he continued, "I don't reckon it's many weeks after we follows Jack to the tomb, when we comes a heap near schedoolin' another funeral, with the general public a-contributin' of the corpse. To be speecific, I refers to a occasion when we-alls comes powerful close to lynchin' Cherokee Hall.

"I don't mind onbosomin' myse'f about it. It's all a misonderstandin'; the same bein' Cherokee's fault complete. We don't know him more'n to merely drink with at that eepock, an' he's that sly an' furtive in his plays, an' covers his trails so speshul, he nacherally breeds sech suspicions that when the stage begins to be stood up reg'lar once a week, an' all onaccountable, Cherokee comes mighty close to culminatin' in a rope. Which goes to show that you can't be too open an' free in your game, an' Cherokee would tell you so himse'f.

1

"This yere tangle I'm thinkin' of ain't more'n a month after Cherokee takes to residin' in Wolfville. He comes trailin' in one evenin' from Tucson, an' onfolds a layout an' goes to turnin' faro-bank in the Red Light. No one remarks this partic'lar, which said spectacles is frequent. The general idee is that Cherokee's on the squar' an' his game is straight, an' of course public interest don't delve no further into his affairs.

"Cherokee, himse'f, is one of these yere slim, silent people who ain't talkin' much, an' his eye for color is one of them raw grays, like a new bowie.

"It's perhaps the third day when Cherokee begins to struggle into public notice. Thar's a felon whose name is Boone, but who calls himse'f the 'Stingin' Lizard,' an' who's been pesterin' 'round Wolfville, mebby, it's a month. This yere Stingin' Lizard is thar when Cherokee comes into camp; an' it looks like the Stingin' Lizard takes a notion ag'in Cherokee from the jump.

"Not that this yere Lizard is likely to control public feelin' in the matter: none whatever. He's some onpop'lar himse'f. He's too toomultuous for one thing, an' he has a habit of molestin' towerists an' folks he don't know at all, which palls on disinterested people who has dooties to perform. About once a week this Lizard man goes an' gets the treemers, an' then the camp has to set up with him till his visions subsides. Fact is, he's what you-alls East calls 'a disturbin' element,' an' we makes ready to hang him once or twice, but somethin' comes up an' puts it off, an' we sorter neglects it.

"But as I says, he takes a notion ag'in Cherokee. It's the third night after Cherokee gets in, an' he's ca'mly behind his box at the Red Light, when in peramb'lates this Lizard. Seems like Cherokee, bein' one of them quiet wolves, fools up the Lizard a lot. This Lizard's been hostile an' blood-hungry all day, an' I reckons he all at once recalls Cherokee;

an', deemin' of him easy, he allows he'll go an' chew some mane some for relaxation.

"If I was low an' ornery like this Lizard, I ain't none shore but I'd be fooled them days on Cherokee myse'f. He's been fretful about his whiskey, Cherokee has, —puttin' it up she don't taste right, which not onlikely it don't; but beyond pickin' flaws in his nose-paint thar ain't much to take hold on about him. He's so slim an' noiseless besides, thar ain't none of us but figgers this yere Stingin' Lizard's due to stampede him if he tries; which makes what follows all the more impressive.

"So the Lizard projects along into the Red Light, whoopin' an' carryin' on by himse'f. Straightway he goes up ag'inst Cherokee's layout.

"'I don't buy no chips,' says the Lizard to Cherokee, as he gets in opposite. 'I puts money in play; an' when I wins I wants money sim'lar. Thar's fifty dollars on the king coppered; an' fifty dollars on the eight open. Turn your kyards, an' turn 'em squar'. If you don't, I'll peel the ha'r an' hide plumb off the top of your head.'

"Cherokee looks at the Lizard sorter soopercillus an' indifferent; but he don't say nothin'. He goes on with the deal, an', the kyards comin' that a-way, he takes in the Lizard's two bets.

"Durin' the next deal the Lizard ain't sayin' much direct, but keeps cussin' an' wranglin' to himse'f. But he's gettin' his money up all the time; an' with the fifty dollars he lose on the turn, he's shy mebby four hundred an' fifty at the close.

"'Bein' in the hole about five hundred dollars,' says the Lizard, in a manner which is a heap onrespectful, 'an' so that a wayfarin' gent may not be misled to rooin utter, I now rises to ask what for a limit do you put on this deadfall anyhow?'

"'The bridle's plumb off to you, *amigo*,' says Cherokee,

an' his tones is some hard. I notices it all right enough, 'cause I'm doin' business at the table myse'f at the time, an' keepin' likewise case on the game. 'The bridle's plumb off for you,' says Cherokee, 'so any notion you entertains in favor of bankruptin' of yourse'f quick may riot right along.'

"'You're dead shore of that?' says the Lizard with a sneer. 'Now I reckons a thousand-dollar bet would scare this puerile game you deals a-screechin' up a tree or into a hole, too easy.'

"'I never likes to see no gent strugglin' in the coils of error,' says Cherokee, with a sneer a size larger than the Lizard's; 'I don't know want wads of wealth them pore old clothes of yours conceals, but jest the same I tells you what I'll do. Climb right onto the layout, body, soul, an' roll, an' put a figger on your worthless se'f, an' I'll turn you for the whole shootin' match. You're in yere to make things inter-estin', I sees that, an' I'll voylate my business principles an' take a night off to entertain you.' An' yere Cherokee lugs out a roll of bills big enough to choke a cow.

"'I goes you if I lose,' says the Stingin' Lizard. Then as-soomin' a sooperior air, he remarks: 'Mebby it's a drink back on the trail when I has misgivin's as to the rectitood of this yere brace you're dealin'. Bein' public-sperited that away, in my first frenzy I allows I'll take my gun an' abate it a whole lot. But a ca'mer mood comes on, an' I decides, as not bein' so likely to disturb a peace-lovin' camp, I re-moves this trap for the onwary by merely bustin' the bank. Thar,' goes on the Stingin' Lizard, at the same time dumpin' a large wad on the layout, 'thar's even four thousand dol-lars. Roll your game for that jest as it lays.'

"'Straighten up your dust,' says Cherokee, his eyes gettin' a kind of gleam into 'em, 'straighten up your stuff an' get it some'ers. Don't leave it all spraddled over the scene. I turns for it ready enough, but we ain't goin' to argue none as to where it lays after the kyard falls.'

"The rest of us who's been buckin' the game moderate an' right cashes in at this, an' leaves an onobstructed cloth to the Stingin' Lizard. This yere's more caution than good nacher. As long as folks is bettin' along in limits, say onder fifty dollars, thar ain't no shootin' likely to ensoo. But whenever a game gets immoderate that a-way, an' the limit's off, an' things is goin' that locoed they begins to play a thousand, an' over on a kyard an' scream for action, gents of experience stands ready to go to duckin' lead an' dodgein' bullets instanter.

"But to resoome: The Stingin' Lizard lines up his stuff, an' the deal begins. It ain't thirty seconds till the bank wins, an' the Stingin' Lizzard is the wrong side of the layout from his money. He takes it onusual ugly, only he ain't sayin' much. He sa'nters over to the bar, an' gets a big drink. Cherokee is rifflin' the deck, but I notes he's got his gray eye on the Stingin' Lizard, an' my respect for him increases rapid. I sees he ain't goin' to get the worst of no deal, an' is organized to protect his game plumb through if this Lizard makes a break.

"'Do you-all know where I hails from?' asks the Stingin' Lizard, comin' back to Cherokee after he's done hid his drink.

"'Which I shorely don't,' says Cherokee. 'I has from time to time much worthless information thrust upon me, but so far I escapes all news of you complete.'

"'Where I comes from, which is Texas,' says the Lizard, ignorin' of Cherokee's manner, the same bein' some insultin', 'they teaches the babies two things, —never eat your own beef, an' never let no kyard-thief down you.'

"'Which is highly thrillin',' says Cherokee, 'as reminiscences of your yooth, but where does you-all get action on 'em in Arizona?'

"'Where I gets action won't be no question long,' says the Lizard, mighty truculent. 'I now announces that this yere game is a skin an' a brace. Tharfore I returns for my money; an', to be frank, I returns a-shootin'.'

"It's at this p'int we-alls who represents the public kicks back our chairs an' stampedes outen range. As the Lizard makes his bluff his hand goes to his artillery like a flash.

"The Lizard's some quick, but Cherokee's too soon for him. With the first move of the Lizard's hand, he searches out a bowie from som'ers back of his neck. I'm some employed placin' myse'f at the time, an' don't decern it none till Cherokee brings it over his shoulder like a stream of white light.

"It's shore great knife-work. Cherokee gives the Lizard aige an p'int, an' all in one motion. Before the Lizard more'n lifts his weepon, Cherokee half slashes his gun-hand off at the wrist; an' then, jest as the Lizard begins to wonder at it, he gets the nine-inch blade plumb through his neck. He's let out right thar.

"'It looks like I has more of this thing to do,' says Cherokee, an' his tone shows he's half-way mournin' over it, 'than any sport in the Territory. I tries to keep outen this, but that Lizard gent would have it.'

"After the killin', Enright an' Doc Peets, with Boggs, Tutt, an' Jack Moore, sorter talks it over quiet, an' allows it's all right.

"'This Stingin' Lizard gent,' says Enright, 'has been projectin' 'round lustin' for trouble now, mebby it's six weeks. It's amazin' to me he lasts as long as he does, an' it speaks volumes for the forbearin', law-abiding temper of the Wolfville public. This Lizard's a mighty oppressive person, an' a heap obnoxious; an' while I don't like a knife none myse'f as a trail out, an' inclines to distrust a gent who does, I s'pose it's after all a heap a matter of taste an' the way your folks brings you up. I leans to the view, gents, that this yere corpse is constructed on the squar'. What do you-all think, Peets?'

"'I entertains idees sim'lar,' says Doc Peets. 'Of course I takes it this kyard-sharp, Cherokee, aims to bury his dead. He nacherally ain't lookin' for the camp to go 'round cleanin' up after him none.'

"That's about how it stands. Nobody finds fault with Cherokee, an' as he ups an' plants the Stingin' Lizard's remainder the next day, makin' the deal with a stained box, crape, an' the full regalia, it all leaves the camp with a mighty decent impression. By first-drink time in the evenin' of the second day, we ain't thinkin' no more about it.

"Now you-all begins to marvel where do we get to the hangin' of Cherokee Hall? We're workin' in towards it now.

"You sees, followin' the Stingin' Lizard's jump into the misty beyond—which it's that sudden I offers two to one them angels notes a look of s'prise on the Stingin' Lizard's face as to how he comes to make the trip—Cherokee goes on dealin' faro same as usual. As I says before, he ain't no talker, nohow; now he says less than ever.

"But what strikes us as onusual is, he saddles up a *pinto* pony he's got over to the corral, an' jumps off every now an' then for two an' three days at a clatter. No one knows where he p'ints to, more'n he says he's due over in Tucson. These yere vacations of Cherokee's is all in the month after the Stingin' Lizard gets downed.

"It's about this time, too, the stage gets held up sech a scand'lous number of times it gives people a tired feelin'. All by one party, too. He merely prances out in onexpected places with a Winchester; stands up the stage in an onconcerned way, an' then goes through everythin' an' everybody, from mail-bags to passengers, like the grace of heaven through a camp-meetin'. Nacheral, it all creates a heap of disgust.

"'If this yere industrious hold-up keeps up his lick,' says Texas Thompson about the third time the stage gets rustled, 'an' heads off a few more letters of mine, all I has to say is my wife back in Laredo ain't goin' to onderstand it none. She ain't lottin' much on me nohow, an' if the correspondence between us gets much more fitful, she's goin' p'intin' out for a divorce. This deal's liable to turn a split for me in my domestic affairs.'

"An' that's the way we-alls feels. This stage agent is shorely in disrepoot some in Wolfville. If he'd been shakin' up Red Dog's letter-bags, we wouldn't have minded so much.

"I never does know who's the first to think of Cherokee Hall, but all at once it's all over camp. Talkin' it over, it's noticed mighty soon that, come right to cases, no one knows his record, where he's been or why he's yere. Then his stampedin' out of camp like he's been doin' for a month is too many for us.

"'I puts no trust in them Tucson lies he tells, neither,' says Doc Peets. 'Whatever would he be shakin' up over in Tucson? His game's yere, an' this theery that he's got to go scatterin' over thar once a week is some gauzy.'

"'That's whatever,' says Dan Boggs, who allers trails in after Doc Peets, an' plays the same system emphatic. An' I says myse'f, not findin' no fault with Boggs tharfor, that this yere Peets is the finest-eddicated an' levelest-headed sharp in Arizona.

"'Well,' says Jack Moore, who as I says before does the rope work for the Stranglers, 'if you-alls gets it settled that this faro gent's turnin' them tricks with the stage an' mail-bags, the sooner he's swingin' to the windmill, the sooner we hears from our loved ones at home. What do you say, Enright?'

"'Why,' says Enright, all thoughtful, 'I reckons it's a case. S'pose you caper over where he feeds at the O.K. House an' bring him to us. The signs an' signal-smokes shorely p'ints to this yere Cherokee as our meat; but these things has to be done in order. Bring him in, Jack, an', to save another trip, s'pose you bring a lariat from the corral at the same time.'

"It don't take Moore no time to throw a gun on Cherokee where he's consoomin' flapjacks at the O.K. House, an' tell him the committee needs him at the New York Store. Cherokee don't buck none, but comes along, passive as a tabby cat.

"'Whatever's the hock kyard to all this?' he says to Jack Moore. 'Is it this Stingin' Lizard play a month ago?'

"'No,' says Moore, "tain't quite sech ancient hist'ry. It's stage coaches. Thar's a passel of people down yere as allows you've been rustlin' the mails.'

"Old Man Rucker, who keeps the O.K. House, is away when Moore rounds up his party. But Missis Rucker's thar, an' the way that old lady talks to Enright an' the committee is a shame. She comes over to the store, too, along of Moore an' Cherokee, an' prances in an' comes mighty near stampedin' the whole outfit.

"'See yere, Sam Enright,' she shouts, wipin' her hands on her bib, 'what be you-alls aimin' for to do? Linin' up, I s'pose, to hand the only decent man in town?'

"'Ma'am,' says Enright, 'this yere sharp is 'cused of stand in' up the stage them times recent over by Tucson. Do you know anythin' about it?'

"'No; I don't,' says Missis Rucker. 'You don't reckon, now, I did it none, do you? I says this, though; it's a heap sight more likely some drunkard a-settin' right yere on this committee stops them stages than Cherokee Hall.'

"'Woman's nacher's that emotional,' says Enright to the rest of us, 'she's oncapable of doin' right. While she's the loveliest of created things, still sech is the infirmities of her intellects, that gov'ment would bog down in its most impor-tant functions, if left to woman.'

"'Bog down or not,' says Missis Rucker, gettin' red an' heated, 'you fools settin' up thar like band of prairie-dogs don't hang this yere Cherokee Hall. 'Nother thing, you ain't goin' to hang nobody to the windmill ag'in nohow. I has my work to do, an' thar's enough on my hands, feedin' sech swine as you-all three times a day, without havin' to cut down dead folks outen my way every time I goes for a bucket of water. You-alls takes notice now; you don't hang nothin' to the windmill no more. As for this yere Cherokee, he ain't stopped no more stages than I be.'

"'But you sees yourse'f, ma'am, you hasn't the slightest evidence tharof,' says Enright, tryin' to soothe her down.

"'I has, however, what's a mighty sight better than evidence,' says Missis Rucker, 'an' that's my firm convictions.'

"'Well, see yere,' says Cherokee, who's been listenin' all peaceful, 'let me in on this. What be you-alls doin' this on? I reckons I'm entitled to a look at your hand for my money.'

"Enright goes on an' lays it off for Cherokee; how he's outen camp every time the stage is robbed, an' the idee is abroad he does it.

"'As the kyards lay in the box,' says Cherokee, 'I don't reckon thar's much doubt but you-alls will wind up the deal by hangin' me?'

"'It's shorely five to one that a-way,' says Enright. 'Although I'm bound to say it ain't none decisive as yet.'

"'The trooth is,' says Cherokee, sorter thoughtful, 'I wasn't aimin' to be hung none this autumn. I ain't got time, gents, for one thing, an' has arranged a heap diff'rent. In the next place, I never stands up no stage.'

"'That's what they all says,' puts in Boggs, who's a mighty impatient man. 'I shorely notes no reason why we-alls can't proceed with this yere lynchin' at once. S'pose this Cherokee ain't stood up no stage; he's done plenty of other things as merits death. It strikes me thar's a sight of onnecessary talk yere.'

"'If you ain't out workin' the road,' says Doc Peets to

Cherokee, not heedin' of Bogg's petulance, 'them stage-robbin' times, s'pose you onfolds where you was at?"

"Well, son, not to string this yere story out longer'n three drinks, yere is how it is: This Cherokee it looks like is softhearted that a-way, —what you calls romantic. An' it seems likewise that shovin' the Stingin' Lizard from shore that time sorter takes advantage an' feeds on him. So he goes browsin' 'round the postmaster all casooal, an' puts questions. Cherokee gets a p'inter about some yearlin' or other in Tucson this Stingin' Lizard scnds moncy to an' makcs good for, which he finds the same to be fact on caperin' over. It's a nephy or some sech play. An' the Stingin' Lizard has the young one staked out over thar, an' is puttin' up for his raiment an' grub all reg'lar enough.

"'Which I yereafter backs this infant's play myse'f,' says Cherokee to the barkeep of the Oriental Saloon over in Tucson, which is the party the Stingin' Lizard pastures the young one on. 'You're all right, Bill,' goes on this Cherokee to the barkeep, 'but now I goes back of the box for this infant boy, I reckons I'll saw him off onto a preacher, or some sharp sim'lar, where he gets a Christian example. Whatever do you think?'

"The barkeep says himse'f he allows it's the play to make. So he an' Cherokee goes surgin' 'round, an' at last they camps the boy—who's seven years comin' grass—on the only pulpitsharp in Tucson. This gospel-spreader says he'll feed an' bed down the boy for some sum; which was shore a giant one, but the figgers I now forgets.

"Cherokee give him a stack of blues to start his game, an' is now pesterin' 'round in a co't tryin' to get the young one counter-branded from the Stingin' Lizard's outfit into his, an' given the name of Cherokee Hall. That's what takes him over to Tucson them times, an' not stage-robbin'.

"Two days later, in fact, to make shore all doubts is over, Cherokee even rings in said divine on us; which the divine tells the same story. I don't reckon now he's much of a preacher neither; for he gives Wolfville one whirl for luck over in the warehouse back of the New York Store, an' I shore hears 'em as makes a mighty sight more noise, an' bangs the Bible twice as hard, back in the States. I says so to Cherokee; but he puts it up he don't bank none on his preachin'.

"'What I aims at,' says Cherokee, 'is some one who rides herd on the boy all right, an' don't let him stampede off none into vicious ways.'

"'Why don't you keep the camp informed of this yere orphan an' the play you makes?' says Enright, at the time it's explained to the committee, —the time they trees Cherokee about them stages.

"'It's that benev'lent an' mushy,' says Cherokee, 'I'm plumb ashamed of the deal, an' don't allow to go postin' no notices tharof. But along comes this yere hold-up business, an', all inadvertent, tips my hand; which the same I stands, however, jest the same.'

"'It's all right,' says Enright, some disgusted though; 'but the next time you makes them foundlin' asylum trips, don't walk in the water so much. Leave your trail so Wolfville sees it, an' then folks ain't so likely to jump your camp in the dark an' take to shootin' you up for Injuns an' sim'lar hostiles.'

"'But one thing more,' continues Enright, 'an' then we orders the drinks. Jack Moore is yereby instructed to present the compliments of the committee to Rucker, when he trails in from Tucson; which he also notifies him to hobble his wife yereafter durin' sessions of this body. She's not to go draggin' her lariat 'round loose no more, settin' law an' order at defiance durin' sech hours as is given to business by the Stranglers."

2

Tucson Jennie's Heart.

"**W**IIYEVER ain't I married?' says you." The Old Cattleman repeated the question after me as he settled himself for one of our many "pow-wows," as he described them. "Looks like you've dealt me that conundrum before. Why ain't I wedded? The answer to that, son, is a long shot an' a limb in the way.

"Now I reckons the reason why I'm allers wifeless a whole lot is mainly due to the wide pop'larity of them females I takes after. Some other gent sorter gets her first each time, an' nacherally that bars me. Bill Jenks's wife on that occasion is a spec'men case. That's one of the disapp'intments I onfolds to you. Now thar's a maiden I not only wants, but needs; jest the same, Bill gets her. An' it's allers sim'lar; I never yet holds better than ace-high when the stake's a lady.

"It's troo," he continued, reflectively puffing his pipe. "I was disp'sitioned for a wife that a-way when I'm a colt. But that's a long time ago; I ain't in line for no sech gymnastics no more; my years is 'way ag'in it.

"You've got to ketch folks young to marry 'em. After they gets to be thirty years they goes slowly to the altar. If you aims to marry a gent after he's thirty you has to blindfold him an' back him in. Females, of course, ain't so obdurate. No; I s'pose this yere bein' married is a heap habit, same as tobacco an' jig-juice. If a gent takes a hand early, it's a good game, I makes no sort of doubt. But let

13

him get to millin' 'round in the thirties or later, an' him not begun none as yet; you bet he don't marry nothin'.

"Bar an onexplainable difference with the girl's old man," he went on with an air of thought, "I s'pose I'd be all married right now. I was twenty, them times. It's 'way back in Tennessee. Her folks lives about 'leven miles from me out on the Pine Knot Pike, an' once in two weeks I saddles up an' sorter sidles over. Thar's jest her old pap an' her mother an' her in the fam'ly, an' it's that far I allers made to stay all night. Thar's only two beds, an' so I'm put to camp along of the old man the times I stays.

"Them days I'm 'way bashful an' behind on all social plays, an' am plenty awe-struck about the old folks. I never feels happy a minute where they be. The old lady does her best to make me easy an' free, too. Comes out when I rides up, an' lets down the bars for my hoss, an' asks me to rest my hat the second I'm in the door.

"Which matters goes on good enough ontil mebby it's the eighth time I'm thar. I remembers the night all perfect. Me an' the girl sets up awhile, an' then I quits her an' turns in. I gets to sleep a-layin' along the aige of the bed, aimin' to keep 'way from the old man, who's snorin' an' thrashin' 'round an' takin' on over in the middle.

"I don't recall much of nothin' ontil I comes to, a-holdin' to the old man's y'ear with one hand an' a-hammerin' of his features with t'other. I don't know yet, why. I s'pose I'm locoed an' dreamin', an allows he's a b'ar or somethin' in my sleep that a-way, an' tries to kill him.

"Son, it's 'way back a long time, but I shudders yet when I reflects on that old man's language. I jumps up when I realizes things, grabs my raiment, an', gettin' my hoss outen the corral, goes p'intin' down the pike more'n a mile 'fore I even stops to dress. The last I sees of the old man he's buckin' an' pitchin' an' tossin', an' the females a-holdin' of him, an' he reachin' to get a Hawkins's rifle as hangs over the door. I never goes back no more, 'cause he's mighty vindictive about it. He tries to make it a grandjury matter next co't-time.

"Speakin' of nuptials, however, you can't tell much about women. Thar's a girl who shorely s'prises us once in a way out in Wolfville. Missis Rucker, who runs the O. K. Restauraw, gets this female from Tucson to fry flap-jacks an' salt hoss, an' he'p her deal her little gastronomic game. This yere girl's name is Jennie—Tucson Jennie. She looks like she's a nice, good girl, too; one of them which its's easy to love, an' in less'n two weeks thar's half the camp gets smitten.

"It affects business, it's that bad. Cherokee Hall tells me thar ain't half the money gets changed in at faro as usual, an' the New York Store reports gents goin' broke ag'in biled shirts, an' sim'lar deadfalls daily. Of course this yere first frenzy subsides a whole lot after a month.

"All this time Jennie ain't sayin' a word. She jest shoves them foolish yooths their *enchilades* an' *chile con carne*, an' ignores all winks an' looks complete.

"Thar's a party named Jim Baxter in camp, as' he set in to win Jennie hard. Jim tries to crowd the game an' get action. It looks like he's due to make the trip too. Missis Rucker is backin' his play, an' Jennie herse'f sorter lets him set 'round in the kitchen an' watch her work; which this yere is license an' riot itse'f compared with how she treats others. Occasionally some of us sorter tries to stack up for Jim an' figger out where he stands with the game.

"'How's it goin', Baxter?' Enright asks one day.

"'It's too many for me,' says Jim. 'Sometimes I thinks I corrals her, an' then ag'in it looks like I ain't in it. Jest now I'm feelin' some dejected.'

"'Somethin' oughter be schemed to settle this yere,' says Enright. 'It keeps the camp in a fever, an' mebby gets serious an' spreads.'

"'If somebody would only prance in,' says Doc Peets,'an' shoot Jim up some, you'd have her easy. Females is like a rabbit in a bush-pile, you has to shake things up a lot to make 'em come out. Now, if Jim is dyin' an' she cares for him, she's shorely goin' to show her hand.'

"I wants to pause right yere to observe that Doc Peets is the best-eddicated sharp I ever encounters in my life. An' what he don't know about squaws is valueless as information. But to go on with the deal.

"'That's right,' says Cherokee Hall, 'but of course it ain't goin' to do to shoot Jim up none.'

"'I don't know,' says Jim; 'I stands quite a racket if I'm shore it fetches her.'

"'What for a game,' says Cherokee, 'would it be to play like Jim's shot? Wouldn't that make her come a-runnin' same as if it's shore 'nough?'

"'I don't see why not,' says Enright.

"Well, the idee gains ground like an antelope, an' at last gets to be quite a conspir'cy. It's settled we plays it, with Dave Tutt to do the shootin'.

"'An' we makes the game complete,' says Jack Moore, 'by grabbin' Dave immediate an' bringin' of him before the committee, which convenes all reg'lar an' deecorous in the Red Light for said purpose. We-alls must line out like we're goin' to hang Dave for the killin'; otherwise it don't look nacheral nohow, an' the lady detects it's a bluff.'

"We gets things all ready, an' in the middle of the afternoon, when Jennie is draggin' her lariat 'round loose an' nothin' much to do—'cause we ain't aimin' to disturb her none in her dooties touchin' them flapjacks an' salt hoss—we-alls assembles over in the New York Store. As a preliminary step we lays Jim on some boxes, with a wagon-cover over him, like he's deceased.

"'Cl'ar things out of the way along by Jim's head,' says Jack Moore, who is takin' a big interest. 'We wants to fix things so Jen can swarm in at him easy. You hear me! she's goin' to come stampedin' in yere like wild cattle when she gets the news.'

"When everythin's ready, Tutt an' Jack, who concloods it's well to have a good deal of shootin', bangs away with their guns about four times apiece.

"'Jest shootin' once or twice,' says Jack, 'might arouse her s'picions. It would be a heap too brief for the real thing.'

"The minute the shootin' is ceased we-alls takes Tutt an' surges over to the Red Light to try him; a-pendin' of which Dan Boggs sa'nters across to the O. K. Restauraw an' remarks, all casooal an' careless like:

"'Dave Tutt downs Jim Baxter a minute back; good clean gun-play as ever I sees, too. Mighty big credit to both boys this yere is. No shootin' up the scenery an' the bystanders; no sech slobberin' work; but everythin' carries straight to centers.'

"'Where is he?' says Jennie, lookin' breathless an' sick.

"'Jim's remainder is in the New York Store,' says Dan.

"'Is he hurt?' she gasps.

"'I don't reckon he hurts none now,' say Dan, ''cause he's done cashed in his stack. Why! girl, he's dead; eighteen bullets, caliber forty-five, plumb through him.'

"'No, but Dave! Is Dave shot?' Tucson Jennie says, a-wringin' of her small paws.

"'Now don't you go to feeling' discouraged none,' says Dan, beginnin' to feel sorrry for her. 'We fixes the wretch so his murderin' sperit won't be an hour behind Jim's gettin' in. The Stranglers has him in the Red Light, makin' plans to stretch him right now.'

"We-alls has consoomed drinks all 'round an' Enright is in the chair, an' we're busy settin' up a big front about hearin' the case, when Tucson Jennie, with a scream as scares up surroundin' things to sech a limit that five ponies hops out of the corral an' flies, comes chargin' into the Red Light, an' the next instant she drifts 'round Tutt's neck like so much snow.

"'What for a game do you call this, anyhow?' says Jack Moore, who's a heap scand'lized. 'Is this yere maiden playin' anythin' on this camp?'

"'She's plumb locoed with grief,' says Dan B oggs, who follers her in, 'an' she's done got 'em mixed in her mind. She thinks Dave is Baxter.'

"'That's it,' says Cherokee. 'Her mind's stampeded with the shock. Me an' Jack takes her over to Jim's corpse, an' that's shore to revive her.' An' with that Cherokee an' Jack goes up to lead her away.

"'Save him, Mister Enright; save him!' she pleads, still clingin' to Tutt's neck like the loop of a lariat. 'Don't let 'em hang him! Save him for my sake!'

"'Hold on, Jack,' says Enright, who by now is lookin' some thoughtful. 'Jest everybody stand their hands yere till I counts the pot an' notes who's shy. It looks like we're cinchin' the hull onto the wrong bronco. Let me ask this female a question. Young woman,' he says to Tucson Jennie, 'be you fully informed as to whose neck you're hangin' to?'

"'It's Dave's, ain't it?' she says, lookin' all tearful in his face to make shore.

"Enright an' the rest of us don't say nothin', but gazes at each other. Tutt flushes up an' shows pleased both at once. But all the same he puts his arms 'round her like the deadgame gent he is.

"'What'll you-alls have, gents?" Enright says at last, quiet an' thoughtful. 'The drinks is on me, barkeep.'

"'Excuse me,' says Doc Peets, 'but as the author of this yere plot, I takes it the p'ison is on me. Barkeep, set out all your bottles.'

"'Gents,' says Jack Moore, 'I'm as peaceful a person as

ever jingled a spur or pulled a gun in Wolfville; but as I reflects on the active part I takes in these yere ceremonies, I
won't be responsible for results if any citizen comes between
me an' payin' for the drinks. Barkeep, I'm doin' this
myse'f.'

"Well, it's hard enoomeratin' how many drinks we do
have. Jim Baxter throws away the wagon cover an' comes
over from the New York Store an' stands in with us. It gets
to be a orgy.

"'Of course it's all right,' says Enright, 'the camp wins
with Tutt instead of Baxter; that's all. It 'lustrates one of
them beautiful characteristics of the gentler sex, too. Yere's
Baxter, to say nothin' of twenty others, as besieges an' be-
leaguers this yere female for six weeks, an' she scorns 'em.
Yere's Tutt, who ain't makin' a move, an' she grabs him.
It is sech oncertainties, gents, as makes the love of woman
valuable.'

"'Yo-alls should have asked me,' says Faro Nell, who
comes in right then an' rounds up close to Cherokee. 'I
could tell you two weeks ago Jennie's in love with Tutt.
Anybody could see it. Why! she's been feedin' of him twice
as good grub as she does anybody else.'"

Drawing of a Cowboy
by Frederick Remington

3

The Man from Red Dog.

"**L**ET me try one of them thar seegyars."

It was the pleasant after-dinner hour, and I was on the veranda for a quiet smoke. The Old Cattleman had just thrown down his paper; the half-light of the waning sun was a bit too dim for his eyes of seventy years.

"Whenever I beholds a seegyar," says the old fellow, as he puffed voluminously at the *principe* I passed over, "I thinks of what that witness says in the murder trial at Socorro.

"'What was you-all doin' in camp yourse'f,' asks the jedge of this yere witness, 'the day of the killin'?'

"'Which,' says the witness, oncrossin' his laigs an' lettin' on he ain't made bashful an' oneasy by so much attentions bein' shown him, 'which I was a-eatin' of a few sardines, a-drinkin' of a few drinks of whiskey, a-smokin' of a few seegyars, an' a-romancin' 'round.'"

After this abrupt, not to say ambiguous reminiscence, the Old Cattleman puffed contentedly a moment.

"What murder trial was this you speak of?" I asked. "Who had been killed?"

"Now I don't reckon I ever does know who it is gets downed," he replied. "This yere murder trial itse'f is news to me complete. They was waggin' along with it when I trails into Socorro that time, an' I merely sa'nters over to the co't that a-way to hear what's goin' on. The jedge is sorter gettin' in on the play while I'm listenin'.

21

"'What was the last words of this yere gent who's killed?' asks the jedge of this witness.

"'As nearly as I keeps tabs, jedge,' says the witness, 'the dyin' statement of this person is: "Four aces to beat."'

"'Which if deceased had knowed Socorro like I does,' says the jedge, like he's commentin' to himse'f, 'he'd shorely realized that sech remarks is simply sooicidal."

Again the Old Cattleman relapsed into silence and the smoke of the *principe*.

"How did the trial come out?" I queried. "Was the accused found guilty?"

"Which the trial itse'f," he replied, "don't come out. Thar's a passel of the boys who's come into town to see that jestice is done, an' bein' the round-up is goin' for'ard at the time, they nacherally feels hurried an' pressed for leesure. They-alls oughter to be back on the range with their cattle. So the fifth day, when things is loiterin' along at the trial till it looks like the law has hobbles on, an' the word goes round it's goin' to be a week yet before the jury gets action on this miscreant who's bein' tried, the boys becomes plumb aggravated an' wearied out that a-way; an' kickin' in the door of the calaboose, they searches out the felon, swings him to a cottonwood not otherwise engaged, an' the right prevails. Nacherally the trial bogs down right thar."

After another season of silence and smoke, the Old Cattle man struck in again.

"Speakin' of killin's, while I'm the last gent to go fosterin' idees of bloodshed, I'm some discouraged jest now by what I've been readin' in that paper about a dooel between some Eytalians, an' it shorely tries me the way them aliens plays hoss. It's obvious as stars on a cl'ar night, they never means fight a little bit. I abhors dooels, an' cowers from the mere idee. But, after all, business is business, an' when folks fights em' the objects of the meetin' oughter be blood. But the way these yere European shorthorns fixes it, a gent shorely runs a heap more resk of becomin' a angel abrupt, attendin' of a Texas cake-walk in a purely social way.

"Do they ever fight dooels in the West? Why, yes—some. My mem'ry comes a-canterin' up right now with the details of an encounter I once beholds in Wolfville. Thar ain't no time much throwed away with a dooel in the South west. The people's mighty extemporaneous, an' don't go browsin' 'round none sendin' challenges in writin', an' that sort of flapdoodle. When a gent notices the signs a-gettin' about right for him to go on the war-path, he picks out his meat, surges up, an' declar's himse'f. The victim, who is most likely a mighty serious an' experienced person, don't copper the play by makin' vain remarks, but brings his gatlin' into play surprisin'. Next it's bang! bang! bang! mixed up with flashes an' white smoke, an' the dooel is over complete. The gent who still adorns our midst takes a drink on the house, while St. Peter onbars things a lot an' arranges gate an' seat checks with the other in the realms of light. That's all thar is to it. The tide of life ag'in flows onward to the eternal sea, an' nary ripple.

"Oh, this yere Wolfville dooel! Well, it's this away. The day is blazin' hot, an' business layin' prone an' dead—jest blistered to death. A passel of us is sorter pervadin' 'round the dance-hall, it bein' the biggest an' coolest store in camp. A monte game is strugglin' for breath in a feeble, fitful way in the corner, an' some of us is a-watchin'; an' some a-settin' 'round loose a-thinkin'; but all keepin' mum an' still, 'cause it's so hot.

"Jest then some gent on a hoss goes whoopin' up the street a-yellin' an' a-whirlin' the loop of his rope, an' allowin' generally he's havin' a mighty good time.

"'Who's this yere toomultuous man on the hoss?' says Enright, a-regardin' of him in a displeased way from the door.

"'I meets him up the street a minute back,' says Dan Boggs, 'an' he allows he's called "The Man from Red Dog."

He says he's took a day off to visit us, an' aims to lay waste the camp some before he goes back.'

"About then the Red Dog man notes old Santa Rosa, who keeps the Mexican *baile* hall, an' his old woman, Marie, a-fussin' with each other in front of the New York Store. They's locked horns over a drink or somethin', an' is pow-wowin' mighty onamiable.

"'Whatever does this yere Mexican fam'ly mean,' says the Red Dog man, asurveyin' of 'em plenty scornful, 'a-draggin' of their domestic brawls out yere to offend a suf-ferin' public for? Whyever don't they stay in their wic-keyup an' fight, an' not take to puttin' it all over the American race which ain't in the play none an' don't thirst tharfor? How-ever, I unites an' reeconciles this divided household easy.'

"With this the Red Dog man drops the loop of his lariat 'round the two contestants an' jumps his bronco up the street like it's come outen a gun. Of course Santa Rosa an' Marie goes along on their heads permiscus.

"They goes coastin' along ontil they gets pulled into a mesquite-bush, an' the rope slips offen the saddle, an' thar they be. We-alls goes over from the dance-hall, extricatin' of 'em, an' final they rounds up mighty hapless an' weak, an' can only walk. They shorely lose enough hide to make a pair of leggin's.

"'Which I brings 'em together like twins,' says the Red Dog man, ridin' back for his rope. 'I offers two to one, no limit, they don't fight none whatever for a month.'

"Which, as it shorely looks like he's right, no one takes him. So the Red Dog man leaves his bluff a-hangin' an' goes into the dance-hall, a-givin of it out cold an' clammy he meditates libatin'.

"'All promenade to the bar,' yells the Red Dog man as he goes in. 'I'm a wolf, an' it's my night to howl. Don't 'rouse me, barkeep, with the sight of merely one bottle; set 'em all up. I'm some fastidious about my fire-water an' likes a chance to select.'

"Well, we'alls takes our inspiration, an' the Red Dog man tucks his onder his belt an' then turns round to Enright.

"'I takes it you're the old he-coon of this yere outfit?' says the Red Dog man, soopercilious-like.

"'Which, if I ain't,' says Enright, 'it's plenty safe as a play to let your wisdom flow this a-way till the he-coon gets yere.'

"'If thar's anythin',' says the Red Dog man, 'I turns from sick, it's voylence an' deevastation. But I hears sech complaints constant of this yere camp of Wolfville, I takes my first idle day to ride over an' line things up. Now yere I be, an' while I regrets it, I finds you-alls is a lawless, onregenerate set, a heap sight worse than roomer. I now takes the notion—for I sees no other trail—that by next drink time I climbs into the saddle, throws my rope 'round this den of sin, an' removes it from the map.'

"'Nacherally,' says Enright, some sarcastic, 'in makin' them schemes you ain't lookin' for no trouble whatever with a band of tarrapins like us.'

"'None whatever,' says the Red Dog man, mighty confident. 'In thirty minutes I distributes this yere hamlet 'round in the landscape same as them Greasers; which feat becomin' hist'ry, I then canters back to Red Dog.'

"'Well,' says Enright, 'it's plenty p'lite to let us know what's comin' this a-way.'

"'Oh! I ain't tellin' you none,' says the Red Dog man, 'I simply lets fly this hint, so any of you-alls as has got bric-a-brac he values speshul, he takes warnin' some an' packs it off all safe.'

"It's about then when Cherokee Hall, who's lookin' on, shoulders in between Enright an' the Red Dog man, mighty positive. Cherokee is a heap sot in his idees, an' I sees right off he's took a notion ag'in the Red Dog man.

"'As you've got a lot of work cut out,' says Cherokee, eyein' the Red Dog man malignant, 's'pose we tips the canteen ag'in.'

"'I shorely goes you,' says the Red Dog man. 'I drinks with friend, an' I drinks with foe; with the pard of my bosom an' the shudderin' victim of my wrath all sim'lar.'

"Cherokee turns out a big drink an' stands a-holdin' of it in his hand. I wants to say right yere, this Cherokee's plenty guileful.

"'You was namin',' says Cherokee, 'some public improvements you aims to make; sech as movin' this yere camp 'round some, I believes?'

"'That's whatever,' says the Red Dog man, 'an' the holycaust I 'nitiates is due to start in fifteen minutes.'

"'I've been figgerin' on you,' says Cherokee, 'an' I gives you the result in strict confidence without holdin' out a kyard. When you-all talks of tearin' up Wolfville, you're a liar an' a hossthief, an' you ain't goin' to tear up nothin'.'

"'What's this I hears!' yells the frenzied Red Dog man, reachin' for his gun.

"But he never gets it, for the same second Cherokee spills the glass of whiskey straight in his eyes, an' the next he's anguished an' blind as a mole.

"'I'll fool this yere human simoon up a lot,' says Cherokee, a-hurlin' of the Red Dog man to the floor, face down, while his nine-inch bowie shines in his hand like the sting of a wasp. 'I shore fixes him so he can't get a job clerkin' in a store,' an' grabbin' the Red Dog man's ha'r, which is long as the mane of a pony, he slashes it off close in one motion.

"'Thar's a fringe for yor leggin's, Nell,' remarks Cherokee, a-turnin' of the crop over to Faro Nell. 'Now, Doc,' Cherokee goes on to Doc Peets, 'take this yere Red Dog stranger over to the Red Light, fix his eyes all right, an' then tell him, if he thinks he needs blood in this, to take his

Winchester an' go north in the middle of the street. In twenty minutes by the watch I steps outen the dance-hall door a-lookin' for him. P'int him to the door all fair an' squar'. I don't aim to play nothin' low on this yere gent. He gets a chance for his ante.'

"Doc Peets sorter accoomilates the Red Dog man, who is cussin' an' carryin' on scand'lous, an' leads him over to the Red Light. In a minute word comes to Cherokee as his eyes is roundin' up all proper, an' that he's makin' war-medicine an' is growin' more hostile constant, an' to heel himse'f. At that Cherokee, mighty ca'm, sends out for Jack Moore's Winchester, which it an' 'eights-quar',' latest model.

"'Oh, Cherokee!' says Faro Nell, beginnin' to cry, an' curlin' her arms 'round his neck. I'm 'fraid he's goin' to down you. Ain't thar no way to fix it? Can't Dan yere settle with this Red Dog man?'

"'Cert,' says Dan Boggs, 'an' I makes the trip too gleeful. Jest to spar' Nell's feelin's, Cherokee, an' not to interfere with no gent's little game, I takes your hand an' plays it.'

"'Not none,' says Cherokee; 'this is my deal. Don't cry, Nellie,' he adds, smoothin' down down her yaller h'ar. 'Folks in my business has to hold themse'fs ready to face any game on the word, an' they never weakens or lays down. An' another thing, little girl; I gets this Red Dog sharp shore. I'm in the middle of a run of luck; I holds fours twice last night, with a flush an' a full hand out ag'in 'em.'

"Nell at last lets go of Cherokee's neck, an' bein' a female an' timid that a-way, allows she'll go, an' won't stop to see the shootin' none. We applauds the idee, thinkin' she might shake Cherokee some if she stays; an' of course a gent out shootin' for his life needs his nerve.

"Well, the twenty minutes is up; the Red Dog man gets his rifle offen his saddle an' goes down the middle of the street. Turnin' up his big sombrero, he squar's 'round, cocks his gun, an' waits. Then Enright goes out with Cherokee an'

stands him in the street about a hundred yards from the Red
Dog man. After Cherokee's placed he holds up his hand for
attention an' says:

"'When all is ready I stands to one side an' drops my hat.
You-alls fires at will.'

"Enright goes over to the side of the street, counts 'one,'
'two,' 'three,' an' drops his hat. Bangety! Bang! Bang! goes
the rifles like the roll of a drum. Cherokee can work a Winchester like one of these yere Yankees 'larm-clocks, an' that
Red Dog hold-up don't seem none behind.

"About the fifth fire the Red Dog man sorter steps for'ard
an' drops his gun; an' after standin' onsteady for a second,
he starts to cripplin' down at his knees. At last he comes
ahead on his face like a landslide. Thar's two bullets plumb
through his lungs, an' when we gets to him the red froth is
comin' outen his mouth some plenteous.

"We packs him back into the Red Light an' lays him onto
a monte-table. Bimeby he comes to a little an' Peets asks
him whatever he thinks he wants.

"'I wants you-alls to take off my moccasins an' pack me
into the street,' says the Red Dog man. 'I ain't allowin' for
my old mother in Missoury to be told as how I dies in no
gin-mill, which she shorely 'bominates of 'em. An' I don't
die with no boots on, neither.'

"We-alls packs him back into the street ag'in, an' pulls
away at his boots. About the time we gets 'em off he sags
back convulsive, an' thar he is as dead as Santa Anna.

"'What sort of a game is this, anyhow?' says Dan Boggs,
who, while we stands thar, has been pawin' over the Red
Dog man's rifle. 'Looks like this vivacious party's plumb
locoed. Yere's his hind-sights wedged up for a thousand
yards, an' he's been a-shootin' of cartridges with a hundred
an' twenty grains of powder into 'em. Between the sights
an' the jump of the powder, he's shootin' plumb over
Cherokee an' aimin' straight at him.'

"'Nellie,' says Enright, lookin' remorseful at the girl, who colors up an' begins to cry ag'in, 'did you cold-deck this yere Red Dog sport this a-way?'

"'I'm 'fraid,' sobs Nell, 'he gets Cherokee; so I slides over when you-alls is waitin' an' fixes his gun some.'

"'Which I should shorely concede you did,' says Enright. 'The way that Red Dog gent manip'lates his weepon shows he knows his game; an' except for you a-settin' things up on him, I'm powerful afraid he'd spoiled Cherokee a whole lot.'

"'Well, gents,' goes on Enright, after thinkin' a while, 'I reckons we-alls might as well drink on it. Hist'ry never shows a game yet, an' a woman in it, which is on the squar', an' we meekly b'ars our burdens with the rest.'"

4

Cherokee Hall.

"A N' you can't schedoole too much good about him,"
remarked the Old Cattleman. Here he threw away
the remnant of the *principe*, and, securing his pipe, beat the
ashes there-out and carefully reloaded with cut plug. Inevit-
ably the old gentleman must smoke. His tone and air as he
made the remark quoted were those of a man whose convictions touching the one discussed were not to be shaken.
"No, sir," he continued; "when I looks back'ard down the
trail of life, if thar's one gent who aforetime holds forth in
Wolfville on whom I reflects with satisfaction, it's this yere
Cherokee Hall."

"To judge from his conduct," I said, "in the hard case of
the Wilkins girl, as well as his remark as she left on the
stage, I should hold him to be a person of sensibilities as
well as benevolent impulse."

It was my purpose to coax the old gentleman to further
reminiscence.

"Benev'lent!" retorted the old man. "Which I should shore
admit it! What he does for this yere young Wilkins female
ain't a marker. Thar's the Red Dog man he lets out. Thar's
the Stingin' Lizzard's nephy; he stakes said yooth from infancy. 'Benev'lent!' says you. This party Cherokee is that
benev'lent he'd give away a poker hand. I've done set an'
see him give away his hand in a jack-pot for two hundred
dollars to some gent 'cross the table who's organizin' to go

ag'in him an' can't afford to lose. An' you can onderscore it'; a winnin' poker hand, an' him holdin' it, is the last thing a thorough-bred kyard-sharp'll give away. But as I says, I sees this Cherokee do it when the opp'sition is settin' in hard luck an' couldn't stand to lose.

"How would he give his hand away? Throw it in the dis-kyard an' not play it none; jest nacherally let the gent who's needy that a-way rake in the chips on the low hand. Cherokee mebby does it this fashion so's he don't wound the feelin's of this yere victim of his gen'rosity. Thar's folks who turns sens'tive an' ain't out to take alms none, who's feelin's he spar's that a-way by losin' to 'em at poker what they declines with scorn direct.

"'Benev'lent,' is the way you puts it! Son 'benev'lent' ain't the word. This sport Cherokee Hall ain't nothin' short of char'table.

"Speakin' wide flung an' onrestrained, Cherokee, as I mentions to you before, is the modestest, decentest longhorn as ever shakes his antlers in Arizona. He is slim an' light, an' a ondoubted kyard-sharp from his moccasins up. An' I never knows him to have a *peso* he don't gamble for. Nothin' common, though; I sees him one night when he sets ca'mly into some four-handed poker, five thousand dollars table stake, an' he's sanguine an' hopeful about landin' on his feet as a Cimmaron sheep. Of course times is plenty flush in them days, an' five thousand don't seem no sech mammoth sum. Trade is eager an' values high; aces-up fre-quent callin' for five hundred dollars before the draw. Still we ain't none of us makin' cigarettes of no sech roll as five thousand. The days ain't quite so halcyon as all that neither.

"But what I likes speshul in Cherokee Hall is his jedge-ment. He's every time right. He ain't talkin' much, an' he ain't needin' advice neither, more'n a steer needs a saddle-blanket. But when he concloodes to do things, you can gam-ble he's got it plenty right.

"One time this Cherokee an' Texas Thompson is comin' in from Tucson on the stage. Besides Cherokee an' Texas, along comes a female, close herdin' of two young-ones; which them infants might have been t'rant'lers an' every one a heap happier. Sorter as range-boss of the whole outfit is a lean gent in a black coat. Well, they hops in, an' Cherokee gives 'em the two back seats on account of the female an' the yearlin's.

"'My name is Jones,' says the gent in the black coat, when he gets settled back an' the stage is goin', 'an' I'm an exhortin' evangelist. I plucks brands from the burnin'.'

"'I'm powerful glad to know it,' says Texas, who likes talk. 'Them games of chance which has vogue in this yere clime is some various, an' I did think I shorely tests 'em all; but if ever the device you names is open in Wolfville I overlooks the same complete.'

"'Pore, sinkin' soul!' says the black-coat gent to the female; 'he's a-flounderin' in the mire of sin. Don't you know,' he goes on to Texas, 'my perishin' friend, you are bein' swept downward in the river of your own sinful life till your soul will be drowned in the abyss?'

"'Well, no,' says Texas, 'I don't. I allows I'm makin' a mighty dry ford of it.'

"'Lost! lost! lost!' says the black-coat gent, aleanin' back like he's plumb dejected that a-way an' hope-less. 'It is a stiff-necked gen'ration an' sorely perverse a lot.'

"The stage jolts along two or three miles, an' nothin' more bein' said. The black-coat gent he groans occasionally, which worries Texas; an' the two infants, gettin' restless, comes tumblin' over onto Cherokee an' is searchin' of his pockets for mementoes. Which this is about as refreshin' to Cherokee as bein' burned at the stake. But the mother she leans back an' smiles, an' of course he's plumb he'pless. Finally the black-coat gent p'ints in for another talk.

"'What is your name, my pore worm?' says the black-coat

gent, addressin' of Texas; 'an' whatever avocation has you an' your lost companion?'

"'Why,' says Texas, 'this yere's Hall—Cherokee Hall. He turns faro in the Red Light; an',' continues Texas, a-lowerin' his voice, 'he's as squar' a gent as ever counted a deck. Actooally, pard, you might not think it, but all that gent knows about settin' up kyards, or dealin' double, or any sech sinful scheme, is mere tradition.'

"'Brother,' says the female, bristlin' up an' tacklin' the black-coat gent, 'don't talk to them persons no more. Them's gamblers, an' mighty awful men,' an' with that she snatches away the yearlin's like they's contam'nated.

"This is relief to Cherokee, but the young-ones howl like coyotes, an' wants to come back an' finish pillagin' him. But the mother she spanks 'em, an' when Texas is goin' to give 'em some cartridges outen his belt to amoose 'em, she sasses him scand'lous, an' allows she ain't needin' no attentions from him. Then she snorts at Texas an' Cherokee contemptuous. The young-ones keeps on yellin' in a mighty onmelodious way, an' while Cherokee is ca'm an' don't seem like he minds it much, Texas gets some nervous. At last Texas lugs out a bottle, aimin' to compose his feelins', which they's some harrowed by now.

"'Well, I never!' shouts the woman; 'I shorely sees inebriates ere now, but at least they has the decency not to pull a bottle that a-way before a lady.'

"This stampedes Texas complete, an' he throws the whiskey outen the stage an' don't get no drink.

"It's along late in the mornin' when the stage strikes the upper end of Apache Canyon. This yere canyon is lately reckoned some bad. Nothin' ever happens on the line, but them is the days when Cochise is cavortin' 'round plenty loose, an' it's mighty possible to stir up Apaches any time a-layin' in the hills along the trail to Tucson. If they ever gets a notion to stand up the stage, they's shore due to be in this canyon; wherefore Cherokee an' Texas an' Old Monte who's drivin' regards it s'picious.

"'Send 'em through on the jump, Monte,' says Cherokee, stickin' out his head.

"The six hosses lines out at a ten-mile gait, which rattles things, an' makes the black-coat gent sigh, while the young-ones pours forth some appallin' shrieks. The female gets speshul mad at this, allowin' they's playin' it low down on her fam'ly. But she takes it out in cuffin' the yearlin's now an' then, jest to keep 'em yellin', an' don't say nothin'.

"Which the stage is about half through the canyon, when up on both sides a select assortment of Winchesters begins to bang an' jump permiscus; the same goin' hand-in-hand with whoops of onusual merit. With the first shot Old Monte pours the leather into the team, an' them hosses surges into the collars like cyclones.

"It's lucky aborigines ain't no shots. They never yet gets the phelosophy of a hind sight none, an' generally you can't reach their bullets with a ten-foot pole, they's that high above your head. The only thing as gets hit this time is Texas. About the beginnin', a little cloud of dust flies outen the shoulder of his coat, his face turns pale, an' Cherokee knows he's creased.

"'Did they get you, Old Man?' says Cherokee, some anxious.

"'No,' says Texas, tryin' to brace himse'f. 'I'll be on velvet ag'in in a second. I now longs, however, for that whiskey I hurls overboard so graceful.'

"The Apaches comes tumblin' down onto the trail an' gives chase, a-shootin' an' a-yellin' a heap zealous. As they's on foot, an' as Old Monte is makin' fifteen miles an hour by now, they merely manages to hold their own in the race, about forty yards to the r'ar.

"This don't go on long when Cherokee, after thinkin', says to Texas, 'This yere is the way I figgers it. If we-all

"An' they leaves him thar on the trail."

keeps on, them Injuns is that fervent they runs in on us at the ford. With half luck they's due to down either a hoss or Monte—mebby both; in which event the stage shorely stops, an' it's a fight. this bein' troo, an' as I'm 'lected for war anyhow, I'm goin' to caper out right yere, an' pull on the *baile* myse'f. This'll stop the chase, an' between us, pard, it's about the last chance in the box this pore females an' her offsprings has. An' I plays it for em, win or lose.'

"'Them's my motives,' says Texas, tryin' to pull himse'f together. 'Shall we take this he-shorthorn along?' An' he p'ints where them four tenderfoots is mixed up together in the back of the stage.

"'He wouldn't be worth a white chip,' says Cherokee, 'an' you-all is too hard hit to go, Texas, yourse'f. So take my regards to Enright an' the boys, an' smooth this all you know for Faro Nell. I makes the trip alone.'

"'Not much,' says Texas. 'My stack goes to the center, too.'

"But it don't, though, 'cause Texas has bled more'n he thinks. The first move he makes he tips over in a faint.

"Cherokee picks up his Winchester, an', openin' the door of the stage, jumps plumb free, an' they leaves him thar on the trail.

"It's mebby an hour later when the stage comes into Wolfville on the lope. Texas is still in a fog, speakin' mental, an' about bled to death; while them exhortin' people is outen their minds entire.

"In no time thar's a dozen of us lined out for Cherokee. Do we locate him? Which I should say we shorely discovers him. Thar's a bullet through his laig, an' thar he is with his back ag'in a rock wall, his Winchester to the front, his eyes glitterin', a-holdin' the canyon. Thar never is no Injun gets by him. Of course they stampedes prompt when they hears us a-comin', so we don't get no fight.

"'I hopes you nails one, Cherokee,' says Enright; 'playin' even on this yere laig they shoots.'

"'I win once, I reckons', says Cherokee, 'over behind that big rock to the left.'

"Shore enough he's got one Injun spread out; an', comin' along a little, Jack Moore turns up a second.

"'Yere's another,' says Jack, 'which breaks even on the bullet in Texas.'

"'That's right,' says Cherokee, 'I remembers now thar is two. The kyards is comin' some fast, an' I overlooks a bet.'

"We-alls gets Cherokee in all right, an' next day 'round comes the female tenderfoot to see him.

"'I wants to thank my defender,' she says.

"'You ain't onder no obligations, whatever, ma'am', says Cherokee, risin' up a little, while Faro Nell puts another goose-h'ar piller onder him. 'I simply prefers to do my fightin' in the canyon to doin' it at the ford; that's all. It's only a matter of straight business; nothin' more'n a preference I has. Another thing, ma'am; you-all forgives it, seein' I'm a gent onused to childish ways; but when I makes the play you names, I simply seizes on them savages that away as an excuse to get loose from them blessed children of your'n a whole lot.'"

5

A Wolfville Foundling.

"**D**OES Jack Moore have sand? Son, is this yere query meant for humor by you? Which for mere sand the Mohave desert is a fool to Jack."

The Old Cattleman's face was full of an earnest, fine sincerity. It was plain, too, that my question nettled the old fellow a bit; as might a doubt cast at an idol. But the sharpness had passed from his tone when he resumed:

"Not only is Jack long on sand that a-way, but he's plumb loaded with what you-alls calls 'nitiative. Leastwise that's what one of these yere fernologists allows, who straggles into camp an' goes to thumbin' our bumps one day.

"'Which this young person,' says the bumpsharp, while his fingers is caperin' about on Jack's head, 'is remarkable for his 'nitiative. He's the sort of gent who builds his fire before he gets his wood; an' issues more invites to drink than he receives. Which his weakness, speakin' general, is he overplays.'

"Which this yere bump party might have gone wrong in his wagers a heap of times; but he shorely calls the turn on Jack when he says he's some strong on 'nitiative.

"An' it's this yere proneness for the prematoor, an' nacheral willin'ness to open any pot that a-way, that makes Jack sech a slam-up offishul. Bein' full of 'nitiative, like this fernologist states, Jack don't idle along ontil somethin's happened. Not much; he abates it in the bud.

"Once when most of the outfit's over in Tucson, an' Jack

is sorter holdin' down the camp alone, a band of rustlers
comes trackin' in, allowin' they'll run Wolfville some.
Which, that's where Jack's 'nitiative shows up big. He goes
after 'em readily, like they's antelope. Them hold-ups is a
long majority over Jack, an' heeled; but that Jack stands
thar—right up ag'in the iron—an' tells 'em what he thinks
an' why he thinks it for; makes his minority report onto 'em
all free, like he outnumbers 'em two to one; an' winds up
by backin' the game with his gun in a way that commands
confidence.

"'You-alls hears my remarks,' he says at the close, briefly
flashin' his six-shooters on the outfit; 'thar ain't no band of
bad men in Arizona can tree this town an' me informed.
Now go slow, or I'll jest stretch a few of you for luck. It's
sech consoomin' toil, a-diggin' of sepulchers in this yere
rock-ribbed landscape, or I'd do it anyhow.'

"An' tharapon them rustlers, notin' Jack's got the drop on
'em, kicks up a dense cloud of dust an' is seen no more.

"But bein' replete with sand an' 'nitiative, that a-way,
don't state all thar is good of Jack. Let any pore, he'pless
party cut Jack's trail, an' he's plumb tender. On sech times
Jack's a dove; leastwise he's a dove a whole lot.

"One hot afternoon, Enright an' Doc Peets is away about
some cattle I reckons. Which the rest of us is noomerous
enough; an' we're sorter revolvin' 'round the post-office, a-
waitin' for Old Monte an' the stage. Yere she comes, final,
a-rattlin' an' a-creakin; that old drunkard Monte a-poppin' of
his whip, the six hosses on the canter, an' the whole
shebang puttin' on more dog than a Mexican officer of rev
enoo. When the stage draws up, Old Monte throws off the
mailbags an' the Wells-Fargo box, an' gets down an' opens
the door. But nobody emerges out.

"'Well, I'm a coyote!' says Monte, a heap disgusted,
'wherever is the female?'

"Then we-alls peers into the stage an' thar's only a baby,

Old Monte

with mebby a ten-months' start down this vale of tears, inside; an' no mother nor nothin' along. Jack Moore, jest as I says when I begins, reachin in an' gets him. The baby ain't sayin' nothin', an' sorter takes it out in smilin' on Jack; which last pleases him excessive.

"'He knows me for a hundred dollars!' says Jack. 'I'm an Apache if he ain't allowin' he knows me! Wherever did you get him, Monte?'

"'Give me a drink,' says Monte, p'intin' along into the Red Light. 'This yere makes me sick.'

"After Old Monte gets about four fingers of carnation onder his belt, he turns in an' explains as how the mother starts along in the stage all right enough from Tucson. The last time he sees her, so he puts it up, is at the last station back some twenty miles in the hills; an' he s'poses all the time late, she's inside ridin' herd on her progeny, ontil now.

"'I don't reckon,' says Old Monte, lookin' gloomy-like at the infant, 'that lady is aimin' to saw this yere young-one onto the stage company none?'

"'Don't upset your whiskey frettin' about the company,' says Jack, a-plantin' of the infant on the bar, while we-alls crowds in for a look at him. 'The camp'll play this hand; an' the company ain't goin' to be in it a little bit.'

"'I wish Enright an' Peets was yere,' says Cherokee Hall, 'to be heard hereon; which I shore deems this a grave occasion. Yere we-alls finds ourse'fs possessed of an onexpected child of tender years; an' the question nacheral enough is, whatever'll we do with it?'

"'Let's maverick it,' says Dan Boggs, who's a mighty good man, but onthinkful that a-way.

"'No,' says Cherokee; 'its mother'll come hoppin' along to-morrow, a-yellin'. This yere sot Monte has jest done drove off an' left her some'ers up the trail; she'll come romancin' along in time.'

"'Meanwhile,' says Jack, 'the infant's got to be took care

of, to which dooty I volunteers. Thar's a tenderfoot a-sleepin' in the room back of the dance-hall, an' he's that 'feminate an' effeet, he's got a shore-'nough bed an' some goose-h'ar pillers; which the same I do yereby confiscate to public use to take care of this yearlin'. Is the sentiment pleasin'?'

"'Jack's scheme is right,' says Boggs; 'an' I'm present to announce he's allers right. Let the shorthorn go sleep onder a mesquite-bush; it'll do him good a whole lot.'

"'I'm some doobersome of this play,' says Cherokee. 'Small infants is mighty myster'ous people, an' no livin' gent is ever onto their game an' able to forsee their needs. Do you-all reckon now you can take care of this yere young-one, Jack? Be you equal to it?'

"'Take care of a small baby like this,' says Jack, plenty scornful; 'which the same ain't weighin' twenty pounds? Well, it'll be some funny if I can't. I could break even with him if he's four times as big. All I asks is for you-alls to stand by in crisises an' back the play; an', that settled, you can go make side bets we-alls comes out winners on the deal.'

"'I ain't absolootly shore,' says Dave Tutt, 'bein' some shy of practice with infants myse'f, but jedgin' by his lookin' smooth an' silky, I offers fifty dollars even he ain't weaned none yet.'

"'I won't bet none on his bein' weaned complete,' says Jack, 'but I'll hang up fifty he drinks outen a bottle as easy as Old Monte.'

"'I'll go you once,' says Tutt; 'it's fifty dollars even he grows contemptuous at a bottle, an' disdains it.'

"Which we-alls talks it over an' decides that Jack's to nurse said infant; after which a passel of us proceeds to make a procession for the tenderfoots's bed, which he shorely resigns without a struggle. We packs it back to Jack; an' Cherokee Hall an' Boggs then goes over to the corral an'

lays for a goat to milk her. This yere goat is mighty reluctant, an' refuses to enter into the sperit of the thing; but they
swings an' rastles with her, makes their p'int right along,
an' after a frightful time comes back with 'most a dipper-
full.

"'That's all right,' says Jack, who's done cramped in a
room back of the Red Light, 'now hop out an' tell the barkeep to give you a pint bottle. We-alls has this yere game
payin' div'dends in two minutes.'

"Jack gets his bottle an' fills her up with goat's milk; an'
makes a stopper outen cotten cloth an' molasses for the infant to draw through. Which it's about this time the infant
puts up a yell, an' refuses peace ag'in till Jack gives him
his six-shooter to play with.

"'Which shows my confidence in him,' says Jack. 'Thar's
only a few folks left I'll pass my gun to.'

"Jack gets along with him first-rate, a-feedin' of him the
goat's milk, which he goes for with avidity; tharby nettin'
Jack the fifty from Dave Tutt. Boggs builds a fire so Jack
keeps the milk warm. Jack turns loose that earnest he don't
even go for no grub; jest nacherally has 'em pack it to him.

"'We-alls'll have to stand night gyards on this yere foundlin' to-night, I reckons?" asks Boggs of Jack, when he's
bringin' Jack things.

"'I s'pose most likely we'll have to make a play that a-
way,' says Jack.

"'All right,' says Boggs, tappin' his shirt with his pistol-
finger; 'you-all knows me an' Cherokee. We're in on this
yere any time you says.'

"So a band of us sorter camps along with Jack an' the infant ontil mebby it's second-drink time at night. The infant
don't raise the war-yell once; jest takes it out in goat's milk;
an' in laughin' , an playin' with Jack's gun.

"'Excuse me, gents,' finally says Jack, mighty dignified,
'but I've been figgerin' this thing, an' I allows it's time to

bed this yere young-one down for the night. If you-alls will withdraw some, I'll see how near I comes to makin' runnin' of it. Stay within whoopin' distance, though; so if he tries to stampede or takes to millin' I can get he'p.'

"We-alls lines out an'leaves Jack an' the infant, an' turns in on faro an' poker an' sim'lar devices which is bein' waged in the Red Light. Mebby it's an hour when Jack comes in.

"'Boggs,' he says; 's'pose you-all sets in an' plays my hand a minute with that infant child, while I goes over an' adjourns them frivolities in the dance-hall. It looks like this yere camp is speshul toomultuous to-night.'

"Boggs goes in with the infant, an' Jack proceeds to the *baile* house an' states the case.

"'I don't want to onsettle the reg'lar programme,' says Jack, 'but this yere young-one I'm responsible for, gets that engaged in the sounds of these yere revels, it don't look like he's goin' to sleep none. So if you-alls will call the last waltz, an' wind her up for to-night, it'll shorely be a he'p. The kid's mother'll be yere by sun-up; which her advent that a-way alters the play all 'round, an' matters then goes back to old lines.'

"'Enough said,' says Jim Hamilton, who runs the dance-hall. 'You can gamble this temple of mirth ain't layin' down on what's right, an' tonight's shindig closes right yere. All promenade to the bar. We takes a drink on the house, quits, an' calls it a day.

"Then Jack comes back, a heap grave with his cares, an' relieves Boggs; who's on watch, straddled of a chair, a-eyein' of the infant, who, a-settin' up ag'in a goose-h'ar pillar, is likewise a-eyein' of Boggs.

"'He's a 'way up good infant, Jack,' says Boggs, givin' up his seat.

"'You can bet your life he's a good infant,' says Jack; 'but it shore looks like he don't aim to turn in an' slumber none. Mebby the goat's milk is too invigeratin' for him, an' keeps him awake that a-way.'

"About another hour goes by, an' out comes Jack into the Red Light ag'in.

"'I ain't aimin' to disturb you-alls none,' he says, 'but, gents, if you-alls could close these games yere, an' shet up the store, I'll take it as a personal favor. He can hear the click of the chips, an' it's too many for him. Don't go away; jest close up an' sorter camp 'round quiet.'

"Which we-alls does as Jack says; closes the games, an' then sets 'round in our chairs an' keeps quiet , a-waitin' for the infant to turn in. A half-hour later Jack appears ag'in.

"'It ain't no use, gents,' he says, goin' back of the bar an' gettin' a big drink; 'that child is onto us. He won't have it. You can gamble, he's fixed it up with himse'f that he ain't goin' to sleep none to-night. I allows it's 'cause he's among rank strangers, an' he figgers it's a good safe play to lookout his game for himse'f.'

"'I wonder couldn't we sing him to sleep,' says Cherokee Hall.

"'Nothin' ag'in a try,' says Jack, some desp'rate, wipin' his lips after the drink.

"'S'pose we-alls gives him "The Dyin' Ranger" an' "Sandy Land" for an hour or so, an' see,' says Boggs.

"In we trails. Cherokee lines up on one side of the infant, an' Jack on t'other; an' the rest of us takes chairs an' camps 'round. We starts in an' shore sings him all we knows; an' we keeps it up for hours. All the time, that child is a-settin' thar, a-battin' his eyes an' a-starin', sleepless as owls. The last I remembers is Bogg's voice on 'Sandy Land':

> "'Great big taters on sandy land,
>   Get thar, Eli, if you can.'

"The next thing I'm aware of, thar's a whoop an' a yell outside. We-alls wakes up—all except the infant, who's wide awake all along—an' yere it is; four o'clock in the mornin', an' the mother has come. Comes over on a speshul buckboard from the station where that old inebriate, Monte, drove off an' left her. Well, son, everybody's plumb willin' an' glad to see her. An' for that matter, splittin' even, so's the infant."

6

Jaybird Bob's Joke.

"**W**HATEVER makes this yere Jaybird Bob believe he's a humorist," said the Old Cattleman one afternoon as we slowly returned from a walk, "whatever it is misleads him to so deem himse'f, is shorely too many for me. Doc Peets tells him himse'f one day he's plumb wrong.

"'You-all's nacherally a somber, morose party,' says Doc Peets this time, 'an' nothin' jocose or jocund about you. Your disp'sition, Jaybird, don't no more run to jokes than a prairie-dog's.'

"'Which I would admire to know why not?' says Jaybird Bob.

"'Well,' goes on Doc Peets, 'you thinks too slow—too much like a cow in a swamp. Your mind moves sluggish that a-way, an' sorter sinks to the hocks each step. If you was born to be funny your intellects would be limber an' frivolous.'

"'Bein' all this is personal to me,' says Jaybird Bob, 'I takes leave to regard you as wrong. My jokes is good, highgrade jokes; an' when you-all talks of me bein' morose, it's a mere case of bluff.' An' so Jaybird goes on a-holdin of himse'f funny ontil we-alls has him to bury.

"No; Jaybird ain't his shore'nough name; it's jest a handle to his 'dentity, so we-alls picks it up handy and easy. Jaybird's real name is Graingerford, —Poindexter Graingerford. But the same is cumbersom an' onwieldy a whole lot; so when he first trails into Wolfville we-alls considers among

49

"It's on the spring round-up."

ourse'fs an' settles it's a short cut to call him 'Jaybird Bob,' that a-way. An' we does.

"It's on the spring round-up this yere Jaybird first develops that he regards himse'f witty. It's in the mornin' as we-alls has saddled up an' lines out to comb the range roundabout for cattle. Thar's a tenderfoot along whose name is Todd, an', as he's canterin' off, Jaybird comes a-curvin' up on his bronco an' reaches over an' tails this shorthorn's pony.

"What's tailin' a pony? It's ridin' up from the r'ar an' takin' a half-hitch on your saddlehorn with the tail of another gent's pony, an' then spurrin' by an' swappin' ends with the whole outfit,—gent, hoss, an' all.

"It's really too toomultuous for a joke, an' mebby breaks the pon'ys neck, mebby the rider's. But whether he saves his neck or no, the party whose pony is thus tailed allers emerges thar from deshevelled an' wrought-up, an' hotter than a wolf. So no one plays this yere joke much; not till he's ready to get shot at..

"As I says, this Jaybird watches Todd as he rides off. Bein' new on the range that a-way, Todd don't ride easy. A cow saddle ain't built like these yere Eastern hulls, nohow. The stirrup is set two inches fruther back for one thing, an' it's compiled a heap different other ways. Bein' onused to cow saddles, an' for that matter cow ponies, this Todd lops over for'ard an' beats with his elbows like he's a curlew or somethin' flyin', an' I reckons it's sech proceedin's makes Jaybird allow he's goin' to be funny an' tail Todd's pony.

"As I explains, he capers along after Todd an' reaches over an' gets a handful of the pon'ys tail; an' then wroppin' it 'round his saddle-horn, he goes by on the jump an' spreads Todd an' his bronco permiscus about the scene. This yere Todd goes along the grass on all fours like a jackrabbit.

"Which Todd, I reckons, is the hostilest gent in south-east

Arizona. Before ever he offers to get up, he lugs out his six-shooter an' makes some mighty sincere gestures that away to shoot up Jaybird. but he's slow with his weepon, bein' spraddled out on the grass, an' it gives Dave Tutt an' Enright a chance to jump in between an' stop the deal.

"We-alls picks Todd up, an' rounds up his pony,—which scrambles to its feet an' is now cavortin' about like its mind is overturned,—an' explains to him this yere is a joke. But he's surly an' relentless about it; an' it don't take no hawk to see he don't forgive Jaybird a little bit.

"'Tailin' a gent's pony,' says Todd, 'is no doubt thrillin' amoosement for folks lookin' on, but thar's nothin' of a redeemin' nature in it from the standp'int of the party whose pony's upheaved that a-way. Not to be misonderstood at this yere crisis,' goes on this Todd, 'I wants to announce that from now for'ard life will have but one purpose with me, which'll be to down the next gent whoever tails a pony of mine. The present incident goes as a witticism; but you can gamble the next won't be so regarded.'

"That sorter ends the talk, an' all of us but the cook an' the hoss-hustlers bein' in the saddle by now, we disperses ourse'fs through the scenery to work the cattle an' proceed with the round-up we-alls is on. We notes, though, that tailin' Todd's pony don't go ag'in with safety.

"It's when we-alls rides away that Doc Peets—who's out with the round-up, though he ain't got no cattle brand himse'f—tells Jaybird he's not a humorist, like I already repeats.

"But, as I su'gests, this Jaybird Bob can't believe it none. He's mighty shore about his jokes bein' excellent good jokes; an' while it's plain Todd ain't got no confidence in him an' distrusts him complete since he tips over his bronco that mornin', it looks like Jaybird can't let him alone. An' them misdeeds of Jaybird's keeps goin' on, ontil by the merest mistake—for it's shore an accident if ever one hap-

pens in the cow country—this yere tenderfoot shoots up
Jaybird an' kills him for good.

"It looks to us like it's a speshul Providence to warn folks
not to go projectin' about, engaged in what you might call
physical jests none. Still, this yere removal of Jaybird don't
take place till mighty near the close of the roundup; an' in-
tervenin', he's pirootin' 'round, stockin' the kyards an' settin' up hands on the pore shorthorn continuous.

"One of Jaybird's jokes'—'one of his best,' Jaybird calls
it—rcsults in stampcdin' the herd of cattle we alls is bringin'
along at the time—bein' all cows an' their calves—to a
brandin'-pen. Which thar's two thousand, big an' little, in
the bunch; an' Jaybird's humor puts 'em to flight like so
many blackbirds; an' it takes two days hard ridin' for the
whole outfit to bring 'em together ag'in.

"Among other weaknesses this Todd imports from the
States is, he's afraid of snakes. Rattlesnakes is his abhor-
rence, an' if each is a disembodied sperit he can't want 'em
further off. He's allers alarmed that mebby, somehow, a
rattlesnake will come pokin' in onder his blankets nights,
an' camp with him while he's asleep. An' this yere wretched
Jaybird fosters them delusions.

"'About them serpents,' I overhears Jaybird say to him
one evenin' while we-alls is settin' 'round; —all but Moore
an' Tutt, who's ridin' herd; ''bout them serpents; a gent
can't be too partic'lar. It looks like they has but one hope,
which it's to crawl into a gent's blankets an' sleep some
with him. Which, if he moves or turns over, they simply
emits a buzz an' grabs him: I knows of forty folks who's bit
that a-way by snakes, an' nary a one lives to explain the
game.'

"'Be rattlesnakes thick in Arizona?' I hears Todd say to
this Jaybird.

"'Be they thick?' answers Jaybird. 'Well, I shore wishes
I had whiskey for all the rattlesnakes thar is yereabouts. I

don't want to go overstatin' the census to a gent who is out playin' for information, an' who's learnin' fast, but I s'pose now thar ain't none less than a billion snakes in southeast Arizona alone. If I could saw off the little passel of cattle I has on this range, you can gamble I'd pull my freight to-morrow. It's all right for sech old Cimmarons as Enright, an' sech parties as that sawbones Peets, to go bluffin' about thar' bein' no rattlesnakes to speak of, an' that they couldn't p'ison you to death no how; but you bet I ain't seen forty of my nearest friends cash in of snake-bites, an' not learn nothin'. An' almost every time it's a rattlesnake as comes slidin' into bed with 'em while they's locked in dreams, an' who gets hot an' goes to chewin' of 'em, because they wants to turn out before the snake does. Rattlesnakes that a-way wants to sleep till it's fourth-drink time an' the sun's 'way up yonder. An' when a gent goes to rollin' out of his blankets say at sun-up, it makes 'em monstrous angry to be disturbed; an' the first he knows of where they be an' how they looks on early risin', their teeth's in him up to the gyard, an' before night thar's one less gent to cook for, an' an extra saddle rides along in the grub-wagon with the blankets when they next moves camp.'

"Of course all this is a heap impressive to Todd; an' while Enright an' Peets both tells him Jaybird's havin' fun with him, you can see he's mortal afraid every night when he spreads his blankets, an' he makes a circle about where he sleeps at with a horseha'r lariat he's got from a Mexican, an' who tells him it'll tickle the snakes' necks when they goes to crawl across it, an' make 'em keep away.

"The way this yere Jaybird manages to stampede the bunch that time is this a-way. Jaybird comes ridin' in from the cattle about three hours before sun-up, to turn out Tutt, who is due to take his place on herd. Jaybird's got a rawhide rope that he's drugged about in the grass, which makes it damp an' cold. As Jaybird rides up to camp he sees this Todd rolled in his blankets, snorin' to beat four of a kind.

"Nacherally Jaybird's out to be joyous in a second. He rides up close to this he'pless shorthorn as he lays asleep, an' tosses a loop of his wet rawhide across his countenance where it's turn up in the moonlight. As it settles down cold an' startlin' on Todd's skin, Jaybird yells:

"'Snake, Todd! Thar's a rattlesnake on you bigger'n a dog.'

"Jaybird says later as how this Todd behaves tremendous. He b'iles up into the atmosphere with a howl like a wolf; an', grabbin' a blanket in each hand, he starts out over the plains in a state of frenzy. Which the worst is he charges headlong toward the herd; an' what with them shrieks he volunteers, an' the blankets flappin' an' wavin', thar ain't a cow in the bunch who stays in her right mind a moment. Which she springs to her feet, an', takin' her offspring along, goes surgin' off into the hills for good. You couldn't head or stop 'em then. It's the completest case of stampede I ever turns out to behold.

"No; this yere Todd never gathers the rights of the eepisode. He's that peevish an voylent by nacher no one tells him it's Jaybird; an' onless, in the light of knowin' more, he has since figgered out the trooth, he allows to this day a rattlesnake as big as a roll of blankets tries to recline on his face that time.

"To keep peace in camp an' not let him go to pawin' 'round for real trouble with the festive Jaybird, Enright stands in to cap the game himse'f; an' puts it up in confab with this Todd the next day as how he sees the rattlesnake, an' that it's mighty near bein' a whopper.

"'It's shore,' says Enright, when he an' Todd is conversin' tharon, 'the most giant serpent I ever sees without the aid of licker. An' when he goes streakin' off into the gloom, bein' amazed an' rattled by your cries, he leaves, so far as

I'm concerned, a trail of relief behind. You-all can gamble, I wasn't interruptin; of no sech snake, nor makin' of no pretexts for his detainment.

"'What for was his rattles like?' says Todd; an' he gets pale at the mere sound of Enright's talk.

"'As to them rattles,' says Enright, like he's mighty thoughtful tryin' to recall 'em to mind, 'as to this reptile's rattles, it's that dark that while I sees 'em I couldn't but jest. So far as I notes anythin' they looks like a belt full of cartridges, sorter corrugated an' noomerous.

"Now this yere which I relates, while no doubt burnin' experiences to Todd, is after all harmless enough. An' to people not careful about the basis of their glee it might do some to laugh at. But it all closes up on a play with nothin' gay nor merry in it; leastwise not for Jaybird Bob.

"This yere finish joke of Jaybird's transpires one evinin' as the cook's startin' in to rustle some chuck. The grub-wagon's been stopped in the mouth of Peeled Pine Canyon. Every gent's in camp but this yere tenderfoot Todd. Enright, who's actin' as round-up boss for the outfit—for everybody's cattle's bein' worked together that a-way, like we allers does—has sent Todd peerin' 'round for cattle, 'way off up the valley into which the Peeled Pine Canyon opens. This yere shorthorn's due to be back any time now, 'cause it's only a question of how far up the valley does he go. He don't run no show to be lost, for nothin' less aerial than goats could climb out of the canyon he's in, an' tharfore he's bound to find camp.

"Of course, knowin' every gent's station in the day's ridin', we-alls is plenty aware that this tenderfoot Todd is some'ers above us in the valley. None of the rest of us is turnin' our minds to him probably, except Jaybird Bob. It all of a bump like a buckin' pony strikes Jaybird that he's missin' a onusual chance to be buoyant.

"'What for a play would it be,' says Jaybird, rousin' up

from where he lays watchin' of the cook slice salt hoss for the fryin'-pan, 'what for a game would it be, I says, for a passel of us to lay out up the draw, an' bush-whack this yere ontaught person Todd as he comes ridin' down to camp? We-alls could hop out at him, a-whoopin' an' shoutin', an' bein' wropped up in blankets, he allows it's shore Injuns an' goes plumb locoed.'

"You-all will keep harrowin' away at this Todd party, Jaybird,' says Enright, 'ontil you arises from the game loser. Now I don't reckon none I'd play Apache if I'm you. Thar's too much effort in bein' an Apache that a-way. I'd lay yere an' think up some joke which don't demand so much industry, an' ain't calc'lated to scare an innocent to death.'

"But Jaybird won't listen. He falls into admiration of his scheme; an' at last Tutt an' Jack Moore allows they'll go along an' play they's aborigines with Jaybird an' note how the tenderfoot stands the racket.

"'As long as this yere Jaybird's bound to make the play,' says Jack Moore to Enright, talkin' one side, 'it's a heap better to have the conserv'tive element represented in the deal. So I puts it up, it's a good sage move for me an' Tutts to stand in. We-alls will come handy to pull Jaybird an' this shorthorn apart if they gets their horns locked in the course of them gaities.'

"Enright takes the same view; so Jaybird an' Moore an' Tutt wanders off up the canyon a mile, an' lays in wait surreptitious to head off Todd. Jack tells me the story when him an' Tutt comes ridin' back with the corpse.

"'This is how we does,' says Jack. 'Me an' Tutt an' deceased—which last is Jaybird all right enough—is ensconced behind a p'int of rocks. Jaybird's got his blanket wropped, 'round him so he looks like a savage. It ain't long when we all hears the tenderfoot comin' down the canyon; it's likely he's half-mile away. He's runnin' onto us at a road-gait; an' when he's about two hundred yards off Jaybird turns out a yell to make you shiver, shakes a load or two outen his gun, goes surgin' out from 'round the p'int of rocks, an charges straight at this onthinkin' tenderfoot. It is due to trooth to say, me an' Tutt follows this Jaybird's suit, only not so voylent as to whoops.

"'Does it scare up the tenderfoot? Well, it shorely alarms him a heap. He takes Jaybird for an Injun an' makes no question; which the same is nowise strange; I'd look for him for a savage myse'f, only, bein' in the deal that away I knows it's Jaybird. So, as I remarks, it horrifies the tenderfoot on end, an' at the first sight of Jaybird he whirls his pony an lights out up that valley like antelope.

"'Nacherally we-alls follows; Jaybird leadin', a-whoopin', an' a-shootin' an' throwin' no end of sperit into it. It's a success, this piece of wit is, up to this juncture, an' Jaybird puts a heap of zest into it.

"'The weak spot in all this yere humor grows out of the idees this tenderfoot's been gainin', an' the improvements he's been makin', while stragglin' about in our s'ciety. I onhesitatin'ly states that if this yere joke is pulled off by Jaybird when Todd first enters our midst, it might have been the vict'ry of his life. But Jaybird defers it too long. This tenderfoot has acquired a few Western ways; enough to spoil the fun an' send poor Jaybird acurvin' to his home on high.

"'This is what that shorthorn does which teaches me he's learnin'. While he's humpin' off up the canyon, an' me an' Jaybird an' Tutt is stampedin' along in pursoot, the fugitive throws loose his six-shooter, an without even turnin' his head or lookin' back at us, he onhooks the entire bundle of lead our way.

"Which the worst feature of it is, this backhanded, blind shootin' is a winner. The very first shot smites Jaybird plumb through the hat, an' he goes off his pony without even mentionin' about it to either Tutt or me.

"'That's all thar is to the report. Dave an 'me pulls up our broncos, abandons the joke, lays Jaybird across his saddle like a sack of corn, an' returns to state the case.'

"'Whatever did you-alls do with this frightened stranger?' asks Enright.

"'Which we never does nothin',' says Jack. 'The last I beholds, he's flyin' up the valley, hittin' nothin' but the high places. An' assoomin' his project is to get away, he's succeedin' admirable. As he vanishes, I should jedge from his motions he's reloadin' his gun; an' from the luck he has with Jaybird, Tutt an' me is led to believe thar's no real object in followin' him no further. I don't press my s'ciety on no gent; — shorely not on some locoed tenderfoot that away who's pulled his gun an' is done blazin' away erratic, without purpose or aim.'

"'Don't you an' Tutt know where he is at?' demands Enright.

"'Which we shorely don't,' says Jack. 'If his hoss holds, an' he don't swerve none from the direction he's p'intin' out in when he fades from view, he's goin' to be over in the San Simon country by to-morrow mornin' when we eats our grub; an' that's half way to the Borax desert. If you yearns for my impressions,' concloods Jack, 'drawn from a-seein' of him depart, I'm free to say I don't reckon you-alls is goin' to meet this yere tenderfoot none soon.'

"An' that's about the size of it. Jack calls the turn. Jaybird's last joke alarms this tenderfoot Todd plumb outen Arizona, an' thar ain't none of us ever sees ha'r, horn, nor hoof-mark of him no more. An' he takes with him, this Todd does, the boss pony in our bunch."

7

Boggs's Experience.

"NO; thar's nothin' prolix about Boggs. Which on the contrary, his nacher is shorely arduous that a-way. If it's a meetin' of the committee, for instance, with intent then an' thar to dwell a whole lot on the doin's of some malefactor, Boggs allers gets to a mental show-down ahead of the other gents involved. Either he's out to throw this party loose, or stretch his neck, or run him outen camp, or whatever's deemed exact jestice, long before sech slow-an'shore people as Old Man Enright even looks at their hands. The trooth is, Boggs ain't so strong on jedgement; his long suit is instinct. An' moreover I knows from his drawin' four kyards so much in poker, Boggs is plumb emotional."

At this point in his discourse the Old Cattleman paused and put in several profound minutes in apparent comtemplation of Boggs. Then he went on.

"That's it; Boggs is emotional; an' I shorely reckons which he'd even been a heap religious, only thar's no churches much on Boggs's range. Boggs tells me himse'f he comes mighty near bein' caught in some speritual round-up one time, an' I allers allows, after hearin' Boggs relate the tale, that if he'd only been submerged in what you-alls calls benigner inflooences that a-way, he'd most likely made the fold all right an' got garnered in with the sheep.

"It's jest after Short Creek Dave gets to be one of them 'vangelists. Dave has been exhortin' of Wolfville to leave off its ways, over in the warehouse of the New York Store, an' that same evenin' Boggs, bein' some moved, confides in me how once he mebby half-way makes up his mind he'll be saved.

"'Leastwise,' says Boggs, when he takes me into his past that a-way, 'I allows I'll be religious in the spring after the round-up is over. But I don't; so you can't, after all, call it a religious exper'ence none; nothin' more'n a eepisode.

"'It's winter when I makes them grace-of-heaven determinations,' goes on this Boggs, 'an' the spring round-up is months away. But I allers puts it up I'd shorely filled my hand an' got plumb into the play, only it's a bad winter; an' in the spring the cattle, weak an' starved, is gettin' down an' chillin' to death about the waterholes; an' as results tharof I'm ridin' the hills, a-cussin' an' a-swearin'; an' all 'round it's that rough, an' I'm that profane an' voylent, I reckons towards April probably my soul's buried onder ten foot of cusswords, an' that j'inin' the church in my case is mighty likely to be a bluff. An so I passes it up.

"'You sees,' says Boggs, 'thar's no good tryin' to hold out kyards on your Redeemer. If your heart ain't right it's no use to set into the game. No cold deck goes. He sees plumb through every kyard you holds, an' nothin' but a straight deal does with Him. Nacherally, then, I thinks— bein' as how you can't bluff your way into heaven, an' re-callin' the bad language I uses workin' them cattle—I won't even try. An' that's why, when resolvin' one winter to get religion mebby next June, I persists in my sinful life.

"'It's over to Taos I acquires this religious idee. I'm come new to the camp from some'ers down 'round Seven Rivers in the Pecos country, an' I don't know a gent. Which I'm by nacher gregar'ous; so not knowin' folks that a-way weighs on me; an' the first night I'm thar, I hastens to re-medy this yere evil. I'm the possessor of wealth to a limit, —for I shore despises bein' broke complete, an' generally

keeps as good as a blue stack in my war-bags, —an' I goes
projectin' 'round from dance-hall to *baile*, an' deciminates
my *dinero* an' draws to me nose-paint an' friends. As thar
ain't but three gin-mills, incloosive of the hurdy-gurdy, I'm
goin' curvin' in them grand rounds which I institoots, on a
sort of triangle.

"'Which it can't be said I don't make runnin' of it, however; I don't reckon now it's mor'n an hour before I knows
all Taos, bar Mexicans an' what some folks calls "the better
elements." It also follows, like its lariat does a loose pony,
that I'm some organized by whiskey, not to say confused.

"'It's because I'm confused I'm misled into this yere
pra'r-meetin.' Not that them exercises is due to dim my eternal game none, now nor yereafter; but as I ain't liable to
adorn the play nor take proper part tharin, I'd shorely passed
out an' kept on to the hurdy-gurdy if I'd knowed. As it
stands, I blunders into them orisons inadvertent; but, havin'
picked up the hand, I nacherally continues an' plays it.

"'It's this a-way about them religious excercises: I'm
emerged from the Tub of Blood, an' am p'intin' out for the
dance-hall, when I strikes a wickeyup all lighted, an' singin'
on the inside. I takes it for a joint I ain't seen none as yet,
an' tharupon heads up an' enters. From the noise, I allows
mebby it's Mexican; which Greasers usual puts up a heap of
singin' an' scufflin' an' talkin' in everythin' from monte to
a bull-fight.

"'Once I'm in, I notes it ain't Mexicans an' it ain't
Monte. Good folks though, I sees that; an' as a passel of
'em near the door looks shocked at the sight of me, I'm too
bashful to break out ag'in, but sorter aiges into the nearest
seat an' stands pat.

"'I can tell the outfit figgers on me raisin' the long yell
an' stampedin' 'round to make trouble; so I thinks to myse'f
I'll fool 'em up a lot. I jest won't say a word. So I sets silent as a coyote at noon; an' after awhile the sharp who's

dealin' for 'em goes on with them petitions I interrupts as I comes bulgin' in.

"'Their range-boss says one thing I remembers. It's about castin' your bread upon the waters. he allows you'll get it ag'in an' a band of mavericks with it. It's playin' white chips to win blues; that's what this sharp says.

"'It shorely strikes me as easy. Every time you does good, says this party, Fate is out to play a return game with you; an' it's written you quits winner on all the good you promulgates that a-way.

"'I sets the deal out an' gets some sleepy at it, too. But I won't leave an' scand'lize the congregation; an' as I gives up strong when the plate goes by, I ain't regarded as no setback.

"'When the contreebution-box—which she's a tin plate— comes chargin' by, I'm sorter noddin,' I'm that weary. I notes the jingle of money, an' rouses up, allowin' mebby it's a jack-pot, I reckons.

"'"How hard be you-all in?" I says to the gent next to me, who's gone to the center for a *peso*.

"'"Dollar," says the gent.

"'"Well," I says, "I ain't seen my hand since the draw, but I'll raise you nine blind." An' I boards a ten-dollar bill.

"'When the rest goes, I sorter sidles forth an' lines out for the dance-hall. The fact is I'm needin' what you-alls calls stimulants. But all the same it sticks in my head about castin' good deeds on the water that a-way. It sticks thar yet, for that matter.

"Bein' released from them devotions, I starts to drinkin' ag'in with zeal an' earnestness. An' thar comes a time when all my money's in my boots. Yere's how: I only takes two stacks of reds when I embarks on this yere debauch. Bein' deep an' crafty, an' a new Injun at that agency that a-way, an' not knowin' what game I may go ag'inst, I puts the rest of my bank-roll over in Howard's store. It turns out, too, that every time I acquires silver in change, I commits it to my left boot, which is high an' ample to hold said specie. Why I puts this yere silver money in my boot-laig is shore too many for me. But I feels mighty cunnin' over it at the time, an' regards it as a 'way-up play.

"'As I tells you, thar arrives an hour while I'm in the Tub of Blood when my money's all in my boot, an' thar's still licker to drink. Fact is, I jest meets a gent named Frosty, as good a citizen as ever riffles a deck or pulls a trigger, an' p'liteness demands we-alls puts the nose-paint in play. That's why I has to have money.

"'I don't care to go pullin' off my moccasins in the Tub of Blood, an' makin' a vulgar display of my wealth by pourin' the silver onto the floor. Thar's a peck of it, if thar's *dos reals*; an' sech an exhibition as spillin' it out in the Tub of Blood is bound to mortify me, an' the barkeep an' Frosty, an' most likely lead to makin' remarks. So I concloods I'll round up my silver outside an' then return.

"'"Excuse me," I says to Frosty. "You stay right yere with the bottle, an' I'll be among you ag'in in a minute all spraddled out."

"'I goes wanderin' out back of the Tub of Blood, where it's lonesome, an' camps down by a Spanish-bayonet, an' tugs away to get my boot off an' my *dinero* into circ'lation.

"'An' while I'm at it, sleep an' nose-paint seizes me, an' my light goes plumb out. I rolls over behind the bayonet-bush an' raises an' raises a snore. As for that Frosty, he waits a while; then he pulls his freight, allowin' I'm too deliberate about comin' back, for him.

"'It must have made them coyotes stop an' consider a whole lot about what I be. To show you how good them coyotes is, I wants to tell you: I don't notice it ontil the next day. While I'm curled up to the r'ar of that bush they comes mighty near gnawin' the scabbard offen my gun. Fact; the leather looks like some pup has been chewin' it. But right then I ain't mindin' nothin' so oninterestin' as a coyote bitin' on the leather of my gun.

"'Now this is where that bluff about bread on the waters comes in; an' it falls so pat on the heels of them devotions of mine, it he'ps brand it on my mem'ry. While I'm layin' thar, an' mighty likely while them coyotes is lunchin' offen my scabbard that a-way, along comes a rank stranger they calls Spanish Bill.

"'I learns afterward how this Spanish Bill is hard, plumb through. He's rustled everythin' from a bunch of ponies to the mail-bags, an' is nothin' but a hold-up who needs hangin' every hour. Whatever takes him to where I lays by my bayonet-bush I never knows. He don't disclose nothin' on that p'int afterward, an' mebby he tracks up on me accidental.

"'But what informs me plain that he explores my war-bags for stuff, before ever he concloods to look after my health, is this: Later, when we gets acquainted an' I onfurls my finances onto him, he seems disapp'inted an' hurt.

"The statistics of the barkeep of the Tub of Blood next day, goes to the effect thar I'm shorely out that four hours; an' when Spanish Bill discovers me I'm mighty near froze. Taos nights in November has a heap of things in common with them Artic regions we hears of, where them fur-lined sports goes in pursoot of that North Pole. Bein' froze, an' mebby from an over dab of nose-paint, I never saveys about this yere Spanish Bill meetin' up with me that a-way ontil later. But by what the barkeep says, he drug me into the Tub of Blood an' allows he's got a maverick.

"'"Fix this yere froze gent up somethin' with teeth," says Spanish Bill to the barkeep. "I don't know his name none, but he's sufferin' an' has got to be recovered if it takes the entire check-rack."

"'Which the barkeep stands in an' brings me to. I comes 'round an' can walk some if Spanish Bill goes along steadyin' of me by the collar. Tharupon said Bill rides herd on me down to the Jackson House an' spreads me on some blankets.

"'It's daylight when I begins to be aware my name's Boggs, an' that I'm a native of Kentucky, an' little personalities like that; an' what wakes me up is this Spanish Bill.

"''See yere," says this hold-up, "I'm goin' to turn in now, an' it's time you-all is up. Yere's what you do: Thar's five whiskey-checks on the Tub of Blood, which will he'p you to an appetite. Followin' of a s'fficient quantity of fire-water, you will return to the Jackson House an' eat. I pays for it. I won't be outen my blankets by then; but they knows that Spanish Bill makes good, 'cause I impresses 'em speshul when I comes in.

"''You-all don't know me," goes on this Spanish Bill, as I sets up an' blinks at him some foggy an' blurred, 'an' I don't know you"—which we-alls allows, outen p'liteness, is a dead loss to both. "But my name's Spanish Bill, an' I'm turnin' monte in the Bank Exchange. I'll be thar at my table by first-drink time this evenin'; an' if you sa'nters that a-way at that epock, we'll have a drink; an' bein' as you're busted, of course I stakes you moderate on your way."

"'It's this bluff about me not havin' money puts me in mind later that this Bill must have rustled my raiments when he finds me that time when I'm presided over by coyotes while I sleeps. When he says it, however, I merely remarks that while I'm grateful to him as mockin-birds, money after all ain't no object with me; an', pullin' off my nigh moccasin, I pours some two pounds of specie onto the blankets.

"''Which I packs this in my boot," I observes, "to put myse'f in mind I've got a roll big enough to fill a nose-bag over to Howard's store."

"''An' I'm feelin' the galiest to hear it," says this Spanish Bill; though as I su'gests he acts pained an' amazed, like a gent who's over-looked a bet.

"'Well, that's all thar is to that part. That's where Spanish Bill launches that bread of his'n; an' the way it later turns out it sorter b'ars down on me, an' keeps me rememberin' what that sky scout says at the pra'r-mettin' about the action a gent gets by playin' a good deed to win.

"'It's the middle of January, mebby two months later, when I'm over on the Upper Caliente about fifty miles back of the Spanish Peaks. I'm workin' a bunch of cattle; Cross-K is the brand; y'ear marks a swallow-fork in the left, with the right y'ear onderhacked.'

"What's the good of a y'ear-mark when thar's a brand?" repeated the Old Cattleman after me, for I had interrupted with the question. "Whatever's the good of y'ear-marks? Why, when mixed cattle is in a bunch, standin' so close you can't see no brands on their sides, an' you-all is ridin' through the outfit cuttin' out, y'ear-marks is what you goes by. Cattle turns to look as you comes ridin' an' pesterin' among 'em, an' their two y'ears p'ints for'ard like fans. You gets their y'ear-marks like printin' on the page of a book. If you was to go over a herd by the brands, you wouldn't cut out a steer an hour. But to trail back after Boggs.

"'It's two months later, an' I'm ridin' down a draw one day,' says this Dan Boggs, 'cussin' the range an' the weather, when my pony goes to havin' symptoms. This yere pony is that sagacious that while it makes not the slightest mention of cattle when they's near, it never comes up on deer, or people in the hills, but it takes to givin' of manifestation. This is so I can squar myse'f for whatever game they opens on us.

"'As I says, me an' this yere wise pony is pushin' out into the Caliente when the pony begins to make signs. I brings him down all cautious where we can look across the valley, an' you-all can gamble I'm some astonished to see a gent walkin' along afoot, off mebby a couple hundred yards. He sorter limps an' leans over on one side like he's hurt.

Nacherally I stops an' surveys him careful. It's plenty
strange he's thar at all; an' stranger still he's afoot. I looks
him over for weepons; I wants to note what he's like an'
how he's heeled.

"Nacherally I stops an' surveys him careful."

"'You saveys as well as me it don't do to go canterin' out
to strangers that a-way in the hills; speshully a stranger
who's afoot. He might hunger for your pony for one thing,
an' open a play on you with his gun, as would leave you
afoot an' likewise too dead to know it.

"'I'm allers cautious that a-way, around a party who's lost
his hoss. It locoes him an' makes him f'rocious; I s'pose
bein' afoot he feels he'pless, an' let out an' crazy. A gent
afoot is a heap easier to aggravate, too; an' a mighty sight
more likely to lay for you than when he's in a Texas saddle
with a pony between his knees.

"'Which is why I remarks, that I stacks up this pedestrian careful an' accurate before I goes after him.

"'As I says, he carries on like he's hurt; an' he's packin' a six-shooter. He seems familiar, too; an' while I looks him over I'm wonderin' where I cuts his trail before.

"'As I has the advantage of a Winchester, I at last rides into the open an' gives a whoopee. The party turns, comes limpin' toward me, an' whoever do you allow it is? Which it's shorely Spanish Bill; an' it's right yere he gets action on that bread on the waters he plays in when he recovers me that time in Taos.

"'To make it brief, Spanish Bill tells me that after I leaves Taos he goes over an' deals monte a bit at Wagon Mound. One night a Mexican comes caperin' in, an' Bill gives him a layout or two. At last he makes an alcy bet of fifty dollars on the queen; what the Greasers call the "hoss." The Mexican loses; an' instead of takin' it easy like a sport should, he grabs the money.

"'As was his dooty, Spanish Bill bends his six-shooter over the Mexican. Tharupon he searches out a knife; an' this yere so complicates the business, Bill, to simplify things, plugs the Mexican full of holes.

"'This shootin' is on the squar', an' no one takes hostile notice of it. Spanish Bill goes on layin' out his monte same as usual. Two days later, though, he gets a p'inter the Mexicans is fixin' for him. So that night he moves camp— mebby to where it's a hundred an' sixty miles from Wagon Mound, over on the Vermejo.

"'But it looks like the Greasers hangs to the trail; for the day before I tracks up on him a band of 'em hops outen a dry *arroya*, where they's bush-wackin' for him, an' goes to shootin'. As might be expected, Spanish Bill turns loose, free an' frequent, an' they all shorely has a high, excessive time.

"'The Mexicans downs Spanish Bill's pony, an' a bullet

creases Bill's side; which last is what curves him over an' indooces him to limp when I trails up with him.

"'As Spanish Bill goes down, the Mexicans scatter. The game is too high for 'em. They was shy two people, with another plugged deep an' strong; by which you notes that Bill is aimin' low an' good.

"'After the shootin' Spanish Bill crawls over to a ranch, an', gettin' a pony an' saddle, which he easy does, he breaks back into the hills where I encounters him. It's that mornin' his pony gets tired of the deal, an' bucks him off, an' goes stampedin' back. That's why he's afoot.

"'While he's talkin' all this, I recalls how Spanish Bill rounds me up that night in Taos, so I don't hesitate. I takes him over to my camp. The next mornin' he turns his nose for Texas on my best pony; which is the last I sees or hears of Spanish Bill, unless he's the Bill who's lynched over near Eagle Pass a year later, of which I surmises it's some likely.

"'But whether Bill's lynched or not, it all brings up ag'in what that Gospel-gent says about doin' benev'lences; an' how after many days you dies an' makes a winnin', an' lives on velvet all eternity. An' don't you know this Spanish Bill pickin' me up that night, an' then in less than two months, when he's afoot an' hurt in the hills, gettin' ag'inst me an' drawin' out of the game ahead a saddle, a pony an' safety, makes it seem like that Bible-sharp is right a whole lot?

"'That's how it strikes me,' concloods Boggs. 'An' as I tells you; if so many cattle don't die that spring; an' if I dont give way so frightful in my talk, I'd shorely hunted down a congregation the next June, an' stood in.'"

8

Dawson & Rudd, Partners.

"WHATEVER'S the difference between the East an' the West?" said the Old Cattleman, repeating my question rather for the purpose of consideration than from any failure to understand: "What's the difference between the East an' the West? Which, so far as I notes, to relapse into metaphor, as you-alls says, the big difference is that the East allers shoots from a rest; while the West shoots off hand.

"The West shore learns easy an' is quick to change a system or alter a play. It's plumb swift, the West is; an' what some regards as rough is mere rapidity. The West might go broke at faro-bank in the mornin', an' be rich at roulette in the afternoon; you can't tell. I knows partners in Arizona who rolls out in the gray light of breakin' day an' begins work by dissolvin' an' windin' up the firm's affairs. By dark them same gents is pards ag'in in a new enterprise complete. Folks'll fight at sun-up an' cook their *chili con carne* together at night, an' then sleep onder the same blankets. For which causes thar's no prophets in the West; a Western future that a-way bein' so mighty oncertain no prophet can fasten his lariat.

"Speakin' of pards an' the fog which surrounds what the same is likely to do, makes me think of the onlicensed an' onlooked-for carryin's-on of 'Doby Dawson an' Copper Queen Billy Rudd. Them two gents fosters a feud among themse'fs that splits 'em wide open an' keeps 'em pesterin' each other for years; which the doin's of them locoed people is the scandal of Wolfville while it lasts.

"It's mebby the spring after we erects the Bird Cage Op'ry House, an' Wolfville is gettin' to be considerable of a camp. We-alls is organized for a shore'-nough town, an Jack Moore is a shore-'nough marshal, with Enright for alcalde that a-way, an' thar's a heap of improvements.

"When I first tracks into Wolfville, cows is what you might call the leadin' industry, with whiskey an' faro-bank on the side. But in the days of 'Doby Dawson an' Copper Queen Billy Rudd, ore has been onearthed, the mines is opened, an' Wolfville's swelled tremendous. We-alls even wins a county-seat fight with Red Dog, wherein we puts it all over that ornery hamlet; an' we shorely deals the game for the entire region.

"As I states, it's the spring after we promotes the Bird Cage Op'ry House—which temple of amoosements is complete the fall before—that 'Doby an' Billy turns up in Wolfville. I knows she's spring, for I'm away workin' the round-up at the time, an' them gents is both thar drunk when I comes in.

"'Doby an' Billy's been pards for ten years. They's miner folks, an' 'Doby tells me himse'f one day that him an' Billy has stood in on every mine excitement from Alaska to Lower Californy. An' never once does they get their trails crossed or have a row.

"Them two gents strikes in at Wolfville when the mines is first opened, an' staked out three claims; one for 'Doby, one for Billy, an' one for both of 'em. They's camped off up a draw about half a mile from town, where their claims is, an' has a little cabin an' seems to be gettin' along peace-ful as a church; an' I reckons thar's no doubt but they be.

"When 'Doby an' Billy first comes caperin' into Wolfville they's that thick an' friendly with each other, it's a shame to thieves. I recalls how their relations that a-way excites general admiration, an' Doc Peets even goes so far he calls 'em 'Jonathan an' David.' Which Peets would have kept on callin' 'em' 'Jonathan an' David' plumb through, but Billy gets hostile.

"'It ain't me I cares for,' says Billy,—which he waits on Doc Peets with his gun,—'but no gent's goin' to malign 'Doby Dawson none an' alloode to him as 'Jonathan' without rebooke.'

"Seein' it pains Billy, an' as thar ain't even a white chip in mere nomenclature that a way, of course Doc Peets don't call 'em 'Jonathan an' David' no more.

"''Doby an' Billy's been around mighty likely six months. The camp gets used to 'em an' likes 'em. They digs an' blasts away in them badger-holes they calls shafts all day, an then comes chargin' down to the Red Light at night. After the two is drunk successful, they mutually takes each other home. An as they lines out for their camp upholdin' an' he'pin' of each other, an' both that dead soaked in nose-paint they long before abondons tryin' to he'p themse'fs, I tells you, son, their love is a picture an' a lesson.

"''Which the way them pore, locoed sots,' says Old Man Enright one night, as 'Doby an' Billy falls outen the Red Light together, an' then turns in an' assists each other to rise,—'which the way them pore darkened drunkards rides herd on each other, an' is onse'fish an' generous that a-way, an' backs each other's play, is as good as sermons. You-all young men,' says Enright, turnin' on Jack Moore an' Boggs an' Tutt, 'you-all imatoor bucks whose character ain't really formed none yet, oughter profit plenty by their example.'

"As I remarks, 'Doby an' Billy's been inhabitin' Wolfville for mighty hard on six months when the trouble between 'em first shows its teeth. As Billy walks out one mornin' to sniff the climate some, he remarks a Mexican—which his name is Jose Salazar, but don't cut no figger nohow—sorter 'pro-priatin' of a mule.

"'The same,' as Billy says, in relatin' the casooalty later, 'bein' our star mule.'

"Nacherally, on notin' the misdeeds of this yere Greaser, Billy reaches inside the cabin, an' sorts out a Winchester an' plugs said culprit in among his thoughts; an' tharby brings his mule-rustlin' an' his reflections to a pause some.

"It's two hours later, mebby, when the defunct's daughter—the outfit abides over in Chihuahua, which is the Mexican part of Wolfville—goes to a show-down with 'Doby an' Billy an wants to know does she get the corpse?

"'Shore,' says 'Doby, 'which we-alls has no further use for your paw, an' his remainder is free an' welcome to you. You can bet me an' Billy ain't holdin' out no paternal corpses none on their weepin' offsprings.'

"Followin' of his bluff, 'Doby goes over an' consoles with the Mexican's daughter, which her name's Manuela, an' she don't look so bad neither. Doc Peets, whose jedgements of females is a cinch, allows she's as pretty as a diamond flush, an' you can gamble Doc Peets ain't makin' no blind leads when it's a question of squaws.

"So 'Doby consoles this yere Manuela a whole lot, while Billy, who's makin' coffee an' bakin'-powder biscuit inside, don't really notice he's doin' it. Fact is, Billy's plumb busy. The New York Store havin' changed bakin'-powder onto us the week before—the same redoocin' biscuits to a conundrum for a month after—an' that bakin'-powder change sorter engagin' Billy's faculties wholly, he forgets about deceased an' his daughter complete; that is, complete temporary. Later, when the biscuits is done an' offen his mind, Billy recalls all about it ag'in.

"But 'Doby, who's a good talker an' a mighty tender gent that a-way, jumps in an' comforts Manuela, an' shows her how this mule her paw is stealin' is by way an' far the best mule in camp, an' at last she dries her tears an' allows in her language that she's growin' resigned.

'Doby winds up by he'pin' Manuela home with what's left of her paw.

"'Which it's jest like that 'Doby,' says Billy, when he hears of his partner packin' home his prey that a-way, an' his tones shows he admires 'Doby no limit, 'which it's shorely like him. Take folks in distress, an' you-alls can bet your last chip 'Doby can't do too much for 'em.'

"Billy's disgust sets in like the rainy season, however, when about two months later 'Doby ups an' weds this Mexican girl Manuela. When Billy learns of said ceremony, he declines a seat in the game, an' won't go near them nuptials nohow.

"'An' I declar's myse'f right yere,' says Billy. 'From now for'ard it's a case of lone hand with me. I don't want no more partners. When a gent with whom for ten years I've camped, trailed, an' prospected with, all the way from the Dalls to the Gila, quits me cold an' clammy for a squaw he don't know ten weeks, you can gamble that lets me plumb out. I've done got my med'cine, an' I'm ready to quit.'

"But 'Doby an' Billy don't actooally make no assignment, nor go into what you-all Eastern sharps calls liquidation. The two goes on an' works their claims together, an' the firm name still waves as ''Doby Dawson an' Copper Queen Billy Rudd,' only Billy won't go into 'Doby's new wickeyup where he's got Manuela,—not a foot.

"'Which I might have conquered my native reluctance,' says Billy, 'so to do, an' I even makes up my mind one night—it's after I've got my grub, an' you-alls knows how plumb soft an' forgivin' that a-way a gent is when his stomach's full of grub—to go up an' visit 'em a lot. But as I gets to the door I hears a noise I don't savey; an' when I Injuns up to a crack an' surveys the scene, I'm a coyote if thar ain't 'Doby, with his wife in his lap, singin' to her. That's squar'; actooally singin'; which sech efforts reminds me of ballards by cinnamon b'ars.

"'I ain't none shore,' goes on Billy, as he relates about it to me, 'but I'd stood sech egreegious plays, chargin' it general to 'Doby's gettin' locoed an' mushy; but when this yere ingrate ends his war-song, what do you-all reckon now he does? Turns in an' begins 'pologizin' for me downin' her dad. Which the old hold-up is on the mule an' goin' hellbent when I curls him up. Well, that ends things with me. I turns on my heels an' goes down to the Red Light an' gets drunk plumb through. You recalls it; the time I'm drunk a month, an' Cherokee Hall bars me at faro-bank, allowin' I'm onconscious of my surroundin's.'

"Billy goes on livin' at their old camp, an 'Doby an' Manuela at the new one 'Doby built. This last is mebby four hundred yards more up the draw. Durin' the day 'Doby an' Billy turns in an' works an' digs an' drills an' blasts together as of yore. The main change is that at evenin' Billy gets drunk alone; an' as 'Doby ain't along to he'p Billy home an' need Billy's he'p to get home, lots of times Billy falls by the trail an' puts in the night among the mesquite-bushes an' the coyotes impartial.

"This yere goes on for plumb a year, an' while things is cooler an' more distant between 'em, same as it's bound to be when two gents sleeps in different camps, still 'Doby an' Billy is trackin' along all right. One mornin', however, Billy goes down to the holes they's projectin' over, but no 'Doby shows up. It goes on ontil mighty likely fifth-drink time that forenoon, an' as Billy don't see no trace, sign, nor signal-smoke of his pard, he gets oneasy.

"'It's a fact,' says Billy afterward, 'thar's hours when I more'n half allows this yere squaw of 'Doby's has done took a knife, or some sech weepon, an' gets even with 'Doby, while he sleeps, for me pluggin' her paw about the mule. It's this yere idee which takes me outen the shaft I'm sinkin', an' sends me cavortin' up to 'Doby's camp. I passes a resolution on my way that if she's cashed 'Doby's chips for him that a-way, I'll shorely sa'nter over an' lay waste all Chihuahua to play even for the blow.'

"But as all turns out, them surmises of Billy's is idle. He gets mebby easy six-shooter distance from the door, when he discerns a small cry like a fox-cub's whine. Billy listens, an' the yelp comes as cl'ar on his y'ears as the whistle of a curlew. Billy tumbles.

"'I'm a Chinaman,' says Billy, 'if it ain't a kid!'

"So he backs off quiet an' noiseless ontil he's dead safe, an' then he lifts the long yell for 'Doby. When 'Doby emerges he confirms them beliefs of Billy's; it's a kid shore-'nought.

"'Boy or girl?' says Billy.

"'Boy,' says 'Doby.

"'Which I shorely quits you cold if it's a girl,' says Billy. 'As it is, I stands by you in your troubles. I ain't none s'prised at your luck, 'Doby,' goes on Billy. 'I half foresees some sech racket as this the minute you gets married. However, if it's a boy she goes. I ain't the gent to lay down on an old-time runnin'-mate while luck's ag'in him; an I'll still be your partner an' play out my hand.'

"Of course, 'Doby has to go back to lookout his game. An' as Billy's that rent an' shaken by them news he can't work none, he takes two or three drinks of nose-paint, an' then promulgates as how it's a holiday. Billy feels, too, that while this yere's a blow, still it's a great occasion; an' as he takes to feelin' his whiskey an roominatin' on the tangled state of affairs, it suddenly strikes him he'll jest nacherally close up the trail by the house.

"'Women is frail people an' can't abide noises that a-way', says Billy, 'an' 'Doby's shore lookin' some faded himse'f. I reckons, tharfore, I'll sorter stop commerce along this yere thoroughfar' ontil further orders. What 'Doby an' his squaw needs now is quietood an' peace, an' you can wager all you-alls is worth they ain't goin' to suffer no disturbances.'

"It ain't half an hour after this before Billy's got two signs, both down an' up the trail, warnin' of people to hunt another wagon-track. The signs is made outen pine boards, an' Billy has marked this yere motto onto 'em with a burnt stick:

"'DOBY's GOT A PAPOOSE,

sO

PULL YOUR FREIGHT."

"It ain't no time after Billy posts his warnin's, an' he's still musin' over 'em mighty reflective, when along projects a Mexican with a pair of burros he's packin' freight on. The Mexican's goin' by the notices without payin' the least heed tharto. But this don't do Billy, an' he stands him up.

"'Can you read?' says Billy to the Mexican, at the same time p'intin' to the signs.

"The Mexican allows in Spanish—which the same Billy saveys an' palavers liberal—that he can't read. Then he p'ints out to go by ag'in.

"'No you don't none, onless in the smoke,' says Billy, an' throws a gun on him. 'Pause where you be, my proud Castilian, an' I'll flood your darkened ignorance with light by nacherally readin' this yere inscription to you a whole lot.'

"Tharupon Billy reads off the notice a heap impressive, an winds up by commandin' of the Mexican to line out on the trail back.

"'Vamos!' says Billy. 'Which if you insists on pushin' along through yere I'll turn in an' crawl your hump some.'

"But the Mexican gets ugly as a t'ran'tler at this, an' with one motion he lugs out a six-shooter an' onbosoms the same.

"Billy is a trifle previous with a gun himse'f, an' while the Mexican is mighty abrupt, he gets none the best of Billy. Which the outcome is the Mexican's shot plumb dead in his moccasins, while Billy takes a small crease on his cheek, the same not bein' deadly. Billy then confiscates the burros.

"'Which I plays 'em in for funeral expenses,' says Billy, an' is turnin' of 'em into the corral by his camp jest as 'Doby comes prancin' out with a six-shooter to take part in whatever game is bein' rolled.

"When 'Doby sees Billy's signs that a-way, he's 'fected so he weeps tears. He puts his hands on Billy's shoulder, an' lookin' at him, while his eyes is swimmin', he says:

"'Billy, you-all is the thoughtfullest pard that ever lived.'

"'Doby throws so much should into it, an' him givin' 'way to emotions, it comes mighty near onhingin' Billy.

"'I knows I be,' he says, shakin' 'Doby by the hand for a minute, 'but, Old Man, you deserves it. It's comin' to you, an' you bet your life you're goin' to get it. With some folks this yere would be castin' pearls before swine, but not with you, 'Doby. You can 'preciate a play, an' I'm proud to be your partner.'

"The next few months goes on, an' 'Doby an' Billy keeps peggin' away at their claims, an' gettin' drunk an' rich about equal. Billy is still that reedic'lous he won't go up to 'Doby's camp; but 'Doby comes over an' sees him frequent. The first throw out of the box Billy takes a notion ag'in the kid an' allows he don't want no traffic with him, —none whatever.

"But 'Doby won't have it that a-way, an' when it's about six months old he packs said infant over one mornin' while Billy's at breakfast.

"'Ain't he hell!' says 'Doby, a heap gleeful, at the same time sawin' the infant onto Billy direct.

"Of course Billy has to hold him then. Which he acts like he's a hot tamale, an' shifts him about in his arms. But it's plain he ain't so displeased neither. At last the kid reaches

out swift an' cinches onto Billy's beard that a-way. This delights Billy, while 'Doby keeps trackin' 'round the room too
tickled to set down. All he can remark—an' he does it frequent, like it tells the entire story—is:

"'Billy, ain't he hell?'

"An' Billy ain't none back'ard admittin' he is, an' allows
onhesitatin' it's the hunkiest baby in Arizona.

"'An' I've got dust into the thousands,' remarks Billy,
'which says he's the prize papoose of the reservation, an'
says it ten to one. This yere offspring is a credit to you,
'Doby, an' I marvels you-all is that modest over it.'

"'You can bet it ain't no Siwash,' says 'Doby.' It's clean
strain, that infant is, if I does say it.'

"'That's whatever,' says Billy, looking the infant over an'
beginnin' to feel as proud of it as 'Doby himse'f, 'that's
whatever. An' I'm yere to remark, any gent who can up an
without no talk or boastin' have sech a papoose as that, is
licensed to plume himse'f tharon, an' put on dog over it, the
same without restraint. If ever you calls the turn for the
limit, pard, it's when you has this yere child.'

"At this 'Doby an' Billy shakes hands like it's a ceremony, an' both is grave an' dignified about it. 'Doby puts
it up that usual he's beyond flattery, but when a gent of
jedgement like Billy looks over a play that a-way, an' in-
dorses it, you can bet he's not insensible. Then they shakes
hands ag'in, an' 'Doby says:

"'Moreover, not meanin' no compliments, not tossin' of
no boquets, old pard, me an' Manuela names this young person "Willyum"; same as you-all.'

"Billy comes mighty near droppin' the infant on the floor
at this, an' the small victim of his onthoughtfulness that a-
way yells like a coyote.

"'That settles it,' says Billy. 'A gent who could come
down to blastin' an' drillin'—mere menial tasks, as they
shorely be—on the heels of honor like this, is a mighty sight
more sordid than Copper Queen Billy Rudd. 'Doby, this
yere is a remarkable occasion, an' we cel'brates.'

"By this time the infant is grown plumb hostile, an' is

howlin' to beat the band; so' Doby puts it up he'll take him
to his mother an' afterwards he's ready to join Billy in an
orgy.

"'I jest nacherally stampedes back to the agency with this
yere Willyum child,' says 'Doby, 'an' then we-alls repairs
to the Red Light an' relaxes.'

"They shorely does. I don't recall no sech debauch—that
is, none so extreme an' broadcast—since Wolfville and Red
Dog engages in them Thanksgivin' exercises.

"'Doby an' Billy, as time goes by, allers alloods to the
infant as 'Willyum,' so's not to get him an' Billy mixed; an'
durin' the next two years, while Billy still goes shy so far
as trackin' over to 'Doby's ranch is concerned, as soon as
he walks, Willyum comes down the canyon to see Billy
every day.

"Oh, no, Billy ain't none onforgivin' to Manuela for
ropin' up 'Doby an' weddin' him that a-way; but you see
downin' her paw for stealin' the mule that time gets so it
makes him bashful an' reluctant.

"'It ain't that I'm timorous neither, nor yet assoomin'
airs,' this yere Billy says to me when he brings it up himse'f
how he don't go over to 'Doby's, 'but I'm never no hand
to set 'round an' visit free an' easy that a-way with the pos-
terity of a gent which I has had cause to plant. This yere
ain't roodness; it's scrooples,' says Billy, an' so it's plumb
useless for me to go gettin' sociable with 'Doby's wife.'

"It's crowdin' close on two years after the infant's born
when 'Doby an' Billy gets up their feud which I speaks of
at the beginnin'. Yere's how it gets fulminated. Billy's
loafin' over by the post-office door one evenin', talkin' to
Tutt an' Boggs an' a passel of us, when who comes projectin' along, p'intin' for the New York Store, but 'Doby's
wife an' Willyum. As they trails by, Willyum sees Billy—
Willyum can make a small bluff at talkin' by now—an',
p'intin' his finger at Billy, he sags back on his mother's
dress like he aims to halt her, an' says:

"'Pop-pa! Pop-pa!' meanin' Billy that a-way; although the
same is erroneous entire, as every gent in Wolfville knows.

"Which if Willyum's forefinger he p'ints with is a Colt's forty-four, an' instead of sayin' 'Pop-pa!' he onhooks the same at Billy direct, now I don't reckon Billy could have been more put out. 'Doby's wife drags Willyum along at the time like he's a calf goin' to be branded, an' she never halts or pauses. But Billy turns all kinds of hues, an' is that prostrated he surges across to the Red Light an' gets two drinks alone, never invitin' nobody, before he realizes. When he does invite us he admits frank he's plumb locoed for a moment by the shock.

"'You bet!' says Billy, as he gets his third drink, the same bein' took in common with the pop'lace present, 'you bet! thar ain't a gent in camp I'd insult by no neglect; but when Willyum makes them charges an' does it publicly, it onhinges my reason, an' them two times I don't invite you-alls, I'm not responsible.'

"We-alls sees Billy's wounded, an' tharfore it's a ha'r-line deal to say anythin'; but as well as we can we tells him that what Willyum says, that a-way, bein' less'n two year old, is the mere prattle of a child, an' he's not to be depressed by it.

"'Sech breaks,' says Dan Boggs, 'is took jocose back in the States.'

"'Shore!' says Texas Thompson, backin' Boggs's play; 'them little bluffs of infancy, gettin' tangled that a-way about their progenitors, is regarded joyous in Laredo. Which thar's not the slightest need of Billy bein' cast down tharat.'

"'I ain't sayin' a word, gents,' remarks Billy, an' his tones is sad. 'You-alls means proper an' friendly. But I warns the world at this time that I now embarks on the spree of my life. I'm goin' to get drunk an' never hedge a bet; an' my last requests, the same bein' addressed to the bar-keep, personal, is to set every bottle of bug-juice in the shebang on the bar, thar to repose within the reach of all ontil further orders.'

"It's about an hour later, an' Billy, who's filed away a quart of fire-water in his interior by now, is vibratin' between the Red Light an' the dancehall, growin' drunk an' dejected even up. It's then he sees 'Doby headin' up the street. 'Doby hears of his son Willyum's wild play from his wife, an' it makes him hot that a-way. But he ain't no notion of blamin' Billy; none whatever.

"However, 'Doby don't have entire charge of the round-up, an' he has to figger with Billy right along.

"''Doby,' shouts Billy, as he notes his pard approachin', while he balances himse'f in his moccasins a heap difficult, ''Doby, your infant Willyum is a eediot. Which if I was the parent of a fool papoose like Willyum, I'd shorely drop him down a shaft a whole lot an' fill up the shaft. He won't assay two ounces of sense to the ton, Willyum won't: an' he ain't worth powder an' fuse to work him. Actooally, that pore imbecile baby Willyum, don't know his own father.'

"Which the rage of 'Doby is beyond bounds complete. For about half a minute him an' Billy froths an' cusses each other out scand'lous, an' then comes the guns. The artillery is a case of s'prise, the most experienced gent in Wolfville not lookin' for no gun-play between folks who's been pards an' blanket-mates for years.

"However, it don't last long; it looks like both gets sorter conscience-stricken that a-way, an' lets up. Still, while it's short, it's long enough for Billy to get his laig busted with one of 'Doby's bullets, an' it all lays Billy up for Doc Peets to fuss with for over three months.

"While Billy's stretched out, an' Doc Peets is ridin' herd on his laig, 'Doby keeps as savage as an Apache an' don't come near Billy. The same, however, ain't full proof of coldness, neither; for Billy's done give it out he'll down 'Doby if he pokes his head in the door, an' arranges his guns where he can work 'em in on the enterprise easy.

"But Willyum don't take no stand-off. The last thing Willyum's afraid of is Billy; so he comes waltzin' over each day, clumsy as a cub cinnamon on his short laigs, an' makes himse'f plumb abundant. He plays with Billy, an' he sleeps with Billy, Willyum does; an' he eats every time the nigger, who's come over from the corral to lookout Billy's domestic game while he's down, rustles some grub.

"'Doby's disgusted with Willyum's herdin' round with Bill that a-way, bein' sociable an' visitin' of him, an' he lays for Willyum an' wallops him. When Billy learns of it—which he does from Willyum himse'f when that infant p'ints in for a visit the day after—he's as wild as a mountain lion. Billy can't get out none, for his laig is a heap fragmentary as yet,—'Doby's bullet gettin' all the results which is comin' that time, —but he sends 'Doby word by Peets, if he hears of any more punishments bein' meted to Willyum, he regards it as a speshul affront to him, an' holds 'Doby responsible personal as soon as he can hobble.

"'Tell him,' says Billy, 'that if he commits any further atrocities ag'in this innocent Willyum child, I'll shore leave him too dead to skin.'

"'This yere Billy's gettin' locoed entire,' says Enright, when he's told of Billy's bluff. 'The right to maul your immediate descendants that a-way is guaranteed by the constitootion, an' is one of them things we-alls fights for at Bunker Hill. However, I reckons Billy's merely blowin' his horn; bein' sick an' cantankerous with his game knee.'

"Billy gets well after a while, an' him an' 'Doby sorter plans to avoid each other. Whatever work they puts in on the claim they holds in partnership, they hires other gents to do. Personal, each works the claim he holds himse'f, which keeps 'em asunder a whole lot, an' is frootful of peace.'

"Deep inside their shirts I allers allows these yere persons deems high an' 'fectionate of one another right at the time they's hangin' up their hardest bluffs an' carryin' on most hostile. Which trivial incidents discloses this.

"Once in the Red Light, when a party who's new from Tucson, turns in to tell some light story of Billy,—him not bein' present none,—'Doby goes all over this yere racontoor like a landslide, an' retires him from s'ciety for a week. An' 'Doby don't explain his game neither; jest reprimands this offensive Tucson gent, an' lets it go as it lays. Of course, we-alls onderstands it's 'cause 'Doby ain't puttin' up with no carpin' criticism of his old pard; which the same is nacheral enough.

"Don't you-all ever notice, son, how once you takes to fightin' for a party an' indorsin' of his plays, it gets to be a habit,—same, mebby, as fire-water? Which you lays for his detractors an' pulls on war for him that a-way long after you ceases to have the slightest use for him yourse'f. It's that a-way with 'Doby about Billy.

"An' this yere Billy's feelin's about 'Doby is heated an' sedulous all sim'lar. 'Doby gets laid out for a week by rheumatics, which he acquires years before—he shore don't rope onto them rheumatics none 'round Wolfville, you can gamble! said camp bein' saloobcrous that a way over on the Nevada plateaus, an' while he's treed an' can't come down to his claim, a passel of sharps ups an' mavericks it; what miners calls 'jumps it.' Whatever does Billy do? Paints for war prompt an' enthoosiastic, takes his gun, an' the way he stampedes an' scatters them marauders don't bother him a bit.

"But while, as I states, this yere trick of makin' war-med'cine which 'Doby an' Billy has, an' schedoolin' trouble for folks who comes projectin' 'round invadin' of the other's rights, mebby is a heap habit, I gleans from it the idee likewise that onder the surface they holds each other in esteem to a p'int which is romantic.

"'Doby an' Billy lives on for a year after 'Doby plugs Billy in the laig, keepin' apart an' not speakin'. Willyum is got so he puts in most of his nights an' all of his days with Billy; which the spectacle of Billy packin' Willyum about camp nights is frequent. 'Doby never 'pears to file no protest; I reckons he looks on it as a fore-ordained an' hopeless play. However, Billy's a heap careful of Willyum's morals, an' is shorely linin' him up right.

"Once a new barkeep in the dance-hall allows he'll promote Willyum's feelin's some with a spoonful of nose-paint.

"'No, you don't,' says Billy, plenty savage; 'an' since the matter comes up I announces cold that, now or yereafter, the first gent who saws off nose-paint on Willyum, or lays for the morals of this innocent infant to corrupt 'em, I'll kill an' skelp him so shore as I packs gun or knife.'

"'Which shows,' said Dan Boggs later, when he hears of Billy's blazer, 'that this yere Billy Rudd is a mighty high-minded gent, an' you-alls can play it to win he has my regards. He can count me in on this deal to keep Willyum from strong drinks.'

"'I thinks myse'f he's right,' says Cherokee Hall. 'Willyum is now but three years old, which is shore not aged. My idee would be to raise Willyum, an' not let him drink a drop of nose-paint ever, merely to show the camp what comes of sech experiments.'

"But Billy's that pos'tive an' self-reliant he don't need no encouragement about how he conducts Willyum's habits; an', followin' his remarks, Willyum allers gets ignored complete on invitations to licker. Packin' the kid 'round that a-way shortens up Billy's booze a lot, too. He don't feel so free to get tanked expansive with Willyum on his mind an' hands that a-way.

"It's shorely a picture, the tenderness Billy lavishes on Willyum. Many a night when Billy's stayin' late, tryin' to win himse'f outen the hole, I beholds him playin' poker, or mebby it's farobank, with Willyum curled up on his lap an' shirt-front, snorin' away all sound an' genial, an' Billy makin' his raises an' callin' his draw to the dealer in whispers, for fear he wakes Willyum.

"But thar comes a time when the feud is over, an' 'Doby an' Billy turns in better friends than before. For a month mebby thar's a Mexican girl—which she's a cousin that a-way or some kin to 'Doby's wife—who's been stayin' at 'Doby's house, sorter backin' their play.

"It falls out frequent this Mexican girl, Marie, trails over to Billy's, roundin' up an' collectin' of Willyum to put another shirt onto him, or some sech benefit. Billy never acts like he's impressed by this yere girl, an', while he relinquishes Willyum every time, he growls an' puts it up he's malev'lent over it.

"But the señorita is game, an' don't put no store by Billy's growls. She ropes up Willyum an' drags him away mighty decisive. Willyum howls an' calls on Billy for aid, which most likely is pain to Billy's heart; but he don't get it none. The señorita harnesses Willyum into a clean shirt, an' then she throws Willyum loose on the range ag'in, an' he drifts back to Billy.

"It's the general view that Billy never once thinks of wedlock with the señorita if he's let alone. But one day Doc Peets waxes facetious.

"'In a month,' says Peets to Billy, while we-alls is renooin' our sperits in the Red Light, 'this yere Marie'll quit comin' over for Willyum.'

"'Why?' says Billy, glarin' at Peets s'picious.

"'Cause,' replies Peets, all careless, ''cause you ups an' weds her by then. I sees it in your eye. Then, when she's thar for good, I reckons she nacherally quits comin' over.'

"'Oh, I don't know,' says Texas Thompson, who's takin' in Doc Peets' remark; 'I don't allow Billy's got the nerve to marry this yere Marie. Not but what she's as pretty as an antelope. But think of 'Doby. He jest never would quit chewin' Billy's mane if he goes pullin' off any nuptial ceremonies with his wife's relative that a-way.'

"Billy looks hard as granite at this. He ain't sayin' nothin', but he gets outside of another drink in a way which shows his mind's made up, an' then he goes p'intin' off towards his camp, same as a gent who entertains designs.

"'I offers three to one,' says Cherokee Hall, lookin' after Billy sorter thoughtful that a-way, 'that Billy weds this yere Mexican girl in a week; an' I'll go five hundred dollars even money he gets her before night.'

"'An' no takers,' says Doc Peets, 'for I about thinks you calls the turn.'

"An' that's what happens. In two hours after this impulsive Billy prances out of the Red Light on the heels of Texas

Thompson's remarks about how hostile 'Doby would be if he ever gets Marie, he's done lured her before the *padre* over in Chihuahua, an' the *padre* marries 'em as quick as you could take a runnin'-iron an' burn a brand on a calf.

"Which this is not all. Like they was out to add to the excitement a whole lot, I'm a Mohave if 'Doby an' his wife don't turn loose an' have another infant that same day.

"I never sees a gent get so excited over another gent's game as Billy does over 'Doby's number two. He sends his new wife up to 'Doby's on the run, while he takes Willyum an' comes pirootin' back to the Red Light to brace up. Billy's shore nervous an' needs it.

"'My pore child,' says Billy to Willyum about the third drink—Willyum is settin' on a montetable an' payin' heed to Billy a heap decorous an' respectful for a three-year-old—'my pore child,' says Billy that a-way, 'you-all is ag'in a hard game up at your paw's. This yere is playin' it plumb low on you, Willyum. It looks like they fills a hand ag'in you, son, an' you ain't in it no more at 'Doby's; who, whatever is your fool claims on that p'int a year ago, is still your dad ondoubted. But you-all knows me, Willyum. You knows that talk in Holy Writ. If your father an' mother shakes you, your Uncle Billy takes you up. I'm powerful 'fraid, Willyum, you'll have to have action on them promises.'

"Willyum listens to Billy plenty grave an' owly, but he don't make no observations on his luck or communicate no views to Billy except that he's hungry. This yere ain't relevant none, but Billy at once pastures him out on a can of sardines an' some crackers, while he keeps on bein' liberal to himse'l about whiskey.

"'I don't feel like denyin' myse'f nothin', 'he says. 'Yere I gets married, an' in less'n an hour my wife is ravaged away at the whoop of dooty to ride herd on another gent's fam'ly; leavin' me, her husband, with that other gent's aban-

doned progeny on my hands. This yere's gettin' to be a
boggy ford for Billy Rudd, you bet.'

"But while Billy takes on a heap, he don't impress me
like he's hurt none after all. When Doc Peets trails in from
'Doby's, where he's been in the interests of science that a-
way, Billy at once drug him aside for a pow-wow. They
talks over in one corner of the Red Light awhile, then Billy
looks up like one load's offen his mind, an' yells:

"'Barkeep, it's another boy. Use my name freely in urgin'
drinks on the camp.'

"Then Billy goes on whisperin' to Doc Peets an' layin'
down somethin', like his heart's sot on it. At last Doc says:

"'The best way, Billy, is for me to bring 'Doby over.'
With this Doc Peets gets onto his pony at the door an' goes
curvin' back to 'Doby's.

"'It's a boy,' says Billy to the rest of us after Doc Peets
lines out, 'an' child an' mother both on velvet an' winnin'
right along.'

"These yere events crowdin' each other that a-way—first
a weddin' an' then an infant boy—has a brightenin' effect
on public sperit. It makes us feel like the camp's shorely
gettin' a start. While we-alls is givin' way to Billy's desire
to buy whiskey, Peets comes back, bringin' 'Doby.

"Thar's nothin' what you-alls calls dramatic about 'Doby
an' Billy comin' together. They meets an' shakes, that's all.
They takes a drink together, which shows they's out to be
friends for good, an' then Billy says:

"'But what I wants partic'lar, 'Doby, is that you makes
over to me your son Willyum. He's shore the finest young-
one in Arizona, an' Marie an' me needs him to sorter organize on.'

"'Billy,' says 'Doby, 'you-all an' me is partners for years,
an' we're partners yet. We has our storm cloud, an' we has
also our eras of peace. Standin' as we do on the brink of
one of said eras, an' as showin' sincerity, I yereby commits

to you my son Willyum. Yereafter, when he calls you
"Pop," it goes, an' the same will not be took invidious.'

"'Doby,' replies Billy, takin' him by the hand, 'this yere
day 'lustrates the prophet when he says: "In the midst of life
we're in luck." If you-all notes tears in my eyes I'm responsible for 'em. Willyum's mine. As I r'ars him it will be with
you as a model. Now you go back where dooty calls you.
When you ceases to need my wife, Marie, send her back to
camp, an' notify me tharof. Pendin' of which said notice,
however,' concloods Billy, turnin' to us after 'Doby starts
back, 'Willyum an' me entertains.'"

9

Bill Hoskins's Coon.

"**N**OW I thoroughly saveys," remarked the Old Cattle-man reflectively, at a crisis in our conversation when the talk turned on men of small and cowardly measure, "I thoroughly saveys that taste for battle that lurks in the deefiles of folk's nacher like a wolf in the hills. Which I reckons now that I myse'f, is one of the peacefullest people as ever belts on a weepon; but in my instincts—while I never jestifies or follows his example—I cl'arly apprehends the emotions of a gent who convenes with another gent all sim'lar, an' expresses his views with his gun. Sech is human nacher onrestrained, an' the same, while deplorable, is not s'prisen'.

"But this yere Olson I has in my mem'ry don't have no sech manly feelin's as goes with a gun play. Olson is that cowardly he's even furtive; an' for a low-flung measly game let me tell you-all what Olson does. It's shorely ornery.

"It all arises years ago, back in Tennessee, an' gets its first start out of a hawg which is owned by Olson an' is downed by a gent named Hoskins—Bill Hoskins. It's this a-way.

"Back in Tennessee in my dream-wreathed yooth, when livestock goes projectin' about permiscus, a party has to build his fences 'bull strong, hawg tight, an' hoss high,' or he takes results. Which Hoskins don't make his fences to conform to this yere rool none; leastwise they ain't hawg tight as is shown by one of Olson's hawgs.

"The hawg comes pirootin' about Hoskins's fence, an' he

93

goes through easy; an' the way that invadin' animal turns Bill's potatoes bottom up don't hinder him a bit. He shorely loots Bill's lot; that's whatever.

But Bill, perceivin' of Olson's layin' waste his crop, reaches down a 8-squar' rifle, 30 to the pound, an' stretches the hawg. Which this is where Bill falls into error. Layin' aside them deeficiencies in Bill's fence, it's cl'ar at a glance a hawg can't be held responsible. Hawgs is ignorant an' tharfore innocent; an' while hawgs can be what Doc Peets calls a 'casus belli,' they can't be regarded as a foe legitimate.

"Now what Bill oughter done, if he feels like this yere hawg's done put it all over him, is to go an' lay for Olson. Sech action by Bill would have been some excessive, — some high so to speak; but it would have been a line shot. Whereas killin' the hawg is 'way to one side of the mark; an' onder.

"However, as I states, Bill bein' hasty that a-way, an' oncapable of perhaps refined reasonin', downs the pig, an' stands pat, waitin' for Olson to fill his hand, if he feels so moved.

"It's at this pinch where the cowardly nacher of this yere Olson begins to shine. He's ugly as a wolf about Bill copperin' his hawg that a-way, but he don't pack the nerve to go after Bill an' make a round-up of them grievances. An' he ain't allowin' to pass it up none onrevenged neither. Now yere's what Olson does; he 'sassinates Bill's pet raccoon.

"That's right, son, jest massacres a pore, confidin' raccoon, who don't no more stand in on that hawg-killin' of Bill's, than me an' you, —don't even advise it.

"Which I shorely allows you saveys all thar is to know about a raccoon. No? Well, a raccoon's like this: In the first place he's plumb easy, an' ain't lookin' for no gent to hold out kyards or ring a cold deck on him. That's straight; a raccoon is simple-minded that a-way; an' his impressive trait is, he's meditative. Besides bein' nacherally thoughtful, a raccoon is a heap melancholy, —he jest sets thar an' absorbs melancholy from merely bein' alive.

"But if a raccoon is melancholy or gets wropped in thought that a-way, it's after all his own play. It's to his credit that once when he's tamed, he's got mountainous confidence in men, an' will curl up to sleep where you be an' shet both eyes. He's plumb trustful; an' moreover, no matter how mournful a raccoon feels, or how plumb melancholy he gets, he don't pester you with no yarns.

"I reckons I converses with this yere identical raccoon of Bill's plenty frequent; when he feels blue, an' ag'in when he's at his gailiest, an' he never remarks nothin' to me except p'lite general'ties.

If this yere Olson was a dead game party who regards himse'f wronged, he'd searched out a gun, or a knife, or mebby a club, an' pranced over an' rectified Bill a whole lot. But he's too timid an' too cowardly, an' afraid of Bill. So to play even, he lines out to bushwhack this he'pless, oninstructed raccoon. Olson figgers to take advantage of what's cl'arly a loop-hole in a raccoon's constitootion.

"Mebby you never notices it about a raccoon, but once he gets interested in a pursoot, he's rigged so he can't quit none ontil the project's a success. Thar's herds an' bands of folks an' animals who's fixed sim'lar. They can start, an' they can't let up. Thar's bull-dogs: They begins a war too easy; but the c'pacity to quit is left out of bull-dogs entire. Same about nose-paint with gents I knows. They capers up to whiskey at the begginnin like a kitten to warm milk; an they never does cease no more. An' that's how the kyards falls to raccoons.

"Knowin' these yere deefects in raccoons, this Olson plots to take advantage tharof; an' by playin' it low on Bill's raccoon, get even with Bill about the dead hawg. Which Bill wouldn't have took a drove of hawgs; no indeed! not the whole Fall round-up of hawgs in all of West Tennessee, an' lose that raccoon.

"It's when Bill's over to Pine Knot layin' in tobacker, an' nose-paint an' corn meal, an' sech necessaries, when Olson stands in to down Bill's pet. He goes injunnin' over to Bill's an' finds the camp all deserted, except the raccoon's thar, settin', battin' his eyes mournful an' lonesome on the doorstep. This Olson camps down by the door an' fondles the raccoon, an' strokes his coat, an' lets him search his pockets with his black hands ontil he gets that friendly an' confident about Olson he'd told him anythin'. It's then this yere miscreant, Olson, springs his game.

"He's got a couple of crawfish which he's fresh caught at the Branch. Now raccoons regards crawfish as onusual good eatin'. For myse'f, I can't say I deems none high of craw-fish as viands, but raccoons is different; an' the way they looks at it, crawfish is pie.

"This Olson brings out his two crawfish an' fetchin' a jar of water from the spring, he drops in a crawfish an' incites an' aggravates Zekiel—that's the name of Bill's raccoon—to feel in an' get him a whole lot.

"Zekiel ain't none shy on the play. He knows crawfish like a gambler does a red chip; so turnin' his eyes up to the sky, like a raccoon does who's wropped in pleasant anticipa-tions that a-way, he plunges in his paw an' gets it.

"Once Zekiel acquires him, the pore crawfish don't last as long as two-bits at faro-bank. When Zekiel has him plumb devoured he turns his eyes on Olson, sorter thankful, an' 'waits developments.

"Olson puts in the second crawfish, an' Zekiel takes him into camp same as t'other. It's now that Olson onfurls his plot on Zekiel. Olson drops a dozen buckshot into the jar of water. Nacherally, Zekiel, who's got his mind all framed up touchin' crawfish, goes after the buckshot with his fore foot. But it's differenct with buckshot; Zekiel can't pick 'em up.

He tries an' tries with his honest, simple face turned up to heaven, but he can't make it. All Zekiel can do is feel 'em with his foot, an' roll 'em about on the bottom of the jar.

"Now as I remarks prior, when a raccoon gets embarked that a-way, he can't quit. He ain't arranged so he can cease. Olson, who's plumb aware tharof, no sooner gets Zekiel started on them buckshot, than knowin' that nacher can be relied on to play her hand out, he sa'nters off to his wick-eyup, leavin' Zekiel to his fate. Bill won't be home till Monday, an' Olson knows that before then, onless Zekiel is interrupted, he'll be even for that hawg Bill drops. As Olson comes to a place in the trail where he's goin' to lose sight of Bill's camp, he turns an' looks back. The picture is all his revenge can ask. Thar sets Zekiel on the doorstep, with his happy countenance turned up to the dome above an' feelin' them buckshot 'round, an' allowin' he's due to ketch a crawfish every moment.

"Which it works out exactly as the wretched Olson figgers. The sun goes down, an' the Sunday sun comes up an' sets ag'in; an' still pore Zekiel is planted by the jar, with his hopeful eyes on high, still feelin' of them buckshot. He can't quit no more'n if he's loser in a poker game; Zekiel can't. When Bill rides up to his door about second-drink time Monday afternoon, Olson is shorely even on that hawg. Thar lays Zekiel, dead. He's jest set thar with them buckshot an' felt himse'f to death.

"But speakin' of the sapiency of Bill Hoskins's Zekiel," continued the old gentleman as we lighted pipes and lapsed into desultory puffing, "while Zekiel for a raccoon is some deep, after all you-all is jest amazed at Zekiel 'cause I calls your attention to him a whole lot. If you was to go into camp with 'em, an' set down an' watch 'em you'd shorely be s'prised to note how level-headed all animals be.

"Now if thar's anythin' in Arizona for whose jedgement I don't have respect nacheral, it's birds. Arizona for sech folks as you an' me, an' coyotes an' jack-rabbits, is a good range. Sech as we-alls sorter fits into the general play an' gets action for our stacks. But whatever a bird can find entrancin' in some of them Southwestern deserts is allers too many for me.

"As I su'gests, I former holds fowls, who of free choice continues a residence in Arizona, as imbeciles. Yet now an' then I observes things that makes me oncertain if I'm onto a bird's system; an' if after all Arizona is sech a dead kyard for birds. It's possible a gent might be 'way off on birds an' the views they holds of life. He might watch the play an' esteem 'em loser, when from a bird's p'int of view they's makin' a killin', an' even callin' the turn every deal.

"What he'ps to open my eyes a lot on birds is two Road Runners Doc Peets an' me meets up with one afternoon comin' down from Lordsburg. These yere Road Runners is a lanky kind of prop'sition, jest a shade off from spring chickens for size. Which their arrangements as to neck an' laigs is onrestricted an' liberal, an' their long suit is runnin' up an' down the sun-baked trails of Arizona with no object. Where he's partic'lar strong, this yere Road Runner, is in waitin' ontil some gent comes along, same as Doc Peets an' me that time, an' then attachin' of himse'f to said cavalcade an' racin' along ahead. A Road Runner keeps up this exercise for miles, an' be about the length of a lariat ahead of your pony's nose all the time. When you-all lets out a link or two an' stiffens your pony with the spur, the Road Runner onbuckles sim'lar an' exults tharat. You ain't goin' to run up on him while he can wave a laig, you can gamble your last chip, an' you confers favors on him by sendin' your pony at him. Thar he stays, rackin' along ahead of you ontil satiated. Usual thar's two Road Runners, an' they clips it along side by side as if thar's somethin' in it for 'em; an' I reckons, rightly saveyed, thar is. However, the profits to Road Runners of them excursions ain't obvious,

none whatever; so I won't try to set 'em forth. Them journeys they makes up an' down the trail shore seems aimless
to me.

"But about Doc Peets an' me pullin' out from Lordsburg
for Wolfville that evenin': Our ponies is puttin' the landscape behind 'em at a good road-gait when we notes a brace
of them Road Runners with wings half lifted, pacin' to
match our speed along the trail in front. As Road Runners
is frequent with us, our minds don't bother with 'em none.
Now an' then Doc an' me can see they converses as they
goes speedin' along a level or down a slope. It's as if one
says to t'other, sometin' like this yere:

"'How's your wind, Bill? Is it comin' easy?'

"'Shore,' it would seem like Bill answers. 'Valves never
is in sech shape. I'm on velvet; how's your laigs standin'
the pace, Jim?'

"'Laigs is workin' like they's new oiled,' Jim replies
back; 'it's a plumb easy game. I reckons, Bill, me an' you
could keep ahead of them mavericks a year if we-alls feels
like it.'

"Bet a blue stack on it,' Bill answers. 'I deems these yere
gents soft. Before I'd ride sech ponies as them, I'd go projectin' 'round some night an' steal one.'

"'Them ponies is shorely a heap slothful' Jim answers.

"At this mebby them Road Runners ruffles their feathers
an' runs on swifter, jest to show what a slow racket keepin'
ahead of me an' Peets is. An' these yere locoed birds keeps
up sech conversations for hours.

"Mind I ain't sayin' that what I tells you is what them
Road Runers really remarks; but I turns it over to you-all the
way it strikes me an' Doc at the time. What I aims to relate,
however, is an incident as sheds light o how wise an' foxy
Road Runners be.

"Doc Peets an' me, as I states, ain't lavishin' no onreasonable notice on these yere birds, an' they've been scat-

terin' along the trail for mebby it's an hour, when one of 'em comes to a plumb halt, sharp. The other stops likewise an' rounds up ag'inst his mate; an' bein' cur'ous to note what's pesterin' 'em, Peets an' me curbs to a stand-still. The Road Runner who stops first—the same bein' Bill—is lookin' sharp an' interested-like over across the plains.

"'Rattlesnake,' he imparts to his side partner.

"'Where's he at?' says the side partner, which is Jim, 'where's this yere snake at, Bill? I don't note no rattle snake.'

"'Come round yere by me,' Bill says. 'Now on a line with the top of yonder mesa an' a leetle to the left of that soap-weed; don't you-all see him quiled up thar asleep?'

"'Which I shorely does,' says Jim, locatin' the rattlesnake with his beady eye, 'an' he's some sunk in slumber. Bill, that serpent is our meat.'

"'Move your moccasins easy,' says Bill, 'so's not to turn him out. Let's rustle up some flat cactuses an' corral him.'

"Tharupon these yere Road Runners turns in mighty dili-gent; an' not makin' no more noise than shadows, they goes pokin' out on the plains ontil they finds a flat cactus which is dead; so they can tear off the leaves with their bills. Doc Peets an' me sets in our saddles surveyin' their play; an' the way them Road Runners goes about the labors of their snake killin' impresses us it ain't the first bootch-ery of the kind they appears in. They shorely don't need no soopervisin'.

"One after the other, Jim an' Bill teeters up, all silent, with a flat cactus leaf in their beaks, an' starts to fence in the rattlesnake with 'em. They builds a corral of cactus all about him, which the same is mebby six-foot across. Them engineerin' feats takes Jim an' Bill twenty minutes. But they completes 'em; an' thar's the rattlesnake, plumb surrounded.

"These yere cactuses, as you most likely saveys, is thorny no limit; an' the spikes is that sharp, needles is futile to 'em. Jim an' Bill knows the rattlesnake can't cross this thorny corral.

"An' it's plain to me an' Peets them Road Runners is aware of said weaknesses of rattlesnakes, an' is bankin' their play tharon. We-alls figgers, lookin' on, that Jim an' Bill aims to put the rattlesnake in prison; leave him captive that a-way in a cactus calaboose. But we don't size up Jim an' Bill accurate at all. Them two fowls is shorely profound.

"No sooner is the corral made, than Jim an' Bill, without a word of warnin', opens up a war-jig 'round the outside; flappin' their pinions an' screechin' like squaws. Nacherally the rattlesnake wakes up. The sight of them two Road Runners, Jim an' Bill, cussin' an' swearin' at him, an' carryin' on that a-way scares him.

"It's trooth to say Bill an' Jim certainly conducts themse'fs scand'lous. The epithets they heaps on that pore ignorant rattlesnake, the taunts they flings at him, would have done Apaches proud.

"The rattlesnake buzzes an' quils up, an' onsheaths his fangs, an' makes bluffs to strike Bill an' Jim, but they only hops an' dances about, thinkin' up more ornery things to say. Every time the rattlesnake goes to crawl away—which he does frequent—he strikes the cactus thorns an' pulls back. By an' by he sees he's elected an' he gets that enraged he swells up till he's big as two snakes; Bill an' Jim maintainin' their sass. Them Road Runners is abreast of the play every minute, you can see that.

"At last comes the finish, an' matters gets dealt down to the turn. The rattlesnake suddenly crooks his neck, he's so plumb locoed with rage an' fear, an' socks his fangs into himse'f. That's the fact; bites hise'f, an' never lets up till he's dead.

"It don't seem to astound Jim an' Bill none when the rattlesnake 'sassinates himse'f that a-way, an' I reckons they has this yere sooicide in view. They keeps pesterin' an' projectin' about ontil the rattlesnake is plumb defunct, an' they emits a whirlwind of new whoops, an' goes over to one side an' pulls off a skelp dance. Jim an' Bill is shorely cel'bra- tin' a vic'try.

"After the skelp dance is over, Bill an' Jim tiptoes over mighty quiet an' sedate, an' Jim takes their prey by the tail an' yanks it. After the rattlesnake's drug out straight, him an' Bill runs their eyes along him like they's sizin' him up. With this yere last, however, it's cl'ar the Road Runners re- gards the deal as closed. They sa'nters off down the trail, arm in arm like, conversin' in low tones so Peets an' me never does hear what they says. When they's in what they takes to be the c'rrect p'sition, they stops an' looks back at me an' Peets. Bill turns to Jim like he's sayin':

"'Thar's them two short-horns ag'in. I wonders if they ever aims to pull their freight, or do they reckon they'll pitch camp right yere?'"

10

Crawfish Jim.

"**D**ON'T I never tell you the story of the death of Crawfish Jim?"

The Old Cattleman bent upon me an eye of benevolent inquiry. I assured him that the details of the taking off of Crawfish Jim were as a sealed book to me. But I would blithely listen.

"What was the fate of Crawfish Jim?" I asked. The name seemed a promise in itself.

"Nothin' much for a fate, Crawfish's ain't," rejoined the Old Cattleman. "Nothin' whatever compared to some fates I keeps tabs onto. It was this a-way: Crawfish Jim was a sheep-man, an' has a camp out in the foothills of the *Tres Hermanas*; mebby it's thirty miles back from Wolfville. This yere Crawfish Jim was a pecooliar person; plumb locoed, like all sheep-men. They has to be crazy or they wouldn't pester 'round in no sech disrepootable pursoots as sheep.

"You-all has seen these yere gents as makes pets of snakes. Mebby it's once in a thousand times you cuts the trail of sech a party. Snakes is kittens to him, an' he's likely to be packin' specimens 'round in his clothes any time.

"That's the way with this Crawfish Jim. I minds talkin' to him at his camp one day when I'm huntin' a bunch of cattle. The first I notes, a snake sticks his head outen Crawfish's shirt, an' looks at me malev'lent and distrustful. Another protroods its nose out up by Crawfish's collar.

"'Which you shore seems ha'nted of snakes?' I says, steppin' back an' p'intin' at the reptiles.

"'Them's my dumb companions,' says Crawfish Jim. 'They shares my solitood.'

"'You-all do seem some pop'lar with 'em,' I observes, for I saveys at once he's plumb off his mental reservation; an' when a party's locoed that a-way it makes him hostile if you derides his little game or bucks his notions.

"I takes grub with Crawfish that same day; good chuck, too; mainly sheep-meat, salt-hoss, an' bakin'-powder biscuit. I watches him some narrow about them snakes he's infested with; I loathin' of 'em, an' not wantin' 'em to transfer no love to me, nor take to enlivenin' my secloosion none.

"Well, son, this yere Crawfish Jim is as a den of serpents. I reckons now he has a plumb dozen mowed away in his raiment. Thar's no harm in 'em; bein' all bull-snakes, which is innocuous an' without p'ison, fangs, or convictions.

"When Crawfish goes to cook, he dumps these folks outen his clothes, an' lets em' hustle an' play 'round while grub's gettin'.

"'These yere little animals,' he says, 'likes their reecreations same as humans, so I allers gives 'em a play-spell while I'm busy round camp.'

"'Don't they ever stampede off none?' I asks.

"'Shorely not,' says Crawfish. 'Bull-snakes is the most domestical snake thar is. If I'd leave one of these yere tender creatures out over night he'd die of homesickness.'

"When Crawfish gets ready to b'ile the coffee, he tumbles the biggest bull-snake I'd seen yet outen the coffee-pot onto the grass. Then he fills the kettle with water, dumps in the coffee, an' sets her on the coals to stew.

"'This yere partic'lar snake,' says Crawfish, 'which I calls him Julius Caesar, is too big to tote 'round in my shirt, an' so he lives in the coffee-pot while I'm away, an' keeps camp for me.'

"'Don't you yearn for no rattlesnakes to fondle?' I inquires, jest to see what kyard he'd play.

"'No,' he says, 'rattlesnakes is all right—good, sociable, moral snakes enough; but in a sperit of humor they may bite you or some play like that, an' thar you'd be. No; bull-snakes is as 'fectionate as rattles, an' don't run to p'ison. You don't have no inadvertencies with 'em.'

"'Can't you bust the fangs outen rattlesnakes?' I asks.

"'They grows right in ag'in,' says Crawfish, 'same as your finger-nails. I ain't got no time to go scoutin' a rattlesnake's mouth every day, lookin' up teeth, so I don't worry with 'em, but plays bull-snakes straight. This bein' dentist for rattlesnakes has resks, which the same would be foolish to assoom.'

"While grub's cookin' an' Crawfish an' me's pow-wowin', a little old dog Crawfish has—one of them no-account fice-dogs—comes up an' makes a small uprisin' off to one side

Crawfish Jim

with Julius Caesar. The dog yelps an' snaps, an' Julius Caesar blows an' strikes at him, same as a rattlesnake. However, they ain't doin' no harm, an' Crawfish don't pay no heed.

"'They's runnin' blazers on each other,' says Crawfish, 'an' don't mean nothin'. Bimeby Caribou Pete—which the same is the dog—will go lie down an' sleep; an' Julius

Caesar will quile up ag'in him to be warm. Caribou, bein'
a dog that a-way, is a warm-blood animal, while pore Julius
has got cold blood like a fish. So he goes over an' camps
on Caribou, an' all the same puts his feet on him for to be
comfortable.'

"Of course, I'm a heap interested in this yere snake knowledge, an' tells Crawfish so. But it sorter coppers my appetite, an' Crawfish saves on sheep-meat an' sow-belly by his
discourse powerful. Thinkin' an' a-lookin' at them blessed
snakes, speshul at Julius Caesar, I shore ain't hungry much.
But as you says: how about Crawfish Jim gettin' killed?

"One day Crawfish allows all alone by himse'f he'll hop
into Wolfville an' buy some stuff for his camp,—flour,
whiskey, tobacker, air-tights, an' sech.

"What's air-tights? Which you Eastern shorthorns is shore
ignorant. Air-tights is can peaches, can tomatters, an'
sim'lar bluffs.

"As I was sayin', along comes poor old Crawfish over to
Wolfville; rides in on a burro. That's right, son; comes
loafin' along on a burro like a Mexican. These yere sheep-
men is that abandoned an' vulgar they ain't got pride to ride
a hoss.

"Along comes Crawfish on a burro, an' it's his first visit
to Wolfville. Yeretofore the old Cimmaron goes over to Red
Dog for his plunder, the same bein' a busted low-down
camp on the Lordsburg trail, which once holds it's a rival
to Wolfville. It ain't, however; the same not bein' of the
same importance, commercial, as a prairie-dog town.

"This time, however, Crawfish p'ints up for Wolfville.
An' to make himse'f loved, I reckons, whatever does he do
but bring along Julius Caesar.

"I don't reckon now he ever plays Julius Caesar none on
Red Dog. Mighty likely this yere was the bull-snake's first
engagement. I clings to this notion that Red Dog never sees
Julius Caesar; for if she had, them drunkards which inhabits

said camp wouldn't have quit yellin' yet. Which Julius
Caesar, with that Red Dog whiskey they was soaked in,
would have shore given 'em some mighty heenous visions.
Fact is, Crawfish told Jack Moore later he never takes Julius
Caesar nowhere before.

"But all the same Crawfish prances into camp on this yere
occasion with Julius bushwacked 'way 'round back in his
shirt, an' sech vacant spaces about his person as ain't otherwise occupied a 'nourishin' of minor bull-snakes plenty
profuse.

"Of course them snakes is all holdin' back, bein', after
all, timid cattle; an' so none of us s'spects Crawfish is packin' any sech s'prises. None of the boys about town knows
of Crawfish havin' this bull-snake habit but me, nohow. So
the old man stampedes 'round an' buys what he's after, an'
all goes well. Nobody ain't even dreamin' of reptiles.

"At last Crawfish, havin' turned his little game for flour,
air-tights, an' jig-juice, as I says, gets into the Red Light,
an' braces up ag'in the bar an' calls for nose-paint all
'round. This yere is proper an' p'lite, an' everybody within
hearin' of the yell lines up.

"It's at this crisis Crawfish Jim starts in to make himse'f
a general fav'rite. Everybody's slopped out his perfoomery,
an' Dan Boggs is jest sayin': 'Yere's lookin' at you, Crawfish,' when that crazy-hoss shepherd sorter swarms 'round
inside his shirt with his hand, an' lugs out Julius Caesar by
the scruff of his neck, a-squirmin' an' a-blowin', an' madder'n a drunken squaw. Once he gets Julius out, he spreads
him 'round profuse on the Red Light bar an' sorter herds
him with his hand to keep him from chargin' off among the
bottles.

"'Gents,' says this locoed Crawfish, 'I ain't no boaster,
but I offers a hundred to fifty, an' stands to make it up to
a thousand dollars in wool or sheep, Julius Caesar is the fattest an' finest serpent in Arizona; also the best behaved.'

"Thar ain't no one takin' Crawfish's bet. The moment he slams Julius on the bar, more'n ten of our leadin' citizens falls to the floor in fits, an' emerges outen one par'xysm only to slump into another. Which we shorely has a general round-up of all sorts of spells.

"'Whatever's the matter of you-all people?' says Crawfish, lookin' mighty aghast. 'Thar's no more harm in Julius Caesar than if he's a full-blown rose.

"Jack Moore, bein' marshal, of course stands his hand. It's his offishul dooty to play a pat hand on bull-snakes an' danger in all an' any forms. An' Jack does it.

"While Crawfish is busy recountin' the attainments of Julius Caesar, a-holdin' of his pet with one hand, Jack Moore takes a snap shot at him along the bar with his six-shooter, an' away goes Julius Caesar's head like a puff of smoke. Then Moore rounds up Crawfish, an', perceivin' of the other bull-snakes, he searches 'em out one by one an' massacres 'em.

"'Call over Doc Peets,' says Jack Moore final, 'an' bring Boggs an' Tutt an' the rest of these yere invalids to.'

"Doc Peets an' Enright both trails in on the lope from the New York Store. They hears Moore's gun-play an' is cur'ous, nacheral 'nough, to know who calls it. Well, they turns in an' brings the other inhabitants outen their fits; pendin' which Moore kills off the last remainin' bull-snake in Crawfish's herd.

"Son, I've seen people mad, an' I've seen 'em gay, an' I've seen 'em bit by grief. But I'm yere to remark I never runs up on a gent who goes plumb mad with sadness ontil I sees Crawfish that day Jack Moore immolates his bull-snake pets. He stands thar, white, an' ain't sayin' a word. Looks for a minute like he can't move. Crawfish don't pack no gun, or I allers allowed we'd had notice of him some, while them bull-snakes is cashin' in.

"But at last he sorter comes to, an' walks out without sayin' nothin'. They ain't none of us regardin' of him much at the time; bein' busy drinkin' an' recoverin' from the shock.

"Now, what do you s'pose this old Navajo does? Lopes straight over to the New York Store—is ca'm as a June day about it, too—an' gets a six-shooter.

"The next information we gets of Crawfish, 'bang!' goes his new gun, an' the bullet cuts along over Jack Moore's head too high for results. New gun that a-way, an' Crawfish not up on his practice; of course he overshoots.

"Well, the pore old murderer never does get a second crack. I reckons eight people he has interested shoots all at once, an' Crawfish Jim quits this earthly deal unanimous. He stops every bullet; eight of 'em, like I says.

"Thar ain't a man of us who don't feel regrets; but what's the use? Thar we be, up ag'inst the deal, with Crawfish clean locoed. It's the only wagon-track out.

"'I shore hopes he's on the hot trail of them bull-snakes of his'n,' says Dan Boggs, as we lays Crawfish out on a monte-table. 'Seems like he thought monstrous well of 'em, an' it would mighty likely please him to run up on 'em where he's gone.

"Whatever did we do? Why, we digs a grave out back of the dance-hall an' plants Crawfish an' his pets tharin.

"'I reckons we better bury them reptiles, too,' says Doc Peets, as we gets Crawfish stretched out all comfortable in the bottom. 'If he's lookin' down on these yere ceremonies it'll make him feel easier.'

"Doc Peets is mighty sentimental an' romantic that a-way, an' allers thinks of the touchin' things to do, which I more'n once notices like-wise, that a gent bein' dead that a-way allers brings out the soft side of Peets's nacher. You bet! he's plumb sympathetic.

"We counts in the snakes. Thar's 'leven of 'em besides Julius Caesar; which we lays him on Crawfish's breast. You can find the grave to-day.

"Shore! we sticks up a headboard. It says on it, the same
bein' furnished by Doc Peets—an' I wants to say Doc Peets
is the best eddicated gent in Arizona—as follows:

> SACRED To the MEMoRY OF
> CRAWFiSh JiM, JuLiuS CAEsAR
> AND
> ELEvEN OtHEr BULL SnAKES
> THEY mEAnT WELL,
> BuT They MISUNDERsTood ExIST-
> ENCE AND DieD.
> THIS BOARD wAS REAREd By AN
> AdMiRInG ciRcLE OF FRieNDS
> wHO WAs wITH DEcEASED
> To THE LAsT.

"An' don't you-all know, son, this yere onfortunate
weedin' out of pore Crawfish that a-way, sorter settles down
on the camp an' preys on us for mighty likely it's a week.
It shorely is a source of gloom. Moreover, it done gives Dan
Boggs the fan-tods. As I relates prior, Boggs is emotional a
whole lot, an' once let him get what you-all calls a shock—
same, for instance, as them bull-snakes—its shore due to set
Boggs's intellects to millin'. An' that's what happens now.
We-alls don't get Boggs bedded down none for ten days, his
visions is that acoote.

"'Which of course,' says Boggs, while we-alls is settin'
up administerin' things to him, 'which of course I'm plumb
aware these yere is mere illoosions; but all the same, as cl'ar
as ever I notes an ace, no matter where I looks at, I discerns
that Julius Caesar serpent a-regardin' me reproachful outen
the atmospher. An' gents, sech spectacles lets me out a heap
every time. You-alls can gamble, I ain't slumberin' none
with no snake-spook that a-way a-gyardin' of my dreams.'

"That's all thar is to the death of Crawfish Jim. Thar ain't no harm in him, nor yet, I reckons, in Julius Caesar an' the rest of Crawfish's fam'ly. But the way they gets tangled up with Wolfville, an' takes to runnin' counter to public sentiment an' them eight six-shooters, Crawfish an' his live-stock has to go."

11

The Grinding
of Dave Tutt.

"YES," said the Old Cattleman, as he took off his sombrero and contemplated the rattlesnake band which environed the crown, "cow-punchers is queer people. They needs a heap of watchin' an' herdin'. I knowed one by the name of Stevenson down on the Turkey Track, as merits plenty of lookin' after. This yere Stevenson ain't exactly ornery; but bein' restless, an' with a disp'sition to be emphatic whenever he's fillin' himse'f up, keepin' your eye on him is good, safe jedgement. He is public-sperited, too, an' sometimes takes lots of pains to please folks an' be pop'lar.

"I recalls once when we're bringin' up a beef herd from the Panhandle country. We're ag'in the south bank of the Arkansaw, tryin' to throw the herd across. Thar's a bridge, but the natifs allows it's plenty weak, so we're makin' the herd swim. Steve is posted at the mouth of the bridge, to turn back any loose cattle that takes a notion to try an' cross that a-way. Thar's nothin' much to engage Steve's faculties, an' he's a-settin' on his bronco, an' both is mighty near asleep. Some women people—from the far East, I reckons—as is camped in town, comes over on the bridge to see us cross the herd. They've lined out clost up to Steve, a-leanin' of their young Eastern chins on the top rail.

"'Which I don't regyard this much,' says one young woman, 'thar's no thrill into it. Whyever don't they do somethin' excitin'?'

"Steve observes with chagrin that this yere lady is dis-

113

pleased; an', as he can't figger nothin' else out quick to entertain her, he gives a whoop, slams his six-shooter off into the scenery, socks his spurs into the pony, an' hops himse'f over the side of the bridge a whole lot into the shallow water below. The jump is some twenty feet an' busts the pony's laigs like toothpicks; also it breaks Steve's collar bone an' disperses his feachers 'round some free an' frightful on account of his sort o' lightin' on his face.

"Well, we shoots the pony: an' Steve rides in the grub wagon four or five days recooperatin'. It's jest the mercy of hell he don't break his neck.

"'Whatever do you jump off for?' I asks Steve when he's comin' 'round.

"'Which I performs said equestrianisms to amoose that she-shorthorn who is cussin' us out,' says Steve. 'I ain't permittin' for her to go back to the States, malignin' of us cow-men.'

"Steve gets himse'f downed a year after, an' strikes out for new ranges in the skies. He's over on the upper Red River when he gets creased. He's settin' into a poker game.

"Steve never oughter gambled none. He is a good cowboy—splendid round-up hand—an' can do his day's work with rope or iron in a brandin' pen with anybody; but comin' right to cases, he don't know no more about playin' poker than he does about preachin'. Actooally, he'd back two pa'r like thar's no record of their bein' beat. This yere, of course, leads to frequent poverty, but it don't confer no wisdom on Steve.

"On this o'casion, when they ships Steve for the realms of light, one of the boys gets a trey-full; Steve being possessed of a heart flush, nine at the head. In two minutes he don't have even his blankets left.

"After he's broke, Steve h'ists in a drink or two an' sours 'round a whole lot; an' jest as the trey-full boy gets into his saddle, Steve comes roamin' along up an' hails him.

"'Pard,' says Steve, a heap gloomy, 'I've been tryin' to school myse'f to b'ar it, but it don't go. Tharfore, I'm yere to say you steals that pa'r of kings as completed my rooin. Comin' to them decisions, I'm goin' to call on you for that bric-a-brack I lose, an' I looks to gain some fav'rable replies.'

"'Oh, you do, do you!' says the trey-full boy. 'Which you-all is a heap too sanguine. Do you reckon I gives up the frootes of a trey-full—as hard a hand to hold as that is? You can go ten to one I won't: not this roundup! Sech requests is preepost'rous!'

"'Don't wax flippant about this yere robbery, says Steve. 'It's enough to be plundered without bein' insulted by gayeties. Now, what I says is this: Either I gets my stuff, or I severs our relations with a gun.' An' tharupon Steve pulls his pistol an' takes hold of the trey-full boy's bridle.

"'If that's one thing makes me more weary than another,' says the trey-full boy, 'it's a gun play; an' to avoid sech exhibitions I freely returns your plunder. But you an' me don't play kyards no more.'

"Whereupon, the trey-full boy gets off his hoss, an' Steve, allowin' the debate is closed, puts up his gun. Steve is preematoor. The next second, 'bang!' goes the trey-full boy's six-shooter, the bullet gets Steve in the neck, with them heavenly results I yeretofore onfolds, an' at first drink time that evenin' we has a hasty but successful fooneral.

"'I don't reckon,' says Wat Peacock, who is range boss, 'thar's need of havin' any law-suits about this yere killin'. I knows Steve for long an' likes him. But I'm yere to announce that them idees he fosters concernin' the valyoo of poker hands, onreasonable an' plumb extrav'gant as they shorely is, absolootely preeclooded Steve's reachin' to old age. An' Steve has warnin's. Once when he tries to get his life insured down in Austin, he's refoosed.

"'"In a five-hand game, table stakes, what is a pair of

aces worth before the draw?" is one of them questions that company asks.

""'Table stakes?" says Steve. "Every chip you've got."

""'That settles it," says the company; "we don't want no sech resk. Thar never is sech recklessness! You won't live a year; you're lucky to be alive right now." An' they declines to insure Steve.'

"However," continued my friend musingly, "I've been puttin' it up to myself, that mighty likely I does wrong to tell you these yere tales. Which you're ignorant of cow folks, an' for me to go onloadin' of sech revelations mebby gives you impressions that's a lot erroneous. Now I reckons from that one eepisode you half figgers cow people is morose an' ferocious as a bunch?"

As the old gentleman gave his tones the inflections of inquiry, I hastened to interpose divers flattering denials. His recitals had inspired an admiration for cow men rather than the reverse.

This setting forth of my approval pleased him. He gave me his word that I in no sort assumed too much in the matter. Cow men, he asserted, were a light-hearted brood; overcheerful, perhaps, at times, and seeking amusement in ways beyond the understanding of the East; but safe, upright, and of splendid generosity. Eager to correct within me any maleffects of the tragedy just told, he recalled the story of a Tucson day of merry relaxation with Dave Tutt. He opined that it furnished a picture of the people of cows in lighter, brighter colors, and so gave me details with a sketchy gladness.

"Which you're acc'rate in them thoughts," he said, referring to my word that I held cow folk to be engaging characters. After elevating his spirit with a clove, he went forward. "Thar ain't much paw an' bellow to a cowboy. Speakin' gen'ral, an' not allowin' for them inflooences which disturbs none—I adverts to mescal an' monte, an' sech abnormalities—he's passive an' easy; no more harm into him than a jack rabbit.

"Of course he has his moods to be merry, an' mebby thar's hours when he's gay to the p'int of over-play. But his heart's as straight as a rifle bar'l every time.

"It's a day I puts in with Dave Tutt which makes what these yere law-sharps calls 'a case in p'int,' an' which I relates without reserve. It gives you some notion of how a cowboy, havin' a leesure hour, onbuckles an' is happy nacheral.

"This yere is prior to Dave weddin' Tucson Jennie. I'm pirootin' 'round Tucson with Dave at the time. Dave's workin' a small bunch of cattle, 'way over near the Cow Springs, an' is in Tucson for a rest. We've been sloshin' 'round the Oriental all day, findin' new virchoos in the whiskey, an' amoosin' ourse'fs at our own expense, when about fifth drink time in the evenin' Dave allows he's some sick of sech revels, an' concloods he'll p'int out among the 'dobys, sort o' explorin' things up a lot. Which we tharupon goes in concert.

"I ain't frothin' at the mouth none to go myse'f, not seein' reelaxation in pokin' about premiscus among a passel of Mexicans, an' me loathin' of 'em from birth; but I goes, aimin' to ride herd on Dave. Which his disp'sition is some free an' various; an' bein' among Mexicans, that a-way, he's liable to mix himse'f into trouble. Not that Dave is bad, none whatever; but bein' seven or eight drinks winner, an' of that Oriental whiskey, too, it broadens him an' makes him feel friendly, an' deloodes him into claimin' acquaintance with people he never does know, an' refoosin' to onderstand how they shows symptoms of doubt. So we capers along; Dave warblin' 'The Death of Sam Bass' in the coyote key.

"The señoras an' señoritas, hearin' the row, would look out an' smile, an' Dave would wave his big hat an' whoop from glee. If he starts toward 'em, aimin' for a powwow—which he does frequent, bein' a mighty amiable gent that a-way—they carols forth a squawk immediate an' shets the door. Dave goes on. Mebby he gives the door a kick or two, a-proclaimin' of his discontent.

"All at once, while we're prowlin' up one of them spacious alleys a Mexican thinks is a street, we comes up on a Eytalian with a music outfit which he's grindin'. This yere music ain't so bad, an' I hears a heap worse strains. As soon as Dave sees him he tries to figger on a dance, but the 'local talent' declines to dance with him.

"'In which event,' says Dave, 'I plays a lone hand.'

"So Dave puts up a small dance, like a Navajo, accompanyin' of himse'f with outcries same as a Injun. But the Eytalian don't play Dave's kind of music, an' the *baile* comes to a halt.

"'Whatever is the matter with this yere tunebox, anyhow?' says Dave. 'Gimme the music for a green-corn dance, an' don't make no delay.'

"'This yere gent can't play no green-corn dance,' I says.

"'He can't, can't he?' says Dave; 'wait till he ropes at it once. I knows this gent of yore. I meets him two years ago in El Paso; which me an' him shorely shakes up that village.'

"'Whatever is his name, then?' I asks.

"'Antonio Marino,' says the Eytalian.

"'Merino?' says Dave; 'that's right. I recalls it, 'cause it makes me think at the jump he's a sheep man, an' I gets plumb hostile.'

"'I never sees you,' says the Eytalian.

"'Yes you do,' says Dave; 'you jest think you didn't see me. We drinks together, an' goes out an' shoots up the camp, arm an' arm.'

"But the Eytalian insists he never meets Dave. This makes Dave ugly a lot, an' before I gets to butt in an' stop it, he outs with his six-shooter, an' puts a hole into the music-box.

"'These yere tunes I hears so far,' says Dave, 'is too frivolous; I figgers that oughter sober 'em down a whole lot.'

"When Dave shoots, the Eytalian party heaves the strap of his hewgag over his head, an' flies. Dave grabs the music-box, keepin' it from fallin', an' then begins turnin' the crank to try it. It plays all right, only every now an' then thar's a hole into the melody like it's lost a tooth.

"'This yere's good enough for a dog!' says Dave, a-twist-in' away on the handle. 'Where's this yere Merino? What-ever is the matter with that shorthorn? Why don't he stand his hand?'

"But Merino ain't noomerous no more; so Dave allows it's a shame to let it go that a-way, an' Mexicans sufferin' for melody. With that he straps on the tune-box, an' roams 'round from one 'doby to another, turnin' it loose.

"'How long does Merino deal his tunes,' says Dave, 'before he c'llects? However, I makes new rooles for the game, right yere. I plays these cadences five minutes; an' then I gets action on 'em for five. I splits even with these Mexi-cans, which is shorely fair.'

"So Dave twists away for five minutes, an' me a-timin' of him, an' then leans the hewgag up ag'in a 'doby, an' starts in to make a round-up. He'll tackle a household, sort o' terrorisin' at 'em with his gun'; an' tharupon the members gets that generous they even negotiates loans an' thrusts them proceeds on Dave. That's right; they're that ambitious to donate.

"One time he runs up on a band of tenderfeet, who's skal-lyhootin' 'round; an' they comes up an' bends their y'ears a-while. They're turnin' to go jest before c'llectin' time.

"'Hold on,' says Dave, pickin' up his Colt's offen the top of the hewgag; 'don't get cold feet. Which I've seen people turn that kyard in church, but you bet you don't jump no game of mine that a-way. You-all line up ag'in the wall thar ontil I tucks the blankets in on this yere outbreak in F flat, an' I'll be with you.'

"When Dave winds up, he goes along the line of them tremblin' towerists, an' they contreebutes 'leven dollars.

"'They aims to go stampedin' off with them nocturnes, an' 'peggios, an' arias, an' never say nothin',' says Dave; 'but they can't work no twist like that, an' me a-ridin' herd; none whatever.'

"Dave carries on sim'lar for three hours; an' what on splits, an' what on bets he wins, he's over a hundred dollars ahead. But at last he's plumb fatigued, an' allows he'll quit an' call it a day. So he packs the tom-tom down to Franklin's office. Franklin is marshal of Tucson, an' Dave turns over the layout an' the money, an' tells Franklin to round up Merino an' enrich him tharwith.

"'Where is this yere Dago?' says Franklin.

"'However do I know?' says Dave. 'Last I notes of him, he's canterin' off among the scenery like antelopes.'

"It's at this p'int Merino comes to view. He starts in to be a heap dejected about that bullet; but when he gets Dave's donation that a-way, his hopes revives. He begins to regyard it as a heap good scheme.

"'But you'll have to cirkle up to the alcalde, Tutt,' says Franklin. 'I ain't shore none you ain't been breakin' some law.'

"Dave grumbles, an' allows Tucson is gettin' a heap too staid for him.

"'It's gettin' so,' says Dave, 'a free American citizen don't obtain no encouragements. Yere I puts in half a day, amassin' wealth for a foreign gent who is settin' in bad luck; an' elevatin' Mexicans, who shorely needs it, an' for a finish I'm laid for by the marshal like a felon.'

"Well, we-all goes surgin' over to the alcalde's. Franklin, Dave an' the alcalde does a heap of pokin' about to see whatever crimes, if any, Dave's done. Which they gets by the capture of the hewgag, an' shootin' that bullet into its bowels don't bother 'em a bit. Even Dave's standin' up them towerists, an' the rapine that ensoos don't worry 'em none; but the question of the music itse'f sets the alcalde to buckin'.

"'I'm shorely depressed to say it, Dave,' says the alcalde, who is a sport named Steele, 'but you've been a-bustin' of ord'nances about playin' music on the street without no license.'

"'Can't we-all beat the game no way?' says Dave.

"'Which I shorely don't see how,' says the alcalde.

"'Nor me neither, says Franklin.

"'Whatever is the matter with counter-brandin' tunes over to Merino's license?' says Dave.

"'Can't do it nohow,' says the alcalde.

"'Well, is this yere ord'nance accordin' to Hoyle an' the Declaration of Independence?' says Dave. 'I don't stand it none onless.'

"'Shore!' says the alcalde.

"'Ante an' pass the buck, then,' says Dave. 'I'm a law-abidin' citizen, an' all I wants is a squar' deal from the warm deck.'

"So they fines Dave fifty dollars for playin' them harmonies without no license. Dave asks me later not to mention this yere outcome in Wolfville, an' I never does. But yere it's different."

12

The Feud of Pickles.

"THAR'S a big crowd in Wolfville that June day."
The Old Cattleman tilted his chair back and challenged my interest with his eye. "The corrals is full of pack mules an' bull teams an' wagon-trains; an' white men, Mexicans, half-breeds an' Injuns is a-mixin' an' meanderin' 'round, a-lyin' an' a-laughin' an' a-drinkin' of Red Light whiskey mighty profuse. Four or five mule skinners has their long limber sixteen-foot whips, which is loaded with dustshot from butt to top, an' is crackin' of 'em at a mark. I've seen one of these yere mule experts with the most easy, delicate, delib'rate twist of the wrist make his whip squirm in the air like a hurt snake; an' then he'll straighten it out with the crack of twenty rifles, an' the buckskin popper cuts a hole in a loose buffalo robe he's hung up; an' all without investin' two ounces of actooal strength. Several of us Wolfville gents is on the sidewalk in front of the O. K. Res tauraw, applaudin' of the good shots, when Dave Tutt speaks up to Jack Moore, next to me, an' says:

"'Jack, you minds that old Navajo you downs over on the San Simon last Fall?'

"'I minds him mighty cl'ar,' says Jack. 'He's stealin' my Alizan hoss at the time, an' I can prove it by his skelp on my bridle now.'

"'Well,' says Dave, p'intin' to a ornery, saddle-colored half-breed who's makin' himse'f some frequent, 'that Injun they calls "Pickles" is his nephy, an' you wants to look out a whole lot. I hears him allow that the killin' of his relatif is mighty rank, an' that he don't like it nohow.'

"'That's all right,' says Jack; 'Pickles an' me has been keepin' cases on each other an hour; an' I'll post you-all private, if he goes to play hoss a little bit, him an' his oncle will be able to talk things over before night.'

"Which it's mighty soon when Pickles comes along where we be.

"'Hello, Jack,' he says, an' his manner is insultin'; 'been makin' it smoky down on the old San Simon lately?'

"'No; not since last fall,' says Jack, plenty light an' free; 'an' now I thinks of it, I b'lieves I sees that Navajo hoss-thief of an oncle of yours when I'm down thar last. I ain't run up on him none lately, though. Where do you all reckon he's done 'loped to?'

"'Can't say, myse'f,' says Pickles, with a kind o' wicked cheefulness; 'our fam'ly has a round-up of itse'f over on B'ar Creek last spring, an' I don't count his nose among 'em none. Mebby he has an engagement, an' can't get thar. Mebby he's out squanderin' 'round in the high grass some'ers. Great man to go 'round permiscus, that Injun is.'

"'You see,' says Jack, 'I don't know but he might be dead. Which the time I speaks of, I'm settin' in camp one day. Something attracts me, an' I happens to look up, an, thar's my hoss, Alizan, with a perfect stranger on him; pitchin' an' buckin', an' it looks like he's goin' to cripple that stranger shore. Pickles, you knows me! I'd lose two hosses rather than have a gent I don't know none get hurt. So I grabs my Winchester an' allows to kill Alizan. But it's a new gun; an' you know what new sights is—coarse as sandburrs; you could drag a dog through 'em—an' I holds too high. I fetches the stranger, "bang!" right back of his left y'ear, an' the bullet comes outen his right y'ear. You can bet the limit, I never am so displeased with my shootin'. The idee of me holdin' four foot too high in a hundred yards! I never is that embarrassed! I'm so plumb disgusted an' ashamed, I don't go near that equestrian stranger till after I finishes my grub. Alizan, he comes up all shiverin' an' sweatin' an' stands thar; an' mebby in a hour or so I strolls out to the deceased. I shorely wearies me a whole lot when I sees him; he's nothin' but a common Digger buck. You can drink on it if I ain't relieved. Bein' a no-account Injun, of course, I don't paw him over much for brands; but do you know, Pickles, from the casooal glance I gives, it strikes me at the time it's mighty likely to be your oncle. This old bronco fancier's skelp is over on my bridle, if you thinks you'd know it.'

"'No,' says Pickles, mighty onconcerned, 'it can't be my oncle nohow. If he's one of my fam'ly, it would be your ha'r on his bridle. It must be some old shorthorn of a Mohave you downs. Let's all take a drink on it.'

"'So we-all goes weavin' over to the Red Light, Jack an' Pickles surveyin' each other close an' interested, that a-way, an' the rest of us on the quee vee, to go swarmin' out of range if they takes to shootin'.

"'It's shore sad to part with friends,' says Pickles, as he secretes his nose-paint, 'but jest the same I must saddle an' stampede out of yere. I wants to see that old villyun, Tom Cooke, an' I don't reckon none I'll find him any this side of Prescott, neither. Be you thinkin' of leavin' camp yourse'f Jack?'

"'I don't put it up I'll leave for a long time,' says Jack. 'Mebby not for a month—mebby it's even years before I go wanderin' off—so don't go to makin' no friendly, quiet waits for me nowhere along the route, Pickles, 'cause you'd most likely run out of water or chuck or something before ever I trails up.'

"It ain't long when Pickles saddles up an' comes chargin' 'round on his little buckskin hoss. Pickles takes to cuttin' all manner of tricks, reachin' for things on the ground, snatch-in' off Mexicans' hats, an' jumpin' his pony over wagon tongues an' camp fixin's. All the time he's whoopin' an yellin' an' carryin' on, an havin' a high time all by himse'f. Which you can see he's gettin' up his blood an' nerve, reg'lar Injun fashion.

"Next he takes down his rope an' goes to whirlin' that. Two or three times he comes flashin' by where we be, an' I looks to see him make a try at Jack. But he's too far back, or thar's too many 'round Jack, or Pickles can't get the distance, or something; for he don't throw it none, but jest keeps yellin' an' ridin' louder an' faster. Pickles shorely puts up a heap or riot that a-way! It's now that Enright calls to Pickles.

"'Look yere, Pickles,' he says, 'I've passed the word to the five best guns in camp to curl you up if you pitch that rope once. Bein' as the news concerns you, personal, I allows it's nothin' more'n friendly to tell you. Then ag'in, I don't like to lose the Red Light sech a customer like you till it's a plumb case of crowd.'

"When Enright vouchsafes this warnin', Pickles swings down an' leaves his pony standin', an' comes over.

"'Do you know, Jack,' he says, 'I don't like the onrespectful tones wherein you talks of Injuns. I'm Injun, part, myse'f, an' I don't like it.'

"'No?' says Jack; 'I s'pose that's a fact, too. An' yet, Pickles, not intendin' nothin' personal, for I wouldn't be personal with a prairie dog, I'm not only onrespectful of Injuns, an' thinks the gov'ment ought to pay a bounty for their skelps, but I states beliefs that a hoss-stealin', skulkin' mongrel of a half-breed is lower yet; I holdin' he ain't even people—ain't nothin', in fact. But to change the subjeck, as well as open an avenoo for another round of drinks, I'll gamble, Pickles, that you-all stole that hoss down thar, an' that the "7K" brand on his shoulder ain't no brand at all, but picked on with the p'int of a knife.'

"When Jack puts it all over Pickles that a-way, we looks for shootin' shore. But Pickles can't steady himse'f on the call. He's like ponies I've met. He'll ride right at a thing as though he's goin' plumb through or over, an' at the last second he quits an' flinches an' weakens. Son, it ain't Pickles' fault. Thar ain't no breed of gent but the pure white who can play a desp'rate deal down through, an' call the turn for life or death at the close; an' Pickles, that a-way, is only half white. So he laughs sort o' ugly at jack's bluff, an' allows he orders drinks without no wagers.

"'An' then, Jack,' he says, 'I wants you to come feed with me. I'll have Missis Rucker burn us up something right.'

"'I'll go you,' says Jack, 'if it ain't nothin' but salt hoss.'

"'I'll fix you-all folks up a feed,' says Missis Rucker, a heap grim, 'but you don't do no banquetin' in no dinin' room of mine. I'll spread your grub in the camp-house, t'other side the corral, an' you-all can then be as sociable an' smoky as you please. Which you'll be alone over thar, an' can conduct the reepast in any fashion to suit yourse'fs. But you don't get into the dinin' room reg'lar, an' go to weedin' out my boarders accidental, with them feuds of yours.'

"After a little, their grub's got ready in the camp house. It's a jo-darter of a feed, with cake, pie, airtights, an' the full game, an' Jack an' Pickles walks over side an' side. They goes in alone an' shets the door. In about five minutes, thar's some emphatic remarks by two six-shooters, an' we-all goes chargin' to find out. We discovers Jack eatin' away all right; Pickles is the other side, with his head in his tin plate, his intellects runnin' out over his eye. Jack's shor subdooed that savage for all time.

"'It don't look like Pickles is hungry none,' says Jack.

"They both pulls their weepons as they sets down, an' puts 'em in their laps; but bein' bred across, that a-way,

Pickles can't stand the strain. He gets nervous an' grabs for his gun; the muzzle catches onder the table-top, an' thar's his bullet all safe in the wood. Jack, bein' clean strain American, has better luck, an' Pickles is got. Shore, it's right an' on the squar'!

"'You sees,' says Dan Boggs, 'this killin's bound to be right from the jump. It comes off by Pickles' earnest desire; Jack couldn't refoose. He would have lost both skelp an' standin' if he had. Which, however, if this yere 'limination of Pickles has got to have a name, my idee is to call her a case of self-deestruction on Pickles' part, an' let it go at that.'"

13

Johnny Florer's Axle Grease.

I T was the afternoon—cool and beautiful. I had been nurs-
ing my indolence with a cigar and one of the large arm-
chairs which the veranda of the great hotel afforded. Now
and then I considered within myself as to the whereabouts
of my Old Cattleman, and was in a half humor to hunt him
up. Just as my thoughts were hardening into decision in that
behalf, a high, wavering note, evidently meant for song,
came floating around the corner of the house, from the veranda on the end. The singer was out of range of eye, but I
knew him for my aged friend. Thus he gave forth:

> "Dogville, Dogville!
> A tavern an' a still,
> That's all thar is in all Dog-ville."

"How do you feel to-day?" I asked as I took a chair near
the venerable musician. "Happy and healthy, I trust?"

"Never feels better in my life," responded the Old Cattleman. "If I was to feel any better, I'd shorely go an' see a
doctor."

"You are a singer, I observe."

"I'm melodious nacheral, but I'm gettin' so I sort o'
stumbles in my notes. Shoutin' an' singin' 'round a passel
of cattle to keep 'em from stampedin' on bad nights has
sp'iled my voice, that a-way. Thar's nothin' so weakenin',
vocal, as them efforts in the open air an' in the midst of
the storms an' the elements. What for a song is that I'm

renderin'? Son, I learns that ballad long ago, back when
I'm a boy in old Tennessee. It's writ, word and music, by
little Mollie Hines, who lives with her pap, old Homer
Hines, over on the 'Possum Trot. Mollie Hines is shore a
poet, an' has a mighty sight of fame, local. She's what
you-all might call a jo-darter of a poet, Mollie is; an' let
anythin' touchin' or romantic happen anywhere along the
'Possum Trot, so as to give her a subjeck, an' Mollie
would be down on it, instanter, like a fallin' star. She
shorely is a verse maker, an' is known in the Cumberland
country as 'The Nightingale of Big Bone Lick.' I remembers when a Shylock over to the Dudleytown bank fore-
closes a mortgage on old Homer Hines, an' offers his settlements at public vandue that a-way, how Mollie prances
out an' pours a poem into the miscreant. Thar's a hundred
an' 'leven verses into it, an' each one like a bullet outen
a Winchester. It goes like this:

"Thar's a word to be uttered to the rich man in his pride.
(Which a gent is frequent richest when it's jest before he died!)
Thar's a word to be uttered to the hawg a-eatin' truck.
(Which a hawg is frequent fattest when it's jest before he's stuck!)

   "Mighty sperited epick, that! You recalls that English
preacher sharp that comes squanderin' 'round the tavern yere
for his health about a month ago? Shore! I knows you
couldn't have overlooked no bet like that divine. Well, that
night in them parlors, when he reads some rhymes in a
book, —whatever is that piece he reads? Locksley Hall;
right you be, son! As I was sayin', when he's through renderin' said Locksley Hall, he comes buttin' into a talk with
me where I'm camped in a corner all cosy as a toad onder
a cabbage leaf, reecoverin' myse'f with licker from them recitals of his, an' he says to me, this parson party does:
   "'Which it's shorely a set-back America has no poets,'
says he.

"'It's evident,' I says, 'that you never hears of Mollie Hines.'

"'No, never once,' he replies; 'is this yere Miss Hines a poet?'

"'Is Mollie Hines a poet!' I repeats, for my scorn at the mere idee kind o' stiffens its knees an' takes to buckin' some. 'Mollie Hines could make that Locksley Hall gent you was readin' from, or even the party who writes Watt's Hymns, go to the diskyard.' An' then I repeats some forty of them stanzas, whereof that one I jest now recites is a speciment.

"What does this pulpit gent say? He see I has him cinched, an' he's plumb mute. He confines himse'f to turnin' up his nose in disgust like Bill Storey does when his father-in-law horsewhips him."

Following this, the Old Cattleman and I wrapped ourselves in thoughtful smoke, for the space of five minutes, as ones who pondered the genius of "The Nightingale of Big Bone Lick"—Mollie Hines on the banks of the 'Possum Trot. At last my friend broke forth with a question.

"Whoever is them far-off folks you-all was tellin' me is related to Injuns?"

"The Japanese," I replied. "Undoubtedly the Indians and the Japanese are of the same stock."

"Which I'm foaled like a mule," said the old gentleman, "a complete prey to inborn notions ag'in Injuns. I wouldn't have one pesterin' 'round me more'n I'd eat offen the same plate with a snake. I shore has aversions to 'em a whole lot. Of course, I never sees them Japs, but I saveys Injuns from feathers to moccasins, an' comparin' Japs to Injuns, I feels about 'em like old Bill Rawlins says about his brother Jim's wife."

"And how was that?" I asked.

The afternoon was lazy and good, and I in a mood to listen to my rambling grey comrade talk of anybody or anything.

"It's this a-way," he began. "This yere Bill an' Jim Rawlins is brothers an' abides in Roanoke, Virginny. They splits up in their yooth, an' Jim goes p'intin' out for the West. Which he shore gets thar, an' nothin' is heard of him for forty years.

"Bill Rawlins, back in Roanoke, waxes a heap rich, an' at last cleans up his game an' resolves he takes a rest. Also he concloods to travel; an' as long as he's goin' to travel, he allows he'll sort o' go projectin' 'round an' see if he can't locate Jim.

"He gets a old an' musty tip about Jim, this Bill Rawlins does, an' it works out all right. Bill cuts Jim's trail 'way out yonder on the Slope at a meetropolis called Los Angeles. But this yere Jim ain't thar none. The folks tells Bill they reckons Jim is over to Virginny City.

"It's a month later, an' Bill is romancin' along on one of them Nevada mountain-meadow trails, when he happens upon a low, squatty dugout, the same bein' a camp rather than a house, an' belongs with a hay ranche. In the door is standin' a most ornery seemin' gent, with long, tangled ha'r an' beard, an' his clothes looks like he's shorely witnessed times. The hands of this ha'ry gent is in his pockets, an' he exhibits a mighty soopercilious air. Bill pulls up his cayouse for a powwow.

"'How far is it to a place where I can camp down for the night?' asks Bill.

"'It's about twenty miles to the next wickeyup,' says the soopercilious gent.

"'Which I can't make it none to-night, then,' says Bill.

"'Not on that hoss,' says the soopercilious gent, for Bill's pony that a-way is plenty played.

"'Mebby, then,' says Bill, 'I'd better bunk in yere.'

"'You can gamble you-all don't sleep yere,' says the soopercilious gent; 'none whatever!'

"'An' why not?' asks Bill.

"'Because I won't let you,' says the soopercilious gent, a-bitin' off a piece of tobacco. 'This is my camp, an' force'ble invasions by casooal hold-ups like you, don't preevail with me a little bit. I resents the introosion on my privacy.'

"'But I'll have to sleep on these yere plains,' says Bill a heap plaintif.

"'Thar's better sports than you-all slept on them plains,' says the soopercilious gent.

"Meanwhile, thar's a move or two, speshully the way he bats his eyes, about this soopercilious gent that sets Bill to rummagin' 'round in his mem'ry. At last he asks:

"'Is your name Rawlins?'

"'Yes, sir, my name's Rawlins,' says the soopercilious gent.

"'Jim Rawlins of Roanoke?'

"'Jim Rawlins of Roanoke,' an' the soopercilious gent reaches inside the door of the dugout, searches forth a rifle an' pumps a cartridge into the bar'l.

"'Stan' your hand, Jim!' says Bill, at the same time slid-in' to the ground with the hoss between him an' his relatif; 'don't get impetyoous. I'm your brother Bill.'

"'What!' says the soopercilious gent, abandonin' them hostile measures, an' joy settlin' over his face. 'What!' he says; 'you my brother Bill? Well, don't that beat grizzly b'ars amazin'! Come in, Bill, an' rest your hat. Which it's simply the tenderness of hell I don't miss you.'

"Whereupon Bill an' Jim tracks along inside an' goes to canvassin' up an' down as to what ensooes doorin' them forty years they've been parted. Jim wants to know all about Roanoke an' how things stacks up in old Virginny, an' he's chuckin' in his questions plenty rapid.

"While Bill's replyin', his eye is caught by a frightful-lookin' female who goes slyin' in an' out, a-organizin' of some grub. She's the color of a saddle, an' Bill can't make out whether she's a white, a Mexican, a Digger Injun or a nigger. An' she's that hideous, this female is, she comes mighty near givin' Bill heart failure. Son, you-all can't have no idee how turrible this person looks. She's so ugly the flies won't light on her. Yes, sir! ugly enough to bring sickness into a fam'ly. Bill can feel all sorts o' horrors stampedin' about in his frame as he gazes on her. Her eyes looks like two bullet holes in a board, an' the rest of her feachers is tetotaciously indeescrib'ble. Bill's intellects at the awful sight of this yere person almost loses their formation, as army gents would say. At last Bill gets in a question on his rapid-fire relatif, who's shootin' him up with queries touchin' Roanoke to beat a royal flush.

"'Jim,' says Bill, sort o' scared like, 'whoever is this yere lady who's roamin' the scene?'

"'Well, thar now!' says Jim, like he's plumb disgusted, 'I hope my gun may hang fire, if I don't forget to introdooce you! Bill, that's my wife.'

"Then Jim goes surgin' off all spraddled out about the noomerous an' manifest excellencies of this female, an' holds forth alarmin' of an' concernin' her virchoos an' loveli ness of face an' form, an' all to sech a scand'lous degree, Bill has to step outdoors to blush.

"'An', Bill,' goes on Jim, an' he's plumb rapturous, that a-away, 'may I never hold three of a kind ag'in, if she ain't got a sister who's as much like her as two poker chips. I'm co'tin' both of 'em mighty near four years before ever I can make up my mind whichever of 'em I needs. They're both so absolootely sim'lar for beauty, an' both that aloorin' to the heart, I simply can't tell how to set my stack down. At last, after four years, I ups an' cuts the kyards for it, an' wins out this one.'

"'Well, Jim,' says Bill, who's been settin' thar shudderin' through them rhapsodies, an' now an' then gettin' a glimpse of this yere female with the tail of his eye: 'Well, Jim, far be it from me, an' me your brother, to go avouchin' views to make you feel doobious of your choice. But candor's got the drop on me an' compels me to speak my thoughts. I never sees this sister of your wife, Jim, but jest the same, I'd a heap sight rather have her.'

"An' as I observes previous," concluded the old gentleman, "I feels about Japs an' Injuns like Bill does about Jim's wife that time. I never sees no Japs, but I'd a mighty sight rather have 'em."

There was another pause after this, and cigars were produced. For a time the smoke curled in silence. Then my friend again took up discussion.

"Thar comes few Injuns investigatin' into Wolfville. Doorin' them emutes of Cochise, an' Geronimo, an' Nana, the Apaches goes No'th and South clost in by that camp of ours, but you bet! they're never that locoed as to rope once at Wolfville! We-all would shorely have admired to entertain them hostiles; but as I su'gests, they're a heap too enlightened to give us a chance.

"Savages never finds much encouragement to come ha'ntin' about Wolfville. About the first visitin' Injuns meets with a contreetemps; though this is inadvertent a-heap an' not designed. This buck, a Navajo, I takes it, from his feathers, has been pirootin' about for a day or two. At last I reckons he allows he'll eelope off into the foothils ag'in. As carryin' out them roode plans which he forms, he starts to scramble onto the Tucson stage jest as Old Monte's c'llectin' up his reins. But it don't go; Injuns is barred. The gyard, who's perched up in front next to Old Monte, pokes this yere aborigine in the middle of his face with the muzzle of his rifle; an' as the Injun goes tumblin', the stage starts, an' both wheels passes over him the longest way. That Injun gives a groan like twenty sinners, an' his lamp is out.

"Old Monte sets the brake an' climbs down an' sizes up the remainder. Then he gets back on the box, picks up his six hosses an' is gettin' out.

"'Yere, you!' says French, who's the Wells-Fargo agent, a-callin' after Old Monte, 'come back an' either plant your game or pack it with you. I'm too busy a gent to let you or any other blinded drunkard go leavin' a fooneral at my door. Thar's enough to do here as it is, an' I don't want no dead Injuns on my hands.'

"'Don't put him up thar an' go sp'ilin' them mail-bags,' howls Old Monte, as French an' a hoss-hustler from inside the corral lays hold of the Navajo to throw him on with the baggage.

"'Then come down yere an' ride herd on the play yourse'f, you murderin' sot!' says French.

"An' with that, he shore cuts loose an' cusses Old Monte frightful; cusses till a cottonwood tree in front of the station sheds all its leaves, an' he deadens the grass for a hundred yards about.

"'Promotin' a sepulcher in this rock-ribbed landscape,' says French, as Jack Moore comes up, kind o' apol'gisin' for his profane voylence at Old Monte; 'framin' up a tomb, I say, in this yere rock-ribbed landscape ain't no child's play, an' I'm not allowin' none for that homicide Monte to put no sech tasks on me. He knows the Wolfville roole. Every gent skins his own polecats an' plants his own prey.'

"'That's whatever!' says Jack Moore, 'an' onless Old Monte is thirstin' for trouble in elab'rate forms, he acquiesces tharin.'

"With that Old Monte hitches the Navajo to the hind axle with a lariat which French brings out, an' then the stage, with the savage coastin' along behind, goes rackin' off to the No'th. Later, Monte an' the passengers hangs this yere remainder up in a pine tree, at an Injun crossin' in the hills, as a warnin'. Whether it's a warnin' or no, we never learns; all that's shore is that the remainder an' the lariat is gone next day; but whatever idees the other Injuns entertains of the play is, as I once hears a lecture sharp promulgate, 'concealed with the customary stoicism of the American savage.'

"Most likely them antipathies of mine ag'in Injuns is a heap enhanced by what I experiences back on the old Jones an' Plummer trail, when they was wont to stampede our herds as we goes drivin' through the Injun Territory. Any little old dark night one of them savages is liable to come skulkin' up on the wind'ard side of the herd, flap a blanket, cut loose a yell, an' the next second thar's a hundred an' twenty thousand dollars' worth of property skally-hootin' off into space on frenzied hoofs. Next day, them same ontootered children of the woods an' fields would demand four bits for every head they he'ps round up an' return to the bunch. It's a source of savage revenoo, troo; but plumb irritatin'. Them Injuns corrals sometimes as much as a hundred dollars by sech treacheries. An' then we-all has to rest over one day to win it back at poker.

"Will Injuns gamble? Shore! an' to the limit at that! Of course, bein', as you saveys, a benighted people that a-way, they're some easy, havin' no more jedgment as to the valyoo of a hand than Steve Stevenson, an' Steve would take a p'ar of nines an' bet 'em higher than a cat's back. We allers recovers our *dinero*, but thar's time an' sleep we lose an' don't get back.

"Yes, indeed, son, Injuns common is as ornery as soapweed. The only good you-all can say of 'em is, they're nacheral-born longhorns, is oncomplainin', an' saveys the West like my black boy saveys licker. One time—this yere is 'way back in my Texas day—one time I'm camped for long over on the Upper Hawgthief. It's rained a heap, an' bein' as I'm on low ground anyhow, it gets that soft an' swampy where I be it would bog a butterfly. For once I'm took sick; has a fever, that a-way. An' lose flesh! shorely you should have seen me! I falls off like persimmons after a frost, an' gets as ga'nt an' thin as a cow in April. So I

allows I'll take a lay-off for a couple of months an' reecoop-
erate some.

"Cossettin' an' pettin' of my health, as I states, I saddles
up an' goes cavortin' over into the Osage nation to visit an
old *compadre* of mine who's a trader thar by the name of
Johnny Florer. This yere Florer is an old-timer with the Osages; been with 'em it's mighty likely twenty year at that
time, an' is with 'em yet for all the notice I ever receives.

"On the o'casion of this ambassy of mine, I has a chance
to study them savages, an' get a line on their char'cters a
whole lot. This time I'm with Johnny, what you-all might
call Osage upper circles is a heap torn by the ontoward rival-
ries of a brace of eminent bucks who's each strugglin' to
lead the fashion for the tribe an' raise the other out.

"Them Osages, while blanket Injuns, is plumb opulent.
thar's sixteen hundred of em, an' they has to themse'fs
1,500,000 acres of as good land as ever comes slippin' from
the palm of the Infinite. Also, the gov'ment is weak-minded
enough to confer on every one of 'em, each buck drawin'
the *dinero* for his fam'ly, a hundred an' forty big iron dollars anyooally. Wherefore, as I observes, them Osages is
plenty strong, financial.

"These yere two high-rollin' bucks I speaks of, who's
strugglin' for the social soopremacy, is in the midst of them
strifes while I'm visitin' Florer. It's some two moons prior
when one of 'em, which we call him the 'Astor Injun,' takes
a heavy fall out of the opp'sition by goin' over to Cherryvale an' buyin' a sooperannuated two-seat Rockaway
buggy. To this he hooks up a span of ponies, loads in his
squaws, an' p'rades 'round from Pawhusky to Greyhoss—
the same bein' a couple of Osage camps—an' tharby re-
dooces the enemy—what we'll name the 'Vanderbilt Injuns'—to desp'ration. The Astor savage shorely has the call
with that Rockaway.

"But the Vanderbilt Osage is a heap hard to down. He

takes one look at the Astor Injun's Rockaway with all its blindin' splendors, an' then goes streakin' it for Cherryvale, like a drunkard to a barbecue. An' he sees the Rockaway an' goes it several better. What do you-all reckon now that savage equips himse'f with? He wins out a hearse, a good big black roomy hearse, with ploomes onto it an' glass winders in the sides.

"As soon as ever this Vanderbilt Injun stiffens his hand with the hearse, he comes troopin' back to camp with it, himse'f on the box drivin',' an' puttin' on enough of lordly dog to make a pack of hounds. Which he shorely squelches the Astors; they jest simply lay down an' wept at sech grandeur. Their Rockaway ain't one, two, three,—ain't in the money.

"An' every day the Vanderbilt Injun would load his squaws an' papooses inside the hearse, an' thar, wropped in their blankets an' squattin' on the floor of the hearse for seats, they would be lookin' out o' the winders at common savages who ain't in it an' don't have no hearse. Meanwhiles, the buck Vanderbilt is drivin' the outfit all over an' 'round the cantonments, the entire bunch as sassy an' as flippant as a coop o' catbirds. It's all the Astors can do to keep from goin' plumb locoed. The Vanderbilts win.

"One mornin', when Florer an' me has jest run our brands onto the fourth drink, an old buck comes trailin' into the store. His blanket is pulled over his head, an' he's pantin' an' givin' it out he's powerful ill.

"'How is my father?' says Johnny in Osage.

"'Oh, my son,' says the Injun, placin' one hand on his stomach, an' all mighty tender, 'your father is plenty sick. Your father gets up this mornin', an' his heart is very bad. You must give him medicine or your father will die.'

"Johnny passes the invalid a cinnamon stick an' exhorts him to chew on that, which he does prompt an' satisfactory, like cattle on their cud. This cinnamon keeps him steady for 'most five minutes.

"'Whatever is the matter with this savage?' I asks of Johnny.

"'Nothin' partic'lar,' says Johnny. 'Last night he comes pushin' in yere an' buys a bottle of Worcestershire sauce; an' then he gets gaudy an' quaffs it all up on a theery she's a new-fangled fire water. He gets away with the entire bottle. It's now he realizes them errors, an' takes to groanin' an' allowin' it gives him a bad heart. Which I should shorely admits as much!'

"'Your father is worse,' says the Osage, as he comes cuttin' in on Johnny ag'in. 'Must have stronger medicine. That medicine,' holdin' up some of the cinnamon, 'that not bad enough.'

"At this, Johnny passes his 'father' over a double handful of black pepper before it's ground.

"'Let my father get away with that,' says Johnny, 'an' he'll feel like a bird. It will make him gay an' full of p'isen, like a rattlesnake in August.'

"Out to the r'ar of Johnny's store is piled up under a shed more'n two thousand boxes of axle grease. It was sent into the nation consigned to Johnny by some ill-advised sports in New York, who figgers that because the Osages as a tribe abounds in wagons, thar must shorely be a market for axle grease. That's where them New York persons misses the ford a lot. Them savages has wagons, troo; but they no more thinks of greasin' them axles than paintin' the runnin' gear. They never goes ag'inst that axle grease game for so much as a single box; said ointment is a drug. When he don't dispose of it none, Johnny stores it out under a shed some twenty rods away, an' regyards it as a total loss.

"'Axle grease,' says Johnny, 'makes a p'int in civilization to which the savage has not yet clambered, an' them optimists, East, who sends it on yere, should have never made no such break.'

"Mebby it's because this axle grease grows sullen an'

feels neglected that a-way; mebby it's the heats of two summers an' the frosts of two winters which sp'iles its disp'sition; shore it is at any rate that at the time I'm thar, that onguent seems fretted to the core, an' is givin' forth a protestin' frangrance that has stood off a coyote an' made him quit at a distance of two hundred yards. You might even say it has caused Nacher herse'f to pause an' catch her breath.

"It's when the ailin' Osage, whose malady is too deep-seated to be reached by cinnamon or pimento, comes frontin' up for a third preescription, that the axle grease idee seizes Johnny.

"'Father,' says Johnny, 'come with me. Your son will now saw off some big medicine on you; a medicine meant for full-blown gents like you an' me. Come, father, come with your son, an' you shall be cured in half the time it takes to run a loop on a lariat.'

"Johnny breaks open one of the axle grease boxes, arms the savage with a chip for a spoon, an' exhorts him to cut in on it a whole lot.

"Son, the odors of them wares is awful; Kansas butter is violets to it; but it never flutters that Osage. He takes Johnny's chip an' goes to work, spadin' that axle grease into his mouth, like he ain't got a minute to live. When he's got away with half the box, he tucks the balance under his blanket an' retires to his teepee with a look of gratitoode on his face. His heart has ceased to be bad, an' them illnesses, which aforetime has him on the go, surrenders to the powers of this yere new medicine like willows to the wind. With this, he goes caperin' out for his camp, idly hummin' a war song, sech is his relief.

"An' here's where Johnny gets action on that axle grease. It shorely teaches, also, the excellence of them maxims, 'Cast your bread upon the waters an' you'll be on velvet before many days.' Within two hours a couple of this sick buck's squaws comes sidlin' up to Johnny an' desires axle

grease. It's quoted as four bits a box, an' the squaws
changes in five pesos an' beats a retreat, carryin' away ten
boxes. Then the fame of this big, new medicine spreads; that
axle grease becomes plenty pop'lar. Other bucks an' other
squaws shows up, changes in their money, an' is made
happy with axle grease. They never has sech a time, them
Osages don't, since the battle of the Hoss-shoe. Son, they
packs it off in blankets, freights it away in wagons. They
turns loose on a reg'lar axle grease spree. In a week every
box is sold, an' thar's orders stacked up on Florer's desk for
two kyar-loads more, which is bein' hurried on from the
East. Even the Injuns' agent gets wrought up about it, an'
begins to bellow an' paw 'round by way of compliments to
Johnny. He makes Johnny a speech.

"'Which I've made your excellent discovery, Mr. Florer,'
says this agent, 'the basis of a .report to the gov'ment at
Washin'ton. I sets forth the mad passion of these yere
Osages for axle grease as a condiment, a beverage, an' a
cure. I explains the tribal leanin' that exists for that speshul
axle grease which is crowned with years, an' owns a
strength which comes only as the cor'lary of hard experience. Axle grease is like music an' sooths the savage breast.
It is oil on the troubled waters of aboriginal existence. Its
feet is the feet of peace. At the touch of axle grease the hostile abandons the war path an' surrenders himse'f. He
washes off his paint an' becometh with axle grease as the
lamb that bleateth. The greatest possible uprisin' could be
quelled with a consignment of axle grease. Mr. Florer, I
congratulate you. From a humble storekeep, sellin' soap,
herrin' an' salt hoss, you takes your stand from now with
the ph'lanthropists an' leaders among men. You have con-
joined Injuns an' axle grease. For centuries the savage has
been a problem which has defied gov'ment. He will do so
no more. Mr. Florer, you have solved the savage with axle
grease.'"

14

How Prince Hal Got Help.

"COME yere, you boy Tom." It was the Old Cattle-man addressing his black satellite. "Stampede up to them rooms of mine an' fetch me my hat; the one with the snakeskin band. My head ain't feelin' none too well, owin' to the barkeep of this hostelry changin' my drinks, an' that rattlesnake band oughter absorb them aches an' clar'fy my roominations a heap. Now, *vamos!*" he continued, as Tom seemed to hesitate, "The big Stetson with the snakeskin on-to it.

"An' how be you stackin' up yours'ef" observed the old gentleman, turning to me as his dark agent vanished in quest of head-gear "Which you shorely looks as worn an' weary as a calf jest branded. It'll do you good to walk a lot; better come with me. I sort o' originates the notion that I'll go swarmin' about permiscus this mornin' for a hour or so, an cirk'late my blood, an' you-all is welcome to attach yourse'f to the scheme. Thar's nothin' like exercise, that away, as Grief Mudlow allows when he urges his wife to take in washin'. You've done heard of Grief Mudlow, the laziest maverick in Tennessee?"

I gave my word that not so much as a rumor of the person Mudlow had reached me. My friend expressed surprise. It was now that the black boy Tom came up with the desired hat. Tom made his approach with a queer backward and forward shuffle, crooning to himself the while:

"Rain come wet me, sun come dry me,
Take keer, white man, don't come nigh me."

"Stop that double-shufflin' an' wing dancin'," re-
monstrated the old gentleman severely, as he took the hat
and fixed it on his head. "I don't want no frivolities an'
merry-makin's 'round me. Which you're always jumpin' an'
dancin' like one of these yere snapjack bugs. I ain't aimin'
at pompousness none, but thar's a sobriety goes with them
years of mine which I proposes to maintain if I has to do it
with a blacksnake whip. So you-all boy Tom, you look out
a whole lot! I'm goin' to break you of them hurdy-gurdy
tendencies, if I has to make you wear hobbles an' frale the
duds off your back besides."

Tom smiled toothfully, yet in conficent fashion, as one
who knows his master and is not afraid.

"So you never hears of Grief Mudlow?" he continued, as
we strolled abroad on our walk. "I reckons mebby you has,
for they shore puts Grief into a book once, commemoratin'
of his laziness. How lazy is he? Well, son, he could beat
Mexicans an' let 'em deal. He's raised away off east, over
among the knobs of old Knox County, Grief is, an' he's that
lazy he has to leave it on account of the hills.

"'She's too noomerous in them steeps an' decliv'ties,'
says Grief. 'What I needs is a landscape where the prevailin'
feacher is the hor'zontal. I was shorely born with a yearnin'
for the level ground.' An; so Grief moves his camp down
on the river bottoms, where thar ain't no hills.

"He's that mis'rable idle an' shiftless, this yere Grief is,
that once he starts huntin' an' then decides he won't. Grief
lays down by the aige of the branch, with his moccasins towards the water. It starts in to rain, an' the storm pounces
down on Grief like a mink on a settin' hen. One of his pards
sees him across the branch an' thinks he's asleep. So he
shouts an' yells at him.

"'Whoopee, Grief!' he sings over to where Grief's layin' all quiled up same as a water-moccasin snake, an' the rain peltin' into him like etarnal wrath; 'wake up thar an' crawl for cover!'

"'I'm awake,' says Grief.

"'Well, why don't you get outen the rain?'

"'I'm all wet now an' the rain don't do no hurt,' says Grief.

"An' this yere lazy Grief Mudlow keeps on layin' thar. It ain't no time when the branch begins to raise; the water crawls up about Grief's feet. So his pard shouts at him some more:

"'Whoopee, you Grief ag'in!' he says. 'If you don't pull your freight, the branch'll get you. It's done riz over the stock of your rifle.'

"'Water won't hurt the wood none,' says Grief.

"'You Grief over thar!' roars the other after awhile; 'your feet an' laigs is half into the branch, an' the water's got up to the lock of your gun.'

"'Thar's no load in the gun,' says Grief, still a-layin', 'an besides she needs washin' out. As for them feet an' laigs, I never catches cold.'

"An' thar that ornery Grief reposes, too plumb lazy to move, while the branch creeps up about him. It's crope up so high, final, that his y'ears an' the back of his head is in it. All Grief does is sort o' lift his chin an' lay squar', to keep his nose out so's he can breath.

"An' he shorely beats the game; for the rain ceases, an' the branch don't rise no higher. This yere Grief lays thar ontil the branch runs down an' he's high an' dry ag'in, an' then the sun shines out a' dries his clothes. It's that same night when Grief has drug himse'f home to supper, he says to his wife, 'Thar's nothin' like exercise,' an' then counsels that lady over his corn pone an' chitlins to take in washin' like I relates."

We walked on in mute consideration of the extraordinary indolence of the worthless Mudlow. Our silence obtained for full ten minutes. Then I proposed "courage" as a subject, and put a question.

"Thar's fifty kinds of courage," responded my companion, "an' a gent who's plumb weak an' craven, that a-way, onder certain circumstances, is as full of sand as the bed of the Arkansaw onder others. Thar's hoss-back courage an' thar's foot courage, thar's day courage an' night courage, thar's gun courage an' knife courage, an' no end of courages besides. An' then thar's the courage of vanity. More'n once, when I'm younger, I'm swept down by this last form of heroism, an' I even recalls how in a sperit of vainglory I rides a buffalo bull. I tells you, son, that while that frantic buffalo is squanderin' about the plains that time, an' me onto him, he feels a mighty sight like the ridge of all the yooniverse. How does it end? It's too long a tale to tell walkin' an' without recooperatifs; suffice it that it ends disastrous. I shall never ride no buffalo ag'in, leastwise without a saddle, onless it's a speshul o'casion.

"No, indeed, that word 'courage' has to be defined new for each case. Thar's old Tom Harris over on the Canadian. I beholds Tom one time at Tascosa do the most b'ar-faced trick; one which most sports of common sens'bilities would have shrunk from. Thar's a warrant out for Tom, an' Jim East the shefriff puts his gun on Tom when Tom's lookin' t'other way.

"'See yere, Harris!' says East, that a-way.

"Tom wheels, an' is lookin' into the mouth of East's six-shooter not a yard off.

"'Put up your hands!' says East.

"But Tom don't. He looks over the gun into East's eye; an' he freezes him. Then slow an' delib'rate, an' glarin' like a mountain lion at East, Tom goes back after his Colt's an' pulls it. He lays her alongside of East's with the muzzle p'intin' at East's eye. An' thar they stands.

"'You don't dar' shoot!' says Tom; an' East don't.

"They breaks away an' no powder burned; Tom stands East off.

"'Warrant or no warrant,' says Tom, 'all the sheriffs that ever jingles a spur in the Panhandle country, can't take me! Nor all the rangers neither!' An' they shore couldn't.

"Now this yere break-away of Tom's, when East gets the drop that time, takes courage. It ain't one gent in a thousand who could make that trip but Tom. An' yet this yere Tom is feared of a dark room.

"Take Injuns;—give 'em their doo, even if we ain't got room for them miscreants in our hearts. On his lines an' at his games, a Injun is as clean strain as they makes. He's got courage, an' can die without battin' an eye or waggin' a y'ear, once it's come his turn. An' the squaws is as cold a prop'sition as the bucks. After a fight with them savages, when you goes 'round to count up an' skin the game, you finds most as many squaws lyin' about, an' bullets through 'em, as you finds bucks.

"Courage is sometimes knowledge, sometimes ignorance; sometimes courage is desp'ration, an' then ag'in it's innocence.

"Once, about two miles off, when I'm on the Staked Plains, an' near the aige where thar's pieces of broken rock, I observes a Mexican on foot, frantically chunkin' up somethin'. He's left his pony standin' off a little, an' has with him a mighty noisy form of some low kind of mongrel dog, this latter standin' in to worry whatever it is the Mexican's chunkin' at, that a-way. I rides over to investigate the war-jig; an' I'm a mesquite digger! if this yere transplanted Castillian ain't done up a full-grown wild cat! It's jest coughin' its last when I arrives. Son, I wouldn't have opened a game on that feline—the same bein' as big as a coyote, an' as thoroughly organized for troubles as a gatling—with anythin' more puny than a Winchester. An' yet that guileless Mexi-

can lays him out with rocks, an regyards sech feats as trivial. An American, too, by merely growlin' towards this
Mexican, would make him quit out like a jack rabbit.

"As I observes prior, courage is frequent the froots of
what a gent don't know. Take grizzly b'ars. Back fifty
years, when them squirrel rifles is preevalent; when a acorn
shell holds a charge of powder, an' bullets runs as light an'
little as sixty-four to the pound, why son! you-all could
shoot up a grizzly till sundown an' hardly gain his disdain.
It's a fluke if you downs one. That sport who can show a
set of grizzly b'ar claws, them times, has fame. They're as
good as a bank account, them claws be, an' entitles said
party to credit in dance hall, bar room an' store, by merely
slammin' 'em on the counter.

"At that time the grizzly b'ar has courage. Whyever does
he have it, you asks? Because you couldn't stop him; he's
out of hoomanity's reach—a sort o' Alexander Selkirk of a
b'ar, an' you couldn't win from him. In them epocks, the
grizzly b'ar treats a gent contemptuous. He swats him, or he
claws him, or he hugs him, or he crunches him, or he quits
him accordin' to his moods, or the number of them engage-
ments which is pressin' on him at the time. An' the last
thing he considers is the feelin's of that partic'lar party he's
dallyin' with. Now, however, all is changed. Thar's rifles,
burnin' four inches of this yere fulminatin' powder, that can
chuck a bullet through a foot of green oak. Wisely directed,
they lets sunshine through a grizzly b'ar like he's a pane of
glass. An', son, them b'ars is plumb onto the play.

What's the finish? To-day you can't get clos't enough to a
grizzly to hand him a ripe peach. Let him glimpse or smell
a white man, an' he goes scatterin' off across hill an' canyon like a quart of licker among forty men. They're shore
apprehensife of them big bullets an' hard-hittin' guns, them
b'ars is; an' they wouldn't listen to you, even if you talks
nothin' but bee-tree an' gives a bond to keep the peace be-

sides. Yes, sir; the day when the grizzly b'ar will stand without hitchin' has deeparted the calendar a whole lot. They no longer attempts insolent an' coarse familiar'ties with folks. Instead of regyardin' a rifle as a rotton cornstalk in disguise, they're as gun-shy as a female institoote. Big b'ars an' little b'ars, it's all sim'lar; for the old ones tells it to the young, an' the lesson is spread throughout the entire nation of b'ars. An' yere's where you observes, enlightenment that a-way means aweakenin' of grizzly-b'ar courage.

"What's that, son? You-all thinks my stories smell some tall! You expresses doubts about anamiles conversin' with one another? That's where you're ignorant. All anamiles talks; they commoonicates the news to one another like hoomans. When I've been freightin' from Dodge down towards the Canadian, I had a eight-mule team. As shore as we're walkin'—as shore as I'm pinin' for a drink, I've listened to them mules gossip by the hour as we swings along the trail. Lots of times I saveys what they says. Once I hears the off-leader tell his mate that the jockey stick is sawin' him onder the chin. I investigates an' finds the complaint troo an' relieves him. The nigh swing mule is a wit; an' all day long he'd be throwin' off remarks that keeps a ripple of laughter goin' up an' down the team. You-all finds trouble creditin' them statements. Fact, jest the same. I've laughed at the jokes of that swing mule myse'f; an' even Jerry, the off wheeler, who's a cynic that a-way, couldn't repress a smile. Shore! anamiles talks all the time; it's only that we-all hoomans ain't eddicated to onderstand.

"Speakin' of beasts talkin', let me impart to you of what passes before my eyes over on the Caliente. In the first place, I'll so far illoomine your mind as to tell you that cattle, same as people—an' speshully mountain cattle, where the winds an' snows don't get to drive 'em an' drift 'em south—lives all their lives in the same places, year after year; an' as you rides your ranges, you're allers meetin' up with the same old cattle in the same canyons. They never moves, once they selects a home.

"As I observes, I've got a camp on the Caliente. Thar's ten ponies in my bunch, as I'm saddlin' three a day an' coverin' a considerable deal of range in my ridin'. Seein' as I'm camped yere some six months, I makes the aquaintance of the cattle for over twenty miles 'round. Among others, thar's a giant bull in Long Canyon—he's shorely as big as a log house. Him an' me is partic'lar friends, only I don't track up on him more frequent than onct a week, as he's miles from my camp. I almost forgets to say that with this yere Goliath bull is a milk-white steer, with long, slim horns an' a face which is the combined home of vain conceit an' utter witlessness. This milky an' semi-ediotic steer is a most abject admirer of the Goliath bull, an' they're allers together. As I states, this mountain of a bull an' his weak-minded follower lives in Long's Canyon.

"Thar's two more bulls, the same bein', as Colonel Sterett would say, also 'persons of this yere dramy.' One is a five-year-old who abides on the upper Red River; an' the other, who is only a three-year-old, hangs out on the Caliente in the vicinity of my camp.

"Which since I've got to talk of an' concernin' them anamiles, I might as well give 'em their proper names. They gets these last all reg'lar from a play-actor party who comes swarmin' into the hills while I'm thar to try the pine trees on his 'tooberclosis,' as he describes said malady, an' whose weakness is to saw off cognomens on everythin' he sees. As fast as he's introdooced to 'em, this actor sport names the Long's Canyon bull 'Falstaff'; the Red River five-year-old 'Hotspur,' bein' he's plumb b'lligerent an' allers makin' war medicine; while the little three-year-old, who inhabits about my camp in the Caliente, he addresses as 'Prince Hal.' The fool of a white steer that's worshippin' about 'Falstaff' gets named 'Pistol,' although thar's mighty little about the weak-

kneed humbug to remind you of anythin' as vehement as a
gun. Falstaff, Pistol, Hotspur an' Prince Hal; them's the ti-
tles this dramatist confers on said cattle.

"Which the West is a great place to dig out new appella-
tions that a-way. Thar's a gentle-minded party comes soarin'
down on Wolfville one evenin'. No, he don't have no real
business to transact; he's out to have a heart-to-heart inter-
view with the great Southwest, is the way he expounds the
objects of his search.

"'An' he's plenty tender,' says Black Jack, who's barkeep
at the Red Light. 'He comes pushin' along in yere this mornin'; an' what do you-all reckon now he wants. Asks for
ice! Now what ever do you make of it! Ice in August, an'
within forty miles of the Mexico line at that. "Pard," I says,
"we're on the confines of the tropics; an' while old Arizona
is some queer, an' we digs for wood an' climbs for water,
an' indulges in much that is morally an' physically the
teetotal reverse of right-side-up-with-care, so far in our
meanderin's we ain't oncovered no glaciers nor cut the trail
of any ice. Which if you've brought snowshoes with you
now, or been figgerin' on a Arizona sleighride, you're settin' in hard luck."'

"Jest as Black Jack gets that far in them statements, this
yere tenderfoot shows in the door.

"'Be you a resident of Wolfville?' asks this shorthorn of
Dave Tutt.

"'I'm one of the seven orig'nal wolves,' says Tutt.

"'Yere's my kyard,' says the shorthorn, an' he beams on
Dave in a wide an' balmy way.

"'Archibald Willingham De Graffenreid Butt,' says Dave,
readin' off the kyard. Then Dave goes up to the side, an'
all solemn an' grave, pins the kyard to the board with his
bowieknife. 'Archibald Willingham De Graffenreid Butt,'
an' Dave repeats the words plumb careful. 'That's your full
an' c'rrect name, is it?'

"The shorthorn allows it is, an' surveys Dave in a woozy way like he ain't informed none of the meanin' of these yere manoovers.

"'Did you-all come through Tucson with this name?' asks Dave.

"He says he does.

"'An' wasn't nothin' said or done about it?' demands Dave; 'don't them Tucson sports take no action?'

"He says nothin' is done.

"'It's as I fears,' says Dave, shakin' his head a heap loogubrious, 'that Tucson outfit is morally goin' to waste. It's worse than careless; it's callous. That's whatever; that camp is callous. Was you aimin' to stay for long in Wolfville with this yere title?' asks Dave at last.

"The shorthorn mentions a week.

"'This yere Wolfville,' explains Dave, 'is too small for that name. Archibald Willingham De Graffenreid Butt! It shorely sounds like a hoss in a dance hall. But it's too long for Wolfville, an' Wolfville even do her best. One end of that name is bound to protrood. Or else it gets all brunkled up like a long nigger in a short bed. However,' goes on Dave, as he notes the shorthorn lookin' a little dizzy, don't 'lose heart. We does the best we can. I likes your looks, an' shall come somewhat to your rescoo myse'f in your present troubles. Gents,' an' Dave turns to where Boggs an' Cherokee an' Texas Thompson is listenin', 'I moves you we suspends the rooles, an' renames this excellent an' well-meanin' maverick, "Butcherknife Bill."'

"'I seconds the motion,' says Boggs. 'Butcherknife Bill is a neat an' compact name. I congratulates our visitin' friend from the East on the ease wherewith he wins it out. I would only make one su'gestion, the same bein' in the nacher of amendments to the orig'nal resolootion, an' which is, that in all games of short kyards, or at sech times as we-all issues invitations to drink, or at any other epoch when time should be saved an' quick attention is desir'ble, said cognomen may legally be redooced to "Butch."'

"'Thar bein' no objections,' says Tutt, 'it is regyarded as the sense of the meetin' that this yere visitin' sharp from the States, yeretofore clogged in his flight by the name of Archibald Willingham De Graffenreid Butt, be yereafter known as "Butcherknife Bill"; or failin' leesure for the full name, as "Butch," or both at the discretion of the co't, with the drinks on Butch as the gent now profitin' by this play. Barkeep, set up all your bottles an' c'llect from Butch.'

"But to go back to my long-ago camp on the Caliente. Prince Hal is a polished an' p'lite sort o' anamile. The second day after I pitches camp, Prince Hal shows up. He paws the grass, an' declar's himse'f, an' gives notice that while I'm plumb welcome, he wants it onderstood that he's party of the first part in that valley, an' aims to so continyoo. As I at once agrees to his claims, he is pacified; then he counts up the camp like he's sizin' up the plunder. It's at this point I signs Prince Hal as my friend for life by givin' him about a foot of bacon-skin. He stands an' chews on that bacon-skin for two hours; an' thar's heaven in his looks.

"It gets so Prince Hall puts in all his spar'time at my camp. An' I donates flapjacks, bacon-skins an' food comforts yeretofore onknown to Prince Hal. He regyards that camp of mine as openin' a new era on the Caliente.

"When not otherwise engaged, Prince Hal stands in to curry my ponies with his tongue. The one he'd been workin' on would plant himse'f rigid, with y'ears drooped, eyes shet, an' tail aquiverin'; an' you-all could see that Prince Hal, with his rough tongue, is jest burnin' up that bronco from foretop to fetlocks with the joy of them attentions. When Prince Hal has been speshul friendly, I'd pass him out a plug of Climax tobacco. Sick? Never once! It merely elevates Prince Hal's sperits in a mellow way, that tobacco does; makes him feel vivid an' gala a whole lot.

"Which we're all gettin' on as pleasant an' oneventful as a litter of pups over on the Caliente, when one mornin' across the divide from Red River comes this yere pugnacious person, Hotspur. He makes his advent r'arin' an' slidin' down the hillside into our valley, promulgatin' insults, an' stampin' for war. You can see it in Hotspur's eye; he's out to own the Caliente.

"Prince Hal is curryin' a pony when this yere invader comes crashin' down the sides of the divide. His eyes burn red, he evolves his warcry in a deep bass voice, an' goes curvin' out onto the level of the valley-bottom to meet the enemy. Gin'ral Jackson couldn't have displayed more promptitood.

"Thar ain't much action in one of them cattle battles. First, Hotspur an' Prince Hal stalks 'round, pawin' up a sod now an' then, an' sw'arin' a gale of oaths to themse'fs. It looks like Prince Hal could say the most bitter things, for at last Hotspur leaves off his pawin' an' profanity an' b'ars down on him. The two puts their fore'ards together an' goes in for a pushin' match.

"But this don't last. Hotspur is two years older, an' overweighs Prince Hal about three hundred pounds. Prince Hal feels Hotspur out, an' sees that by the time the deal goes to the turn, he'll be shore loser. A plan comes into his mind. Prince Hal suddenly backs away, an' keeps on backin' ontil he's cl'ared himse'f from his foe by eighty feet. Hotspur stands watchin'; it's a new wrinkle in bull fights to him. He can tell that this yere Prince Hal ain't conquered none, both by the voylent remarks he makes as well as the plumb defiant way he wears his tail. So Hotspur stands an' ponders the play, guessin' at what's likely to break loose next.

"But the conduct of this yere Prince Hal gets more an' more mysterious. When he's a safe eighty feet away, he jumps in the air, cracks his heels together, hurls a frightful curse at Hotspur, an' turns an' walks off a heap rapid.

Hotspur can't read them signs at all; an' to be frank, no more can I. Prince Hal never looks back; he surges straight ahead, clumbs the hill on the other side, an' is lost in the oak bushes.

"Hotspur watches him out of sight, gets a drink in the Caliente, an' then climbs the hillside to where I'm camped, to decide about me. Of course, Hotspur an' I arrives at a treaty of peace by the bacon-rind route, an' things ag'in quiets down on the Calente.

"It's next mornin' about fourth drink time, an' I'm overhaulin' a saddle an' makin' up some beliefs on several subjects of interest, when I observes Hotspur's face wearin' a onusual an' highly hangdog expression. An' I can't see no cause. I sweeps the scenery with my eye, but I notes nothin', but that's because he thinks he'll save his breath to groan with when dyin'. It's a fact, son; I couldn't see nor hear a thing, an' yet that Hotspur bull stands thar fully aware, somehow, that thar's a warrant out for him.

"At last I'm made posted of impendin' events. Across the wide Caliente comes a faint but f'rocious war song. I glance over that a-way, an' thar through the oak bresh comes Prince Hal. An' although he's a mile off, he's p'intin' straight for this yere invader, Hotspur. At first I thinks Prince Hal's alone, an' I'm marvellin' whatever he reckons he's goin' to a'complish by this return. But jest then I gets a glimmer, far to Prince Hal's r'ar, of that reedic'lous Pistol, the milkwhite steer.

"I beholds it all; Falstaff is comin'; only bein' a dark brown I can't yet pick himout o' the bresh. Prince Hal has travelled over to Long's Canyon an' told the giant Falstaff how Hotspur jumps into the Galiente an' puts it all over him that a-way. Falstaff is lumberin' over—it's a journey of miles—to put this redundant Hotspur back on his reservation. Prince Hal, bein' warm, lively an' plumb zealous to recover his valley, is nacherally a quarter of a mile ahead of Falstaff.

"It's allers a question with me why this yere foolhardy Hotspur don't stampede out for safety. But he don't; he stands thar lookin' onusual limp, an' awaits his fate. Prince Hal don't rush up an' mingle with Hotspur; he's playin' a system an' he don't deviate tharfrom. He stands off about fifty yards, callin' Hotspur names, an' waitin' for Falstaff to arrive.

"An' thar's a by-play gets pulled off. This ranikaboo Pistol, who couldn't fight a little bit, an' who's caperin' along ten rods in the lead of Falstaff, gets the sudden crazy-hoss notion that he'll mete out punishment to Hotspur himse'f, an' make a reputation as a war-eagle with his pard an' patron, Falstaff. With that, Pistol curves his tail like a letter S, and, lowerin' his knittin'-needle horns, comes dancin' up to Hotspur. The bluff of this yere ignoble Pistol is too much. Hotspur r'ars loose an' charges him. This egregious Pistol gets crumpled up, an' Hotspur goes over him like a baggage wagon. The shock is sech that Pistol falls over a wash-bank; an' after swappin' end for end, lands twenty feet below with a groan an' a splash in the Caliente. Pistol is shorely used up, an' crawls out on the flat ground below, as disconsolate a head o' cattle as ever tempts the echoes with his wails.

"But Hotspur has no space wherein to sing his vic'try. Falstaff decends upon him like a fallin' tree. With one rushin' charge, an' a note like thunder, he simply distributes that Hotspur all over the range. Thar's only one blow; as soon as Hotspur can round up his fragments an' get to his hoofs, he goes sailin' down the valley, his eyes stickin' out so he can see his sins. As he starts, Prince Hal, who's been hooppin' about the rim of the riot, blaps his horns to Hotspur's flyin' hocks an' keeps him goin'. But it ain't needed none; that Falstaff actooaly ruins Hotspur with the first charge.

"That night Falstaff, with the pore Pistol jest able to totter, stays with us, an' Prince Hal fusses an' bosses' 'round, sort o' directin' their entertainment. The next afternoon Falstaff gives a deep bellow or two, like he's extendin' 'adios' to the entire Caliente canyon, an' then goes pirootin' off for home in Long's, with Pistol, who looks an' feels like a laughin' stock, limpin' at his heels. That's the end. Four days later, as I'm swingin' 'round the range, I finds Falstaff an' Pistol in Long's Canyon; Prince Hal is on the Caliente; while Hotspur an' his air is both wise an' sad—is tamely where he belongs on the Upper Red. An' now recallin' how I comes to plunge into this yere idyl, I desires to ask you-all, however Prince Hal brings Falstaff to the wars that time, if cattle can't talk?"

Doc Peets

15

How Wolfville Made a Jest.

"IT'S soon after that time I tells you of when Rainbow Sam dies off," and the Old Cattleman assumed the airs of a conversational Froude, "when the camp turns in an' has its little jest with the Signal Service sharp. You sees we're that depressed about Rainbow cashin' in, we needs reelaxation that a-way, so we-all nacheral enough diverts ourse'fs with this Signal party who comes bulgin' up all handy.

"Don't make no mistaken notions about Wolfville bein' a idle an' a dangerous camp. Which on the contrary, Wolfville is shorely the home of jestice, an' a squar' man gets a squar' game every time. Thar ain't no 'bad men' 'round Wolfville, public sentiment bein' obdurate on that p'int. Hard people, who has filed the sights offen their six-shooters or fans their guns in a fight, don't get tolerated, none whatever.

"Of course, thar's gents in Wolfville who has seen trouble an' seen it in the smoke. Cherokee Hall, for instance, so Doc Peets mentions to me private, one time an' another downs 'leven men.

"But Cherokee's by nacher kind o' warm an' nervous, an' bein' he's behind a faro game, most likely he sees more o'casion; at any rate, it's common knowledge that whatever he's done is right.

"He don't beef them 'leven in Wolfville; all I recalls with us, is the man from Red Dog, the Stingin' Lizard, an' mebby a strayed Mexican or so. But each time Cherokee's hand is forced by these yere parties, an' he's exculpated in every gent's mind who is made awar' tharof.

"No; Cherokee don't rely allers on his gun neither. He's a hurryin' knife fighter for a gent with whom knives ain't nacher. Either way, however, gun or knife, Cherokee is a heap reliable; an' you can put down a bet that what he misses in the quadrille he'll shore make up in the waltz with all who asks him to a war dance. But speakin' of knives: Cherokee comes as quick an' straight with a bowie as a rattlesnake; an' not half the buzz about it.

"But jest the same, while thar's gents in camp like Cherokee, who has been ag'inst it more'n onct, an' who wins an' gets away, still Wolfville's as quiet an' sincere an outfit as any christian could ask.

"It's a fact; when Shotgun Dowling capers in an' allows he's about to abide with us a whole lot, he's a notified to hunt another hole the first day.

"'So far from you-all livin' with us, Shotgun,' says Jack Moore, who's depooted to give Shotgun Dowling the run; 'so far from you bunkin' in yere for good, we ain't even aimin' to permit your visits. My notion is that you better pull your freight some instant. Thar's a half-formed thought in the public bosom that if anybody sees your trail to-morry, all hands'll turn in an' arrange you for the grave.'

"'Never mind about arrangin' nothin',' says Shotgun; 'I quits you after the next drink; which libation I takes alone.' An' Shotgun rides away.

"What is the matter with Shotgun? Well, he's one of these yere murderin' folks, goin' about downin' Mexicans merely to see 'em kick, an' that sort of thing, an' all of which no se'f-respectin' outfit stands. He wins out his name 'Shotgun' them times when he's dep'ty marshal over at Prescott.

"'You must be partic'lar an' serve your warrant on a gent before you downs him,' says the Jedge, as he gives Shotgun some papers. 'First serve your warrant, an' then it's legal to kill him; but not without!'

"So Shotgun Dowling takes this yere warrant an' crams it down the muzzle of a shotgun an' hammers her out flat on top them buckshot.

"'Thar you be!' says Dowling. 'I reckons now the warrant gets to him ahead of the lead; which makes it on the level.'

"Tharupon Shotgun canters out an' busts his gent—warrant, lead an' all—an'that gives him the name of 'Shotgun' Dowling.

"But at the time he comes riotin' along into Wolfville, allowin' he'll reside some, he's regyarded hard; havin' been wolfin' 'round, cooperin' Mexicans an' friskin' about general; so, nacheral, we warns him out as aforesaid. Which I, tharfore, ag'in remarks, that Wolfville is a mighty proper an' peaceful place, an' its witticism with this yere Signal Service party needn't be inferred ag'inst it.

"This yere gent has been goin' about casooal, an' his air is a heap high-flown. He's been pesterin' an' irritatin' about the post-office for mighty like an hour, when all at once he crossesover to the Red Light an' squar's up to the bar. He don't invite none of us to licker—jest himse'f'; which onp'liteness is shore received invidious.

"'Gimme a cocktail,' says this Signal person to the barkeep.

"As they ain't mixin' no drinks at the Red Light for man or beast, nor yet at Hamilton's hurdy-gurdy, this sport in yooniform don't get no cocktail.

"'Can't mix no drinks,' says Black Jack.

"'Can't mix no cocktail?' says the Signal sharp. 'Why! what a band of prairie dogs this yere hamlet is! What's the matter with you-all that you can't mix no cocktails? Don't you savey enough?'

"'Do we-all savey enough?' says Black Jack some facetious that a-way. 'Stranger, we simply suffers with what we saveys. But thar's a law ag'in cocktails an' all mixin' of drinks. You sees, a Mexican female over in Tucson is one day mixin' drinks for a gent she's a-harborin' idees ag'in, an' she rings in the loco onto him, an' he goes plumb crazy. Then the Legislatoore arouses itse'f to its peril, that a-way, an' ups an' makes a law abatin' of mixed drinks. This yere bein' gospel trooth, you'll have to drink straight whiskey; an' you might as well drink it outen a tin cup, too.'

"As he says this, Black Jack sets up a bottle an' a tin cup, an' then for a blazer slams a six-shooter on the bar at the same time. Lookin' some bloo tharat, the Signal sharp takes a gulp or two of straight nose-paint, cavilin' hot at the tin cup, an' don't mention nothin' more of cocktails.

"'Whatever is the damage anyhow?' he says to Black Jack, soon as he's quit gaggin' over the whiskey, the same tastin' raw an' vicious to him, an' him with his lady-like throat framed ready for cocktails. 'What's thar to pay?'

"'Narry *centouse*,' says Black Jack, moppin' of the bar complacent. 'Not a soo markee. That drink's on the house, stranger.'

"When the Signal sharp goes out, Enright says he's got pore manners, an' he marvels some he's still walkin' the earth.

"'However,' says Enright, 'I s'pose his livin' so long arises mainly from stayin' East, where they don't make no p'int on bein' p'lite, an' runs things looser.'

"'Whatever's the matter of chasin' this insultin' tenderfoot 'round a lot,' asks Texas Thompson, 'an' havin' amoosement with him? Thar ain't nothin' doin', an' we oughter not begretch a half day's work, puttin' knowledge into this party. If somethin' ain't done forthwith to inform his mind as to them social dooties while he stays in Arizona, you can gamble he won't last to go East no more.'

"As what Texas Thompson says has weight, thar begins to grow a gen'ral desire to enlighten this yere sport. As

Texas su'gests the idee, it follows that he goes for'ard to begin its execootion.

"'But be discreet, Texas,' says Enright, 'an' don't force no showdown with this Signal gent. Attainin' wisdom is one thing, an' bein' killed that a-way is plumb different; an' while I sees no objection to swellin' the general fund of this young person's knowledge, I don't purpose that you-all's goin' to confer no diplomas, an' graduate him into the choir above none with a gun, at one an' the same time.'

"'None whatever,' says Texas Thompson; 'we merely toys with this tenderfoot an' never so much as breaks his crust, or brings a drop of blood, the slightest morsel. He's takin' life too lightly; an' all we p'ints out to do, is sober him an' teach him a thoughtful deecorum.'

"Texas Thompson goes a-weavin' up the street so as to cross the trail of this Signal party, who's headed down. As they passes, Texas turns as f'rocious as forty timber wolves, an' claps his hand on the shoulder of the Signal party.

"'How's this yere?' says Texas, shakin' back his long h'ar. An' he shorely looks hardened, that a-way.

"'How's what?' says the Signal man, who's astonished to death.

"'You saveys mighty well,' says Texas. 'You fails to bow to me, aimin' to insult an' put it all over me in the presence of this yere multitood. Think of it, gents!' goes on Texas, beginnin' to froth, an' a-raisin' of his voice to a whoop, 'think of it, an' me the war-chief of the Panhandle, with forty-two skelps on my bridle, to be insulted an' disdained by a feeble shorthorn like this. It shore makes me wonder be I alive!

"'Stranger,' goes on Texas, turnin' to the Signal party, an' his hand drops on his gun, an' he breathes loud like a buffalo; 'nothin' but blood is goin' to do me now. If I was troo to myse'f at this moment, I'd take a knife an' shorely split you like a mackerel. But I restrains myse'f; also I don't notice no weepons onto you. Go, tharfore, an' heel yourse'f, for by next drink time the avenger'll be huntin' on your trail. I gives you half an hour to live. Not on your account, 'cause it ain't comin' to you; but merely not to ketch no angels off their gyard, an' to allow 'em a chance to organize for your reception. Besides, I don't aim to spring no corpses on this camp., Pendin' hostil'ties, I shall rest myse'f in the Red Light, permittin' you the advantages of the dance hall, where Hamilton'll lend you pen, ink, paper, an' monte table, wharby to concoct your last will. Stranger, *adios*!'

"By the time Texas gets off this talk an' starts for the Red Light, the Signal sport is lookin' some sallow an' perturbed. He's shorely alarmed.

"'See yere, pard,' says Dan Boggs, breakin' loose all at once, like he's so honest he can't restrain himse'f, an' jest as Texas heads out for the Red Light; 'you're a heap onknown to me, but I takes a chance an' stands your friend. Now yere's what you do. You stiffen yourse'f up with a Colt's '44, an' lay for this Texas Thompson. He's a rustler an' a hoss-thief, an' a murderer who, as he says, has planted forty-two, not countin, Injuns Mexicans an' mavericks. He oughter be massacred; an' as it's come your way, why prance in an' spill his blood. This camp'll justify an' applaud the play.'

"'But I can't fight none,' says the Signal party. 'It's ag'in the rooles an' reg'lations of the army.'

"'Which I don't see none how you're goin' to renig,' says Dave Tutt. 'This debauchee is doo to shoot you on sight. Them army rooles shorely should permit a gent to scout off to one side the strict trail a little; partic'lar when it's come down to savin' his own skelp.'

"One way an' another, Tutt an' Boggs makes it cl'ar as paint to the Signal party that thar's only two chances left in the box; either he downs Texas or Texas gets him. The Signal party says it's what he calls a 'dread alternatif.'

"'Which when I thinks of the gore this yere murderous

Thompson already dabbles in,' says Boggs to the Signal party, 'I endorses them expressions. However, you put yourse'f in the hands of me an' Dave, an' we does our best. If you lives through it, the drinks is on you; an' if Texas beefs you—which, while deplorable, is none remote considerin' this yere Texas is a reg'lar engine of destruction —we sees that your remainder goes back to the States successful.'

"The Signal party says he's thankful he's found friends, an' tharupon they-all lines out for the dance hall, where they gets drinks, an' the Signal man, who's some pallid by now, figgers he'll write them letters an' sort o' straighten up his chips for the worst. Boggs observes that it's a good move, an' that Tutt an' he'll take an o'casional drink an' ride herd on his interests while he does.

"Tutt an' Boggs have got their brands onto mebby two drinks, when over comes Doc Peets, lookin' deadly dignified an' severe, an' says:

"'Who-all represents yere for this gent who's out for the blood of my friend, Texas Thompson?'

"'Talk to me an' Tutt,' says Boggs; 'an' cut her short, 'cause it's the opinion of our gent this rancorous Thompson infests the earth too long, an' he's hungerin' to begin his butchery.'

"'Which thar's enough said,' says Peets; 'I merely appears to notify you that in five minutes I parades my gent in front of the post-office, an' the atrocities can proceed. They fights with six-shooters; now what's the distance?'

"'Make it across a blanket,' says Tutt.

"'An' fold the blanket,' breaks in Boggs.

"'You can't make it too clost for my gent,' says Peets. 'As I starts to this yere conference, he says: "Doc, make her six-shooters an' over a handkerchief. I thirsts to shove the iron plumb ag'inst the heart that insults me, as I onhooks my weepon.

"Of course, the poor Signal party, tryin' to write over by a monte table, an' spillin' ink all over himse'f, listens to them remarks, an' it makes him feel partic'lar pensif.

"'In five minutes, then,' says Peets, 'you-all organize your gent an' come a-runnin'. I must canter over to see how Texas is holdin' himse'f. He's that fretful a minute back, he's t'arin' hunks out outen a white-ash table with his teeth like it's ginger-cake, an' moanin' for blood. Old Monte's lookin' after him, but I better get back. Which he might in his frenzy, that a-way, come scatterin' loose any moment, an' go r'arin' about an' killin' your gent without orders. Sech a play would be onelegant an' no delicacy to it; an' I now returns to gyard ag'in it.'

"As soon as Peets is started for the Red Light, Tutt ag'in turns to the Signal party, who's settin' thar lookin' he'pless an' worried, like he's a prairie dog who's come back from visitin' some other dog, an' finds a rattlesnake's done pitched camp in the mouth of his hole.

"'Now then, stranger,' says Tutt, 'if you-all has a'complished that clerical work, me an' Dan will lead you to your meat. When you gets to shootin', aim low an' be shore an' see your victim every time you cuts her loose.'

"The Signal party takes it plumb gray an' haggard, but not seein' no other way, he gets up, an' after stampin' about a trifle nervous, allows, since it's the best he can do, he's ready.

"'Which it is spoke like a man,' says Boggs. 'So come along, an' we'll hunt out this annihilator from Laredo an' make him think he's been caught in a cloudburst.'

"Old Monte has spread a doubled blanket in front of the post-office; an' as Tutt an' Boggs starts with their Signal party, thar's a yell like forty Apaches pours forth from across the street.

"'That's Thompson's war yelp,' says Boggs, explainin' of them clamors to the Signal party. 'Which it would seem from the fervor he puts into it, he's shorely all keyed up.

"As Doc Peets comes out a-leadin' of Texas, it's noticed that Texas has got a tin cup.

"'Whatever's your gent a-packin' of that yootensil for?' demands Tutt, mighty truculent. 'Is this yere to be a combat with dippers?'

"'Oh, no!' says Peets, like he's tryin' to excuse somethin', 'but he insists on fecthin' it so hard, that at last to soothe him I gives my consent.'

"'Well, we challenges the dipper,' says Tutt. 'You-all will fight on the squar', or we removes our gent.'

"'Don't, don't!' shouts Texas, like he's agitated no limit; 'don't take him outen my sight no more. I only fetches the cup to drink his blood; but it's a small detail, which I shore relinquishes before ever I allows my heaven-sent prey the least loophole to escape.'

"When Peets goes up an' takes Texas's cup, the two debates together in a whisper, Texas lettin' on he's mighty hot an' furious. At last Peets says to him:

"'Which I tells you sech a proposal is irreg'lar; but since you insists, of course I names it. My gent yere,' goes on Peets to Boggs an' Tutt, 'wants to agree that the survivor's to be allowed to skelp his departed foe. Does the bluff go?'

"'It's what our gent's been urgin' from the jump,' says Boggs; 'an' tharfore we consents with glee. Round up that outlaw of yours now, an' let's get to shootin'.'

"I don't reckon I ever sees anybody who seems as fatigued as that Signal person when Boggs an' Tutt starts to lead him up to the blanket. His face looks like a cancelled postage-stamp. While they're standin' up their folks, Texas goes ragin' loose ag'in because it's a fight over a blanket an' not a handkerchief, as he demands.

"'What's the meanin' of a cold an' formal racket sech as this?' he howls, turnin' to Peets. 'I wants to go clost to my work; I wants to crowd in where it's warm.'

"'I proposes a handkerchief,' says Peets; 'but Tutt objects

on the grounds that his man's got heart palp'tations or somethin'.'

"'You're a liar,' yells Tutt; 'our gent's heart's as solid as
a sod house.'

"'What do I hear?' shouts Peets. 'You calls me a liar?'

"At this Tutt an' Peets lugs out their guns an' blazes away
at each other six times like the roll of a drum—Texas all the
time yellin' for a weepon, an' cavortin' about in the smoke
that demoniac he'd scare me, only I knows it's yoomerous.
Of course Peets an' Tutt misses every shot, and at the wind-
up, after glarin' at each other through the clouds, Peets says
to Tutt:

"'This yere is mere petulance. Let's proceed with our
dooties. As soon as Texas has killed an' skelped the hold-up
you represents, I'll shoot it out with you, if it takes the autumn.'

"'That's good enough for a dog,' says Tutt, stickin' his
gun back in the scabbard; 'an' now we proceeds with the
orig'nal *baile.*'

"But they don't proceed none. As Tutt turns to his Signal
sharp, who's all but locoed by the shootin', an' has to be de-
tained by Boggs from runnin' away, Jack Moore comes chargin' up on his pony an' throws a gun on the whole outfit.

"'Hands up yere!' he says, sharp an' brief; 'or I provides
the coyotes with meat for a month to come.'

"Everybody's hands goes up; an' it's plain Moore's
comin' ain't no dissapp'intment to the Signal person. He's
that relieved he shows it.

"'Don't look so tickled,' growls Boggs to him, as Moore
heads the round-up for the New York Store; 'don't look so
light about it; you mortifies me.'

"Moore takes the band over to the New York Store, where
Enright's settin' as a jedge. He allows he's goin' to put 'em
all on trial for disturbin' of Wolfville's peace. The Signal
sharp starts to say somethin', when Peets interrupts, an' that

brings Boggs to the front, an' after that a gen'ral uproar breaks loose like a stampede.

"'Gimme a knife, somebody,' howls Texas, 'an' let me get in on this as I should. Am I to be robbed of my revenge like this?'

"But Enright jumps for a old Spencer sevenshooter, an' announces it cold, he's out to down the first gent that talks back to him a second time. This ca'ms 'em, an' the riot sort o' simmers.

"'Not that I objects to a street fight,' says Enright, discussin' of the case; 'but you-all talks too much. From the jabber as was goin' for'ard over that blanket out thar, it shorely reminds me more of a passel of old ladies at a quiltin' bee, than a convocation of discreet an' se'f-respectin' gents who's pullin' off a dooel. To cut her short, the public don't tolerate no sech rackets, an' yereupon I puts Texas Thompson an' this Signal party onder fifty-thousand-dollar bonds to keep the peace.'

"Texas is set loose, with Peets an' Cherokee Hall on his papers; but the Signal sharp, bein' strange in camp, can't put up no bonds.

"'Which as thar's no calaboose to put you into,' says Enright, when he's told by the Signal party that he can't make no bonds; 'an' as it's plumb ag'in the constitootion of Arizona to let you go, I shore sees no trail out but hangin'. I regrets them stern necessities which feeds a pore young man to the halter, but you sees yourse'f the Union must an' shall be preserved. Jack, go over to my pony an' fetch the rope. It's a new half-inch manilla, but I cheerfully parts with it in the cause of jestice.'

"When Moore gets back with the rope, an' everybody's lookin' serious, that a-way, it shakes the Signal party to sech a degree that he camps down on a shoe-box an' allows he needs a drink. Boggs says he'll go after it, when Tutt breaks in an' announces that he's got a bluff to hand up.

"'If I'm dead certain,' says Tutt, surveyin' of the Signal party a heap doubtful; 'if I was shore now that this gent wouldn't leave the reservation none, I'd go that bond myse'f. But I'm in no sech fix financial as makes it right for me to get put in the hole for fifty thousand dollars by no stranger, however intimate we be. But yere's what I'm willin' to do: If this sharp wears hobbles so he can't up an' canter off, why, rather than see a young gent's neck a foot longer, I goes this bail myse'f.'

"The Signal party is eager for hobbles, an' he gives Tutt his word to sign up the documents an' he wont run a little bit.

"'Which the same bein' now settled, congenial an' legal,' says Enright, when Tutt signs up; 'Jack Moore he'ps the gent on with them hobbles, an' the court stands adjourned till further orders.'

"After he's all hobbled an' safe, Tutt an' the Signal party starts over for the post-office, both progressin' some slow an' reluctant because of the Signal party's hobbles holdin' him down to a shuffle. As they toils along, Tutt says:

"'An' now that this yere affair ends so successful, I'd shore admire to know whatever you an' that cut-throat takes to chewin' of each other's manes for, anyway? Why did you refoose to bow?'

"'Which I never refooses once,' says the Signal party; 'I salootes this Texas gent with pleasure, if that's what he needs.'

"'In that case,' says Tutt, 'you make yourse'f comfortable leanin' ag'in this buildin', an' I'll project over an' see if this embroglio can't be reeconciled a lot. Mootual apol'gies an' whiskey, looks like, ought to repair them dissensions easy.'

"So the Signal party leans up ag'in the front of the post-office an' surveys his hobbles mighty melancholy, while Tutt goes over to the Red Light to look up Texas Thompson. It ain't no time when he's headed back with Texas an' the balance of the band.

"'Give us your hand, pard,' says Texas, a heap effoosive, as he comes up to the Signal party; 'I learns from our common friend, Dave Tutt, that this yere's a mistake, an' I tharfore forgives you freely all the trouble you causes. It's over now an' plumb forgot. You're a dead game sport, an' I shakes your hand with pride.'

"'Same yere,' says Doc Peets, also shakin' of the Signal party's hand, which is sort o' limp an' cheerless.

"However, we rips off his hobbles, an' then the outfit steers over to the Red Light to be regaled after all our hard work.

"'Yere's hopin' luck an' long acquaintance, stranger,' says Texas, holdin' up his glass to the Signal party, who is likewise p'lite, but feeble.

"'Which the joyous outcome of this tangle shows,' says Dan Boggs, as he hammers his glass on the bar an' shouts for another all 'round, 'that you-all can't have too much talk swappin', when the objects of the meetin' is to avert blood. How much better we feels, standin' yere drinkin' our nose-paint all cool an' comfortable, an' congrat'latin' the two brave sports who's with us, than if we has a corpse sawed onto us onexpected, an' is driven to go grave-diggin' in sech sun-blistered, sizzlin' weather as this.'

"'That's whatever,' says Dave Tutt; 'an' I fills my cup in approval, you can gamble, of them observations.'"

16

How Jack Rainey Quit.

"CUSTOMARY, we has our social round-ups in the Red Light," observed the Old Cattleman; "which I mentions once it does us for a club. We're all garnered into said fold that time when Dave Tutt tells us how this yere Jack Rainey quits out.

"'Rainey gets downed,' says Tutt, 'mainly because his system's obscoore, an' it chances that a stranger who finds himse'f immeshed tharin takes it plumb ombrageous; an' pendin' explanations, gets tangled up with a pard of Rainey's, goes to a gun play, an' all accidental an' casooal Rainey wings his way to them regions of the blest.

"'Now I allers holds,' goes on Tutt, 'an' still swings an' rattles with that decision, that it's manners to ask strangers to drink; an' that no gent, onless he's a sky-pilot or possesses scrooples otherwise, has a right to refoose. Much less has a gent, bein' thus s'licited to licker, any license to take it hostile an' allow he's insulted, an' lay for his entertainers with weapons.'

"'Well, I don't know, neither,' says Texas Thompson, who's a heap dispootatious an' allers spraddlin' in on every chance for an argyment. 'Thar's a party, now deceased a whole lot—the Stranglers over in Socorro sort o' chaperones this yere gent to a cottonwood an' excloodes the air from his lungs with a lariat for mebby it's an hour—an' this party I'm alloodin' at, which his name is Flowler, is plumb murderous. Now, it's frequent with him when he's selected a victim that a-way, an' while he's bickerin' with him up to the killin' p'int, to invite said sacrifice to take a drink. When they're ag'inst the bar, this yere Fowler we-all strangles would pour out a glass of whiskey an' chuck it in the eyes of that onfortunate he's out to down. Of course, while this party's blind with the nose-paint, he's easy; an' Fowler tharupon c'llects his skelp in manner, form an' time to suit his tastes. Now I takes it that manners don't insist none on no gent frontin' up to a bar on the invite of sech felons as Fowler, when a drink that a-way means a speshul short-cut to the tomb.'

"'All this yere may be troo,' replies Tutt, 'but it's a exception. What I insists is, Texas, that speakin' wide an' free an' not allowin' none for sports of the Fowler brand, it's manners to ask strangers to stand in on what beverages is goin'; an' that it's likewise manners for said strangers to accept; an' it shows that both sides concerned tharin is well brought up by their folks. Sech p'liteness is manners, goin' an' comin', which brings me with graceful swoops back to how Jack Rainey gets shot up.'

"'But, after all,' breaks in Texas ag'in, for he feels wranglesome, 'manners is frequent a question of where you be. What's manners in St. Looey may be bad jedgment in Texas; same as some commoonities plays straights in poker, while thar's regions where straights is barred.'

"'Texas is dead right about his State that a-way,' says Jack Moore, who's heedin' of the talk. 'Manners is a heap more inex'rable in Texas than other places. I recalls how I'm galivantin' 'round in the Panhandle country—it's years ago when I'm young an' recent—an' as I'm ridin' along south of the Canadian one day, I discerns a pony an' a gent an' a fire, an' what looks like a yearlin' calf tied down. I knows the pony for Lem Woodruff's cayouse, an' heads over to say "Howdy" to Lem. He's about half a mile away; when of a sudden he stands up—he's been bendin' over the yearlin' with a runnin' iron in his hand—an' gives a whoop an' makes some copious references towards me with his hands. I wonders what for a game he's puttin' up, an' whatever is all this yere sign-language likely to mean; but I keeps ridin' for'ard. It's then this Woodruff steps over to his pony, an' takin' his Winchester off the saddle, cuts down with it in my direction, an' onhooks her—"Bang!" The bullet raises the dust over about fifty yards to the right. Nacherally I pulls up my pony to consider conduct. While I'm settin' thar tryin' to figger out Woodruff's system, thar goes that Winchester ag'in' an' a streak of dust lifts up, say fifty yards to the left. I then sees Lem objects to me. I don't like no gent to go carpin' an' criticisin' at me with a gun; but havin' a Winchester that a-way, this yere Woodruff can overplay me with only a six-shooter, so I quits him an' rides contemptuous away. As I withdraws, he hangs his rifle on his saddle ag'in' picks up his runnin' iron an' goes back content an' all serene to his maverick.'"

"What is a maverick?" I asked, interrupting my friend in the flow of his narration.

"Why, I s'posed," he remarked, a bit testily at being halted, "as how even shorthorns an' tender-feet knows what mavericks is. Mavericks, son, is calves which gets sep'rated from the old cows, their mothers, an' ain't been branded none yet. They're bets which the round-ups overlooks, an' don't get marked. Of course, when they drifts from their mothers, each calf for himse'f, an' no brands nor y'ear marks, no one can tell whose calves they be. They ain't branded, an' the old cows ain't thar to identify an' endorse 'em, an' thar you stands in ignorance. Them's mavericks.

"It all comes," he continued in further elucidation of mavericks, "when cattle brands is first invented in Texas. The owners, whose cattle is all mixed up on the ranges, calls a meetin' to decide on brands, so each gent'll know his own when he crosses up with it, an' won't get to burnin' powder with his neighbors over a steer which breeds an' fosters doubts. After every party announces what his brand an' y'ear mark will be, an' the same is put down in the book, a old longhorn named Maverick addresses the meetin', an' puts it up if so be thar's no objection, now they all has brands but him, he'll let his cattle lope without markin', an' every gent'll savey said Maverick's cattle because they won't have no brand. Cattle without brands, that a-way, is to belong to Maverick, that's the scheme, an' as no one sees no reason why not, they lets old Maverick's proposal go as it lays.

"An' to cut her short, for obv'ous reasons, it ain't no time before Maverick, claimin' all the onbranded cattle, has herds on herds of 'em; whereas thar's good authority which states that when he makes his bluff about not havin' no brand that time, all the cattle old Maverick has is a triflin' bunch of Mexican steers an' no semblances of cows in his outfit. From which onpromisin', not to say barren, beginnin', Maverick owns thousands of cattle at the end of ten years. It all provokes a heap of merriment an' scorn. An' ever since that day, onmarked an onbranded cattle is called 'mavericks.' But to go back ag'in to what Jack Moore is remarkin' about this yere outlaw, Woodruff, who's been bustin' away towards Jack with his Winchester.

"'It's a week later,' goes on Jack Moore, 'when I encounters this sport Woodruff in Howard's store over in Tascosa. I stands him up an' asks whatever he's shootin' me up for that day near the Serrita la Cruz.

"'"Which I never sees you nohow," replies this yere Woodruff, laughin'. "I never cuts down on you with no Winchester, for if I did, I'd got you a whole lot. You bein' yere all petulant an' irritated is mighty good proof I never is shootin' none at you. But bein' you're new to the Canadian country an' to Texas, let me give you a few p'inters

on cow ettyquette an' range manners. Whenever you notes
a gent afar off with a fire goin' an' a yearlin' throwed an'
hawg-tied ready to mark up a heap with his own private
hieroglyphics, don't you-all go pesterin' 'round him. He
ain't good company, sech a gent ain't. Don't go near him.
It's ag'in the law in Texas to brand calves lonely an' forlorn
that a-way, without stoppin' to herd 'em over to some well-
known corral, an' the punishment it threatens, bein' several
years in Huntsville, makes a gent when he's violatin' it a
hcap misanthropic, an' he don't hunger none for folks to
come ridin' up to see about whatever he reckons he's at.
Mebby later them visitors gets roped up before a co't, or
jury, to tell whatever they may know. So, as I says, an'
merely statin' a great trooth in Texas ettyquette, yereafter on
beholdin' a fellow-bein' with a calf laid out to make, don't
go near him a little bit. It's manners to turn your back onto
him an' ignore him plumb severe. He's a crim'nal, an' any
se'f-respectin' gent is jestified in refoosin' to affiliate with
him. Wherefore, you ride away from every outcast you
tracks up ag'inst who is engaged like you says this onknown
party is the day he fetches loose his Winchester at you over
by the Serrita la Cruz."

"'That's what this Woodruff says,' concloodes Jack,
windin' up his interruption, 'about what's manners in Texas;
an' when it's made explicit that a-way, I sees the force of
his p'sition. Woodruff an' me buys nose-paint for each
other, shakes hearty, an' drops the discussion. But it shorely
comes to this: manners, as Texas declar's, is sometimes born
of geography, an' what goes for polish an' the p'lite play in
St. Looey may not do none for Texas.'

"'Mighty likely,' says Old Man Enright, 'what Texas
Thompson an' Jack Moore interjecks yere is dead c'rrect;
but after all this question about what's manners is 'way to
one side of the main trail. I tharfore su'gests at this crisis
that Black Jack do his best with a bottle, an' when every

gent has got his p'ison, Dave Tutt proceeds for'ard with the killin' of this Jack Rainey.'

"'Goin' on as to said Rainey,' observes Tutt, followin' them remarks of Enright, 'as I explains when Texas an' Moore runs me down with them interestin' outbreaks, Rainey gets ag'inst it over in a jimcrow camp called Lido; an' this yere is a long spell ago.

"'Rainey turns in an' charters every bar in Lido, an' gets his brand onto all the nose-paint. He's out to give the camp an orgy, an' not a gent can spend a splinter or lose a chip to any bar for a week. Them's Jack Rainey's commands. A sport orders his forty drops, an' the barkeep pricks it onto a tab; at the end of a week Jack Rainey settles all along the line, an' the "saturnalia," as historians calls 'em, is over. I might add that Jack Rainey gives way to these yere charities once a year, an the camp of Lido is plumb used tharto an' approves tharof.

"'On this sad o'casin when Jack Rainey gets killed, this yere excellent custom he invents is in full swing. Thar's notices printed plenty big, an' posted up in every drink-shop from the dance hall to the Sunflower saloon; which they reads as follows:

RUIN!   RUIN!   RUIN!

CUT LOOSE!

JACK RAINEY MAKES GOOD

ALL DRINKS

FOR

ONE WEEK.   NAME YOUR POISON!

"'At this yere time, it's about half through Jack Rainey's week, an' the pop'lace of Lido, in consequence, is plumb happy an' content. They're holdin' co't at the time; the same bein' the first jestice, legal, which is dealt out in Lido.'

"'An' do you-all know,' puts in Dan Boggs, who's listnein' to Tutt, 'I'm mighty distrustful of co'ts. You go to holdin' of 'em, an' it looks like everybody gets wrought up to frenzy ontil life where them forums is held ain't safe for a second. I shall shorely deplore the day when a co't goes to openin' its game in Wolfville. It's "*adios*" to liberty an' peace an' safety from that time.'

"'You can go a yellow stack,' remarks Texas Thompson, who sets thar plumb loquacious an' locoed to get in a speech, 'that Boggs sizes up right about them triboonals. They're a disturbin' element in any commoonity. I knowed a town in Texas which is that peaceful it's pastoral—that's what it is, it's like a sheepfold, it's so meek an' easy—ontil one day they ups an' plays a co't an' jedge an' jury on that camp; rings in a herd of law sharps, an' a passel of rangers with Winchesters to back the deal. The town's that fretted tharat it gets full of nose-paint to the brim, an' then hops into the street for gen'ral practice with its guns. In the mornin' the round-up shows two dead an' five wounded, an' all for openin' co't on an outfit which is too frail to stand the strain of so much jestice onexpected.'

"'As I'm engaged in remarkin',' says Tutt, after Boggs an' Texas is redooced to quiet ag'in—Tutt bein' married most likely is used to interruptions, an' is shore patient that a-way—'as I states, they're holdin' co't, an' this day they emancipates from prison a party named Caribou Sam. They tries to prove this Caribou Sam is a hoss-thief, but couldn't fill on the draw, an' so Caribou works free of 'em an' is what they calls "'quitted."

"'As soon as ever the marshal takes the hobbles off this Caribou Sam—he's been held a captif off some'ers an' is packed into Lido onder gyard to be tried a lot—this yere malefactor comes bulgin' into the Sunflower an' declar's for fire-water. The barkeep deals to him, an' Caribou Sam is assuaged.

"'When he goes to pay, a gent who's standin' near shoves back his dust, an' says: "This is Jack Rainey's week—it's the great annyooal festival of Jack Rainey, an' your money's no good."

""But I aims to drink some more *poco tiempo*," says this Caribou Sam, who is new to Lido, an' never yet hears of Jack Rainey an' his little game, "an' before I permits a gent to subsidize my thirst, an' go stackin'in for my base appetites, you can gamble I want to meet him an' make his acquaintance. Where is this yere sport Jack Rainey, an' whatever is he doin' this on?"

"'The party who shoves Caribou's *dinero* off the bar, tells him he can't pay, an' explains the play, an' exhorts him to drink free an' frequent an' keep his chips in his war-bags.

""As I tells you," says this party to Caribou, "my friend Jack Rainey has treed the camp, an' no money goes yere but his till his further commands is known. Fill your hide, but don't flourish no funds, or go enlargin' on any weakness you has for buyin' your own licker. As for seein' Jack Rainey, it's plumb impossible. He's got too full to visit folks or be visited by 'em; but he's upsta'rs on some blankets, an' if his reason is restored by tomorry, you sends up your kyard an' pays him your regyards—pendin' of which social function, take another drink. Barkeep, pump another dose into this stranger, an' charge the same to Jack."

""This yere sounds good," says 'Caribou Sam, "but it don't win over me. Ontil I sees this person Rainey, I shall shorely decline all bottles which is presented in his name. I've had a close call about a bronco I stole to-day, an' when the jury makes a verdict that they're sorry to say the evidence ain't enough to convict, the jedge warns me to be a heap careful of the company I maintains. He exhorts me to live down my past, or failin' which he'll hang me yet. With this bluff from the bench ringin in my y'ears, I shall refoose drinks with all onknown sots, ontil I sees for myse'f they's proper characters for me to be sociable with. Tharfore, barkeep, I renoo my determination to pay for them drinks; at

the same time, I orders another round. Do you turn for me
or no?"

""'Not none you don't," says the friend of Jack Rainey.
"You can drink, but you can't pay—leastwise, you-all can't
pay without gettin' all sort o' action on your money. This
Rainey you're worried about is as good a gent as me, an'
not at all likely to shake the standin' of a common hoss-thief
by merely buyin' his nosepaint."

""'Mine is shorely a difficult p'sition," says Caribou Sam.
"What you imparts is scarce encouragin.' If this yere Rainey
ain't no improvement onto you, I absolootely weakens on
him an' turns aside from all relations of his proposin'. I'm
in mighty bad report as the game stands, an' I tharfore insists ag'in on payin' for my own war medicine, as bein' a
move necessary to protect my attitoodes before the public."

"'With these yere observations, Caribou Sam makes a
bluff at the barkeep with a handful of money. In remonstra-
tin', Jack Rainey's pard nacherally pulls a gun, as likewise
does Caribou Sam. Thar's the customary quantity of
shootin', an' while neither Caribou nor his foe gets drilled,
a bullet goes through the ceilin' an' sort o' sa'nters in a
careless, indifferent way into pore Jack Rainey, where he's
bedded down an' snorin' up above.

"'Shore, he's dead, Rainey is,' concloodes Dave, 'an' his
ontimely takin' off makes Lido quit loser for three days of
licker free as air. He's a splendid, gen'rous soul, Jack
Rainey is; an' as I says at the beginnin', he falls a sacrifice
to his love for others, an' in tryin' at his own expense to
promote the happiness an' lift them burdens of his fellow-
men.'

"'This yere miscreant, Caribou,' says Texas Thompson,
'is a mighty sight too punctilious about them drinks; which
thar's no doubt of it. Do they lynch him?'

"'No,' says Tutt; 'from the calibre of the gun which fires
the lead that snatches Rainey from us, it is cl'ar that it's the

gent who's contendin' with Caribou who does it. Still public opinion is some sour over losin' them three days, an' so Caribou goes lopin' out of Lido surreptitious that same evenin', an' don't wait none on Rainey's obsequies Caribou merely sends regrets by the barkeep of the Sunflower, reiterates the right to pay for them drinks an' Lido sees him no more.'"

17

Colonel Sterett's War Record.

I T had been dark and overcast as to skies; the weather, however, was found serene and balmy enough. As I climbed the steps after my afternoon canter, I encountered the Old Cattleman. He was relocating one of the big veranda chairs more to his comfort, and the better to enjoy his tobacco. He gave me a glance as I came up.

"Them's mighty puny spurs," he observed with an eye of half commiseration, half disdain; "them's shore reedic'lous. Which they'd destroy your standin' with a cow pony, utter. He'd fill up with contempt for you like a water-hole in April. Shore! it's the rowels; they oughter be the size an' shape of a mornin' star, them rowels had. Then a gent might hope for action. An' whyever don't you-all wear leather chapps that a-way, instead of them jimcrow boots an' trousers? They're plumb amoosin', them garments be. No, I onderstands; you don't go chargin' about in the bresh an' don't need chapps, but still you oughter don 'em for the looks. Thar's a wrong an' a right way to do; an' chapps is right. Thar's Johnny Cook of the Turkey Track; he's like you; he contemns chapps. Johnny charges into a wire fence one midnight, sorto' sidles into said boundary full surge; after that Johnny wears chapps all right. Does it hurt him? Son, them wires t'ars enough hide off Johnny, from some'ers about the hock, to make a saddle cover, an' he loses blood sufficient to paint a house. He comes mighty near goin' shy a laig on the deal. It's a lesson on c'rrect costumes that Johnny don't soon forget.

"No, I never rides a hoss none now. These yere Eastern saddles ain't the right model. Which they's a heap too low in the cantle an' too low in the horn. An' them stirrup leathers is too short, an' two inches too far for'ard. I never does grade over-high for ridin' a hoss, even at my best. No, I don't get pitched off more'n is comin' to me'; still, I ain't p'inted out to the tenderfeet as no 'Centaur' as Doc Peets calls 'em. I gets along without buckin' straps, an' my friends don't have to tie no roll of blankets across my saddle-horn, an' that's about the best I can report.

"Texas Thompson most likely is the chief equestr'an of Wolfville. One time Texas makes a wager of a gallon of licker with Jack Moore, an' son! yere's what Texas does. I sees him with these eyes. Texas takes his rope an' ties down a bronco; one the record whereof is that he's that toomultuous no one can ride him. Most gents would have ducked at the name of this yere steed, the same bein' 'Dynamite.' But Texas makes the bet I mentions, an' lays for his onrooly cayouse with all the confidence of virgin gold that a-way.

"Texas ropes an' ties him down an' cinches the saddle into him while he's layin' thar; Tutt kneelin' on his locoed head doorin' the ceremony. Then Tutt throws him loose; an' when he gets up he nacherally rises with Texas Thompson on his back.

"First, that bronco stands in a daze, an' Texas takes advantage of his trance to lay two silver dollars on the saddle, one onder each of his laigs. An' final, you should shorely have beheld that bronco put his nose between his laigs an' arch himse'f an' buck! Reg'lar worm-fence buckin' it is; an' when he ain't hittin' the ground, he's shore abundant in that atmosphere a lot.

"In the midst of these yere flights, which the same is enough to stim'late the imagination of a Apache, Texas, as ca'm an' onmoved as the Spanish Peaks, rolls an' lights a cigarette. Then he picks up the bridle an' gives that roysterin' bronco jest enough of the Mexican bit to fill his mouth with blood an' his mind with doubts, an' stops him. When Texas swings to the ground, them two silver dollars comes jinglin' along; which he holds 'em to the saddle that a-way throughout them exercises. It's them dollars an' the cigarette that raises the licker issue between Jack an' Texas; an' of course, Texas quits winner for the nose-paint."

I had settled by this time into a chair convenient to my reminiscent companion, and relishing the restful ease after a twenty-mile run, decided to prolong the talk. Feeling for subjects, I became tentatively curious concerning politics.

"Cow people," said my friend, "never saveys pol'tics. I wouldn't give a Mexican sheep—which is the thing of lowest valyoo I knows of except Mexicans themse'fs—for the views of any cowpuncher on them questions of state. You can gamble an' make the roof the limit, them opinions, when you-all once gets 'em rounded up, would be shore loodicrous, not to say footile.

"Now, we-all wolves of Wolfville used to let Colonel Strerett do our polit'cal yelpin' for us; sort o' took his word for p'sition an' stood pat tharon. It's in the Red Light this very evenin' when Texas subdoos that bronco, an' lets the whey outen Jack Moore to the extent of said jug of Valley Tan, that Colonel Sterett goes off at a round road-gait on this yere very topic of pol'tics, an' winds up by tellin' us of his attitood, personal, doorin' the civil war, an' the debt he owes some Gen'ral named Wheeler for savin' of his life.

"'Pol'tics,' remarks Colonel Sterett on that o'casion, refillin' his glass for the severaleth time, ''jest nacherally oozes from a editor, as you-all who reads reg'larly the *Coyote* b'ars witness; he's saturated with pol'tics same as Huggins is with whiskey. As for myse'f, aside from my vocations of them tripods, pol'tics is inborn in me. I gets 'em from my grandfather, as tall a sport an' as high-rollin' a statesman as ever packs a bowie or wins the beef at a

shootin' match in old Kaintucky. Yes, sir,' says the Colonel, an' thar's a pensive look in his eyes like he's countin'
up that ancestor's merits in his mem'ry; 'pol'tics with me
that-away is shore congenital.'

"'Congenital!' says Dan Boggs, an' his tones is a heap
satisfact'ry; 'an' thar's a word that's good enough for a dog.
I reckons I'll tie it down an' brand it into my bunch right
yere.'

"'My grandfather,' goes on the Colonel, 'is a Jackson
man; from the top of the deck plumb down to the hock
kyard, he's nothin' but Jackson. This yere attitood of my
grandsire, an' him camped in the swarmin' midst of a Henry
Clay country, is frootful of adventures an' calls for plenty
nerve. But the old Spartan goes through.

"'Often as a child, that old gent has done took me on his
knee an' told me how he meets up first with Gen'ral
Jackson. He's goin' down the river in one of the little old
steamboats of that day, an' the boat is shore crowded. My
grandfather has to sleep on the floor, as any more in the
bunks would mean a struggle for life an' death. Thar's
plenty of bunkless gents, however, besides him, an' as he
sinks into them sound an' dreamless slumbers which is the
her'tage of folks whose conscience run troo, he hears 'em
drinkin' an' talkin' an' barterin' mendacity, an' argyfyin'
pol'tics on all sides.

"'My grandfather sleeps on for hours, an' is only aroused
from them torpors, final, by some sport chunkin' him a
thump in the back. The old lion is sleepin' on his face, that
away, an' when he gets mauled like I related, he wakes up
an' goes to struggle to his feet.

"'"B'ars an' buffaloes!" says my grandfather; "whatever's
that?"

"'"Lay still, stranger," says the party who smites him;
"I've only got two to go."

"'That's what it is. It's a couple of gents playin' seven-up;

and bein' crowded, they yootilizes my grandfather for a table. This sport is swingin' the ace for the opp'site party's jack, an' he boards his kyard with that enthoosiasm it comes mighty clost to dislocatin' my old gent's shoulder. But he's the last Kaintuckian to go interferin' with the reecreations of others, so he lays thar still an' prone till the hand's played out.

""'High, jack, game!' says the stranger, countin' up; "that puts me out an' one over for lannyap."

"'This yere seven-up gents turns out to be General Jackson, an' him an' my grandfather camps down in a corner, drinks up the quart of Cincinnati Rectified which is the stakes, an' becomes mootually acquainted. An', gents, I says it with pride, the hero of the Hoss-shoe, an' the walloper of them English at New Orleans takes to my grandfather like a honeysuckle to a front porch.

"'My grandfather comes plenty near forfeitin' them good opinions of the Gen'ral, though. It's the next day, an' that ancestor of mine an' the Gen'ral is recoverin' themse'fs from the conversation of the night before with a glass or two of tanzy bitters, when a lady, who descends on the boat at Madison, comes bulgin' into the gents' cabin. The captain an' two or three of the boat's folks tries to herd her into the women's cabin; but she withers 'em with a look, breshes 'em aside, an' stampedes along in among the men-people like I explains. About forty of 'em's smokin'; an' as tobacco is a fav'rite weakness of the tribe of Sterett, my grandfather is smokin' too.

""'I wants you-all to make these yere miscreants stop smokin'," says the lady to the captain, who follows along thinkin' mebby he gets her headed right after she's had her run out an' tires down some. "You're the captain of this tub," says the lady, "an' I demands my rights. Make these barb'rous miscreants stop smokin', or I leaves the boat ag'in right yere."

"'The lady's plumb fierce, an' her face which, is stern an' heroic, carries a capac'ty for trouble lurkin' 'round in it, same as one of them bald hornet's nests on a beech limb. Nacherally my grandfather's gaze gets rivited on this lady a whole lot, his pipe hangin' forgetful from his lips. The lady's eyes all at once comes down on my grandfather, partic'lar an' personal, like a milk-crock from a high shelf.

"'"An I mean you speshul," says the lady, p'intin' the finger of scorn at my grandfather. "The idee of you standin' thar smokin' in my very face, an' me atotterin' invalid. It shorely shows you ain't nothin' but a brute. If I was your wife I'd give you p'isen."

"'"Which if you was my wife, I'd shore take it," says my grandfather; for them epithets spurs him on the raw, an' he forgets he's a gent, that a-way, an' lets fly this yere retort before he can give him se'f the curb."

"'The moment my grandfather makes them observations, the lady catches her face—which as I tells you is a cross between a gridiron an' a steel trap—with both her hands, shakes her h'ar down her back, an' cuts loose a scream which, like a b'ar in a hawgpen, carries all before it. Then she falls into the captain's arms an' orders him to pack her out on the deck where she can faint.

"'"Whatever be you-all insultin' this yere lady for?" says a passenger, turnin' on my grandfather like a crate of wildcats. "Which I'm the Roarin' Wolverine of Smoky Bottoms, an' I waits for a reply."

"'My grandfather is standin' thar some confoosed an' wrought up, an' as warm as a wolf, thinkin' how ornery he's been by gettin' acrid with that lady. The way he feels, this yere Roarin' Wolverine party comes for'ard as a boon. The old gent simply falls upon him, jaw an' claw, an' goes to smashin' furniture an' fixin's with him.

"'The Roarin' Wolverine allows after, when him an' my grandfather drinks a toddy an' compares notes, while a jack-

laig doctor who's aboard sews the Roarin' Wolverine's y'ear
back on, that he thinks at the time it's the boat blowin' up.

""'She's shore the vividest skrimmage I ever partic'pates
in," says the Roarin' Wolverine; 'an' the busiest. I wouldn't
have missed it for a small clay farm."

"'But Gen'ral Jackson when he comes back from offerin'
condolences to the lady, looks dignified an' shakes his head
a heap grave.

""'Them contoomelious remarks to the lady," he says to
my grandfather, "lowers you in my esteem a lot. An' while
the way you breaks up that settee with the Roarin' Wolverine goes some towards reestablishin' you, still I shall not
look on you as the gent I takes you for, ontil you seeks this
yere injured female an' crawfishes on that p'isen takin'
bluff."

"'So my grandfather goes out on deck where the lady is
still sobbin' an' hangin' on the captain's neck like the loop
of a rope, an' apol'gizes. Then the lady takes a brace, accepts them contritions, an' puts it up for her part that she
can see my grandfather's a shore-enough gent an' a son of
chivalry; an' with that the riot winds up plumb pleasant all
'round.'

"'If I may come romancin' in yere,' says Doc Peets, sort
o' breakin' into the play at this p'int, 'with a interruption,
I wants to say that I regyards this as a very pretty narratif,
an' requests the drinks onct to the Colonel's grandfather.'
We drinks accordin', an' the Colonel resoomes.

"'My grandfather comes back from this yere expedition
down the Ohio a most voylent Jackson man. An' he's troo
to his faith as a adherent to Jackson through times when the
Clay folks gets that intemp'rate they hunts 'em with dogs.
The old gent was wont, as I su'gests, to regale my childish
y'ears with the story of what he suffers. He tells how he
goes pirootin' off among the farmers in the back counties;
sleepin' on husk beds, till the bedropes cuts plumb through

an' marks out a checkerboard on his frame that would stay for months. Once he's sleepin' in a loft, an' all of a sudden about daybreak the old gent hears a squall that mighty near locoes him, it's so clost an' turrible. He boils out on the floor an' begins to claw on his duds, allowin', bein' he's only half awake that a-way, that it's a passel of them murderin' Clay Whigs who's come to crawl his hump for shore. But she's a false alarm. It's only a Dom'nick rooster who's been perched all night on my grandfather's wrist where his arm sticks outen bed, an' who's done crowed a whole lot, as is his habit when he glints the comin' day. It's them sort o' things that sends a shudder through you, an' shows what that old patriot suffers for his faith.

"'But my grandfather keeps on prevailin' along in them views ontil he jest conquers his county an' carries her for Jackson. Shore! he has trouble at the polls, an' trouble in the conventions. But he persists; an' he's that domineerin' an' dogmatic they at last not only gives him his way, but comes rackin' along with him. In the last convention, he nacherally herds things into a corner, an' thar's only forty votes ag'in him at the finish. My grandfather allers says when relatin' of it to me long afterwards:

"'"An' grandson Willyum, five gallons more of rum would have made that convention yoonanimous."

"'But what he'ps the old gent most towards the last, is a j'int debate he has with Spence Witherspoon, which begins with reecrim'nations an' winds up with the guns. Also, it leaves this yere aggravatin' Witherspoon less a whole lot.

"'"Wasn't you-all for nullification, an' ain't you now for Jackson an' the union?" asks this yere insultin' Witherspoon. "Didn't you make a Calhoun speech over on Mink Run two years ago, an' ain't you at this barbecue, to-day, consoomin' burgoo an' shoutin' for Old Hickory?"

"'"What you-all states is troo," says my grandfather. "But my party turns, an' I turns with it. You-all can't lose Jack

Sterett. He can turn so quick the heels of his moccasins will be in front."

""'Which them talents of yours for change," says Witherspoon, "reminds me a powerful lot of the story of how Jedge Chinn gives Bill Hatfield, the blacksmith, that Berkshire suckin' pig."

""'An' whatever is that story?" asks my grandfather, beginnin' to loosen his bowie-knife in its sheath.

""'Take your paws off that old butcher of your'n," returns this pesterin' Witherspoon, "an' I'll tell the story. But you've got to quit triflin' with that 'leven-inch knife ontil I'm plumb through, or I'll fool you up a lot an' jest won't tell it."

"'Tharupon my grandfather takes his hand offen the knife-haft, an' Witherspoon branches forth:

""'When I recalls how this oncompromisin' outlaw," p'intin' to my grandfather, "talks for Calhoun an' nullification over on Mink Run, an' today is yere shoutin' in a rum-sodden way for the union an' Andy Jackson, as I observes yeretofore, it shore reminds me of the story of how Jedge Chinn give Bill Hatfield that Berkshire shoat. 'Send over one of your niggers with a basket an' let him get one, Bill,' says Jedge Chinn, who's been tellin' Hatfield about the pigs. Next day, Bill mounts his nigger boy, Dick, on a mule, with a basket on his arm, an' Dick lines out for Jedge Chinn's for to fetch away that little hawg. Dick puts him in the basket, climbs onto his mule, an' goes teeterin' out for home. On the way back Dick stops at Hickman's tavern. While he's pourin' in a gill of corn jooce, a wag who's present subtracts the pig an' puts in one of old Hickman's black Noofoundland pups. When Dick gets home to Bill Hatfield's, Bill takes one look at the pup, breaks the big rasp on Dick's head, throws the forehammer at him, an' bids him go back to Jedge Chinn an' tell him that he, Bill, will sally over the first dull day an' p'isen his cattle an' burn his barns. Dick takes the basket full of dog on his arm, an' goes p'intin' for Jedge Chinn. Nacherally, Dick stops at Hickman's tavern so as to mollify his feelin's with that red-eye. This yere wag gets in ag'in on the play, subtracts the pup an' restores the little hawg a whole lot. When Dick gets to Jedge Chinn, he onfolds to the Jedge touchin' them trans-formations from pig to pup. 'Pshaw!' says the Jedge, who's one of them pos'tive sharps that no ghost tales is goin' to shake; 'pshaw! Bill Hatfield's gettin' to be a loonatic. I tells him the last time I has my hoss shod that if he keeps on pourin' down that Hickman whiskey, he'll shorely die, an' begin by dyin' at the top. These yere illoosians of his shows I drives the center.' Then the Jedge oncovers the basket an' turns out the little hawg. When nigger Dick sees him he falls on his knees. 'I'm a chu'ch member, Marse Jedge,' says Dick, 'an' you-all believes what I says. That anamile's con-jured, Jedge. I sees him yere an' I sees him thar; an' Jedge, he's either pig or pup, whichever way he likes.'

"""An', ladies an' gents," concloodes this Whitherspoon, makin' a incriminatin' gesture so's to incloode my grand-father that a-way; "When I reflects on this onblushin' turncoat, Jack Sterett, as I states prior, it makes me think of how Jedge Chinn lavishes that Berkshire shoat on blacksmith Bill Hatfield. Confessin' that afore time he's a nullification pig on Mink Run, he sets yere at this barbecue an' without color of shame declar's himse'f a union pup. Mister Cha'rman, all I can say is, it shore beats squinch owls!"

"'As the story is finished, the trooce which binds my grandfather ends, an' he pulls his bowie-knife an' chases this Witherspoon from the rostrum. He'd had his detractor's skelp right thar, but the cha'rman an' other leadin' sperits interferes, an' insists on them resentments of my grand-father's findin' the usual channel in their expression. With-erspoon, who's got on a new blanket coat, allows he won't fight none with knives as they cuts an' sp'iles your clothes;

he says he prefers rifles an' fifty paces for his. My grandfather, who's the easiest gent to get along with in matters
of mere detail, is agree'ble; an' as neither him nor Witherspoon has brought their weepons, the two vice pres'dents,
who's goin' to act as seconds—the pres'dent by mootual
consent dealin' the game as referee—rummages about an'
borrys a brace of Looeyville rifles from members of the
Black B'ar Glee Club—they're the barytone an' tenor—an'
my grandfather an' the scandal-mongerin' Witherspoon is
stood up.

""""Gents," says the pres'dent, "the words will be, 'Fire-
one-two-three-stop.' It's incumbent on you-all to blaze away
anywhere between the words 'Fire' an' 'Stop'. My partin'
injunctions is, 'May heaven defend the right,' an' be shore
an' see your hindsights as you onhooks your guns."

"'At the word, my grandfather an' Witherspoon responds
prompt an' gay. Witherspoon overshoots, while my grandfather plants his lead in among Witherspoon's idees, an' that
racontoor quits Kaintucky for the other world without a
murmur.

""""I regyards this event as a vict'ry for Jackson an' prin-
ciple," says my grandfather, as he's called on to proceed
with his oration, "an' I'd like to say in that connection, if
Henry Clay will count his spoons when he next comes
sneakin' home from Washin'ton, he'll find he's short Spence
Witherspoon."'

"'Your grandfather's a troo humorist,' says Texas
Thompson, as Colonel Sterett pauses in them recitals of his
to reach the bottle; 'I looks on that last witticism of his
plumb apt.'

"'My grandfather,' resoomes Colonel Sterett, after bein'
refreshed, 'is as full of fun as moneymusk, an' when that
audience gets onto the joke in its completeness, the merriment is wide an yooniversal. It's the hit of the barbecue; an'
in this way, little by little, my grandfather wins his

neighbors to his beliefs, ontil he's got the commoonity all stretched an'hawgtied, an' brands her triumphant for Gen'ral Jackson.'

"'An' does your own pap follow in the footprints of his old gent, as a convincin' an' determined statesman that a-way?' asks Doc Peets.

"'No,' says Colonel Sterett, 'my own personal parent simmers down a whole lot compared to my grandfather. He don't take his pol'tics so much to heart; his democracy ain't so virulent an' don't strike in. His only firm stand on questions of state, as I relates the other day, is when he insists on bein' nootral doorin' the late war. I explains how he talks federal an' thinks reb, an' manages that a-way, to promote a decent average.

"'His nootrality, however, don't incloode the fam'ly none. My brother Jeff—an' I never beholds a haughtier sperit— goes squanderin' off with Morgan at the first boogle call,'

"'That raid of Morgan's' says Enright, his eye brightenin', 'is plumb full of dash an' fire.'

"'Shore,' says the Colonel, 'plumb full of dash an' fire. But Jeff tells me of it later, foot by foot, from the time they crosses the river into Injeanny, till they comes squatterin' across at Blennerhasset's Island into Kaintucky ag'in, an' I sadly, though frankly, admits it looks like it possesses some elements of a chicken-stealin' expedition also. Jeff says he never sees so many folks sincere, an' with their minds made up, as him an' Morgan an' the rest of the Bloo Grass chivalry encounters on that croosade. Thar's an uprisin' of the peasantry, Jeff says, where ever they goes; an' them clods pursooes Jeff an' the others, from start to finish, with hoes an' rakes an' mattocks an' clothes-poles an' puddin'sticks an' other barbarous an' obsolete arms, an' never lets up ontil Jeff an' Morgan an' their gallant comrades is ag'in safe in the arms of their Kaintucky brethren. Their stay in any given spot is trooly brief. That town of Cincinnati makes up a bundle of money big enough to choke a cow to give 'em as a ransom; but Jeff an' Morgan never do hear of it for years. They goes by so plumb swift they don't get notice; an' they fades away in the distance so fast they keeps ahead of the news. However, they gets back to Kaintucky safe an' covered with dust an' glory in even parts; an' as for Jeff speshul, as the harvest of his valor, he reports himse'f the owner of a one-sixth interest in a sleigh which him an' five of his indomitable companions has done drug across the river on their return. But they don't linger over this trophy; dooty calls 'em, so they stores the sleigh in a barn an' rides away to further honors.

"'We never do hear of Jeff none all through that war but once. After he's j'ined Stonewall Jackson, I recalls how he sends home six hundred dollars in confed'rate money with a letter to my father. It runs like this:

> In camp with STONEWALL JACKSON.
> Respected Sir:
>   The slave who bears this will give you from me a treasure of six hundred dollars. I desire that you pay the tavern and whatever creditors of mine you find. To owe debts does not comport with the honor of a cavalier, and I propose to silence all base clamors on that head. I remain, most venerated sir,   Yours to command,
> JEFFERSON STERETT.

"'That's the last we-all hears of my sens'tive an' high-sperited brother ontil after Mister Lee surrenders. It's one mornin' when Jeff comes home, an' the manner of his return shorely displays his nobility of soul, that a-way, as ondiscouraged an ondimmed. No one's lookin' for Jeff partic'lar, when I hears a steamboat whistle for our landin'. I bein' as I am full of the ontamed cur'osity of yooth, goes curvin' out to see what's up. I hears the pilot give the engineer the bells to set her back on the sta'board wheel, an' then on both. The boat comes driftin' in. A stagin' is let down, an' with the tread of a conqueror who should come ashore but my brother Jeff! Thar's nothin' in his hands; he ain't got nothin' with him that he ain't wearin'. An' all he has on is a old wool hat, a hick'ry shirt, gray trousers, an' a pair of copper-rivet shoes as red as a bay hoss. As he strikes the bank, Jeff turns an' sweeps the scene with the eye of a eagle. Then takin' a bogus silver watch outen his pocket, he w'irls her over his head by the leather string an' lets her go out into the river, *kerchunk!*

""""Which I enters into this yere rebellion," says Jeff, flashin' a proud, high glance on me where I stands wonderin', "without nothin', an' I proposes to return with honor ontarnished, an' as pore as I goes in."

"'As me an' Jeff reepairs up to the house, I notes the most renegade-lookin' nigger followin' behind.

""""Whoever's this yere nigger?" I asks.

""""He's my valet," says Jeff.

"'My arm's a heap too slight,' goes on Colonel Sterett, followin' a small libation, 'to strike a blow for the con-fed'racy, but my soul is shorely in the cause. I does try to j'ine, final, an' is only saved tharfrom, an' from what would, ondoubted, have been my certain death, by a reb gen'ral named Wheeler. He don't mean to do it; she's inad-vertent so far as he's concerned; but he saves me jest the same. An' settin' yere as I be, enjoyin' the friendship an' esteem of you-all citizens of Wolfville, I feels more an' more the debt of gratitoode I owes that gallant officer an' man.'

"'However does this Gen'ral Wheeler save you?' asks Dan Boggs. 'Which I'm shore eager to hear.'

"'The tale is simple,' responds the Colonel, 'an' it's a triboote to that brave commander which I'm allers ready to pay. It's in the middle years of the war, an' I'm goin' to school in a village which lies back from the river, an' is about twenty miles from my ancestral home. Thar's a stock-ade in the place which some invadin' Yanks has built, an' thar's about twenty of 'em inside, sort o' givin' orders to

the village an' makin' its patriotic inhabitants either march
or mark time, whichever chances to be their Yankee cap-
rices.

"'As a troo Southern yooth, who feels for his strugglin'
country, I loathes them Yankees to the limit, an' has no
more use for 'em than Huggins has for a temp'rance lecturer.

"'One day a troop of reb cavalry jumps into the village,
an' stampedes these yere invaders plum off the scene. We
gets the news up to the school, an' adjourns in a bunch to
come down town an' cel'brate the success of the Southern
arms. As I arrives at the field of carnage, a reb cavalryman
is swingin' outen the saddle. He throws the bridle of his
hoss to me.

"'"See yere, Bud," he says, "hold my hoss a minute while
I sees if I can't burn this stockade."

"'I stands thar while the reb fusses away with some pine
splinters an' lightwood, strugglin' to inaug'rate a holycaust.
He can't make the landin'; them timbers is too green, that
a-way.

"'While I'm standin' thar, lendin' myse'f to this yere con-
flagratory enterprise, I happens to cast my eyes over on the
hills a mile back from the village, an' I'm shocked a whole
lot to observe them eminences an' summits is bloo with
Yankees comin'. Now I'm a mighty careful boy, an' I don't
allow none to let a ragin' clanjamfrey of them Lincoln hirel-
ings caper up on me while I'm holdin' a reb hoss. So I calls
to this yere incendiary trooper where he's blowin' an' ex-
perimentin' an' still failin' with them flames.

"'"Secesh!" I shouts; "oh, you-all secesh! You'd a mighty
sight better come get your hoss, or them Yanks who's bulgin' along over yonder'll spread your hide on the fence."

"'This reb takes a look at the Yanks, an' then comes an'
gets his hoss. As he gathers up the bridle rein an' swings
into the saddle, a mad thirst to fight, die an' bleed for my

country seizes me, an' I grabs the reb's hoss by the bits an' detains him.

""""Say, Mister," I pleads, "why can't you-all take me with you?"

""""Which you're a lot too young, son," says the reb, takin' another size-up of the Yanks.

""""I ain't so young as I looks," I argues; "I'm jest small of my age."

""""Now, I reckons that's so," says the reb, beamin' on me approvin', "an' you're likewise mighty peart. But I'll tell you, Bud, you ain't got no hoss."

""""That's nothin'," I responds; "which if you-all will only get me a gun, I can steal a hoss, that a-way, in the first mile."

"'Seein' me so ready with them argyments, an' so dead pertinacious to go, this yere trooper begins to act oneasy, like his resolootion gets shook some. At last he gridds his teeth together like his mind's made up.

""""Look yere, boy," he says, "do you know who our Gen'ral is?"

""""No," I says, "I don't."

""""Well," says the reb, as he shoves his feet deep in the stirrups, an' settles in his saddle like he's goin' to make some time; "well, he's a ragin' an' onfettered maverick, named Wheeler; an' from the way he goes skallyhootin' 'round, he's goin' to get us all killed or captured before ever we gets back, an' I don't want no chil'en on my hands."

"'With that this yere soldier yanks the bridle outen my grasp, claps the steel into his hoss's flanks, an' leaves me like a bullet from a gun. For my part, I stands thar saved; saved, as I says, by that Gen'ral Wheeler's repootation with his men.'"

18

Colonel Sterett's Panther Hunt.

"**P**ANTHERS, what we-all calls 'mountain lions,'" observed the Old Cattleman, wearing meanwhile the sapient air of him who feels equipped of his subject, "is plenty furtive, not to say mighty sedyoolous to skulk. That's why a gent don't meet up with more of 'em while pirootin' about in the hills. Them cats hears him, or they sees him, an' him still ignorant tharof; an' with that they bashfully withdraws. Which it's to be urged in favour of mountain lions that they never forces themse'fs on no gent; they're shore considerate, that a-way, an' speshul of themse'fs. If one's ever hurt, you can bet it won't be a accident. However, it ain't for me to go 'round impungin' the motives of no mountain lion; partic'lar when the entire tribe is strangers to me complete. But still a love of trooth compels me to concede that if mountain lions ain't cowardly, they're shore cautious a lot. Cattle an' calves they passes up as too bellicose, an' none of 'em ever faces any anamile more warlike than a baby colt or mebby a half-grown deer. I'm ridin' along the Caliente once when I hears a crashin' in the bushes on the bluff above—two hundred foot high, she is, an' as sheer as the walls of this yere tavern. As I lifts my eyes, a fear-frenzied mare an' colt comes chargin' up an' projects themse'fs over the precipice an' lands in the valley below. They're dead as Joolius Caesar when I rides onto 'em, while a brace of mountain lions is skirtin' up an' down the aige of the bluff they leaps from, mewin' an' lashin' their long tails in hot enthoosiasm. Shore, the cats has been chasin' the mare an' foal, an' they locoes 'em to that extent they don't know where they're headin' an' makes the death jump I relates. I bangs away with my six-shooter, but beyond given' the mountain lions a convulsive start I can't say I does any execootion. They turns an' goes streakin' it through the pine woods like a drunkard to a barn raisin'.

"Timid? Shore! They're that timid seminary girls compared to 'em is as sternly courageous as a passel of buccaneers. Out in Mitchell's canyon a couple of the Lee-Scott riders cuts the trail of a mountain lion and her two kittens. Now whatever do you-all reckon this old tabby does? Basely deserts her offsprings without even barin a tooth, an' the cow-punchers takes 'em gently by their tails an' beats out their joovenile brains. That's straight; that mother lion goes swarmin' up the canyon like she ain't got a minute to live. An' you can gamble the limit that where a anamile sees its children perish without frontin' up for war, it don't possess the commonest roodiments of sand. Sech, son, is mountain lions.

"It's one evenin' in the Red Light when Colonel Sterett, who's got through his day's toil on that *Coyote* paper he's editor of, onfolds concernin' a panther round-up which he pulls off in his yooth.

"'This panther hunt,' says Colonel Sterett, as he fills his third tumbler, 'occurs when mighty likely I'm goin' on sev enteen winters. I'm a leader among my young companions at the time; in fact, I allers is. An' I'm proud to say that my soopremacy that a-way is doo to the dom'nant character of my intellects. I'm ever bright an' sparklin' as a child, an' I recalls how my aptitoode for learnin' promotes me to be regyarded as the smartest lad in my set. If thar's visitors, to the school, or if the selectmen invades that academy to sort o' size us up, the teacher allers plays me on 'em. I'd go to the front for the outfit. Which I'm wont on sech harrowin' o'casions to recite a ode—the teacher's done rote it himse'f—an' which is entitled *Napoleon's Mad Career.* Thar's twenty-four stanzas to it an' while these interlopin' selectmen sets thar lookin' owley an' sagacious, I'd wallop loose with the twenty-four verses, stampin' up and down, an' accompanyin' said recitations with sech a multitood of reckless gestures, it comes plenty clost to backin' everybody plumb outen the room. Yere's the first verse:

> I'd drink an' sw'ar an' r'ar an t'ar
> An' fall down in the mud,
> While the y'earth for forty miles about
> Is kivered with my blood.

"'You-all can see from that speciment that our schoolmaster ain't simply flirtin' with the muses when he originates that epic; no sir, he means business; an' whenever I throws it into the selectmen, I does it jestice. The trustees used to silently line out for home when I finishes, an' never a yeep. It stuns 'em; it shore fills 'em to the brim!

"'As I gazes r'arward,'goes on the Colonel, as by one rapt impulse he uplifts both his eyes an' his nosepaint, 'as I gazes r'arward, I says, on them sunfilled days, an' speshul if ever I gets betrayed into talkin' about 'em, I can hardly t'ar myse'f from the subject. I explains yeretofore, that not only by inclination but by birth, I'm a shore-enough 'ristocrat. This captaincy of local fashion I assoomes at a tender age. I wears the record as the first child to don shoes throughout the entire summer in that neighbourhood; an' many a time an' oft does my yoothful but envy-eaten compeers lambaste me for the insultin' innovation. But I sticks to my moccasins; an' to-day shoes in the Bloo Grass is almost as yooniversal as the licker habit.

"'Thar dawns a hour, however, then my p'sition in the van of Kaintucky *ton* comes within a ace of bein' ser'ously shook. It's on my way to school one dewey mornin' when I gets involved all inadvertent in a onhappy rupture with a polecat. I never does know how the misonderstandin' starts. After all, the seeds of said dispoote is by no means important; it's enough to say that polecat finally has me thoroughly convinced.

Followin' the difference an' my defeat, I'm witless enough to keep goin' on to school, whereas I should have returned homeward an' cast myse'f upon my parents as a sacred trust. Of course, when I'm in school I don't go impartin' my troubles to the other chil'en; I emyoolates the heroism of the Spartan boy who stands to be eat by a fox, an' keeps 'em to myself. But the views of my late enemy is not to be smothered; they appeals to my young companions; who tharupon puts up a most onneedful riot of coughin's an' sneezin's. But nobody knows me as the party who's so pungent.

"'It's a tryin' moment. I can see that, once I'm located, I'm goin' to be as onpop'lar as a b'ar in a hawg pen; I'll come tumblin' from my pinnacle in that proud commoonity as the glass of fashion an' the mold of form. You can go your bottom *peso* the thought causes me to feel plenty perturbed.

"'At this peril I has a inspiration; as good, too, as I ever entertains without the aid of rum. I determines to cast the opprobrium on some other boy an' send the hunt of gen'ral indignation sweepin' along his trail.

"'Thar's a innocent infant who's a stoodent at this temple of childish learnin' an' his name is Riley Bark. This Riley is one of them giant children who's only twelve an' weighs three hundred pounds. An' in proportions as Riley is a son of Anak, physical, he's dwarfed mental; he ain't half as well upholstered with brains as a shepherd dog. That's right; Riley's intellects, is like a fly in a saucer of syrup, they struggles 'round plumb slow. I decides to uplift Riley to the public eye as the felon who's disturbin' that seminary's sereenity. Comin' to this decision, I p'ints at him where he's planted four seats ahead, all tangled up in a spellin' book, an' says in a loud whisper to a child who's sittin' next:

"'Throw him out!'

"'That's enough. No gent will ever realise how easy it is to direct a people's sentiment ontil he take a whirl at the game. In two minutes by the teacher's bull's-eye copper watch, every soul knows it's pore Riley; an' in three, the teacher's done drug Riley out doors by the ha'r of his head an' chased him home. Gents, I look back on that yoothful feat as a triumph of diplomacy; it shore saves my standin' as the Beau Brummel of the Bloo Grass.

"'Good old days, them!' observes the Colonel mournfully, 'an' ones never to come ag'in! My sternest studies is romances, an' the peroosals of old tales as I tells you-all prior fills me full of moss an' mockin' birds in equal parts. I reads deep of *Walter Scott* an' waxes to be a sharp on Moslems speshul. I dreams of the Siege of Acre, an' Richard the Lion Heart; an' I simply can't sleep nights for honin' to hold a tournament an' joust a whole lot for some fair lady's love.

"'Once I commits the error of my career by joustin' with my brother Jeff. This year Jeff is settin' on the bank of the Branch fishin' for bullpouts at the time, an' Jeff don't know I'm hoverin' near at all. Jeffs reedic'lous fond of fishin'; which he'd sooner fish than read *Paradise Lost*. I'm romancin' along, sim'larly bent, when I notes Jeff perched on the bank. To my boyish imagination Jeff at once turns to be a Paynim. I drops my bait box, couches my fishpole, an' emittin' a impromtoo warcry, charges him. Its the work of a moment; Jeff's onhossed an' falls into the Branch.

"'But thar's bitterness to follow vict'ry. Jeff emerges like Diana from the bath an' frales the wamus off me with a club. Talk of puttin' a crimp in folks! Gents when Jeff's wrath is assuaged I'm all on one side like the leanin' tower of Pisa. Jeff actooally confers a skew-gee to my spinal column.

"'A week later my folks takes me to a doctor. That practitioner puts on his specs an' looks me over with jealous care.

"'"Whatever's wrong with him, Doc?" says my father.

"'"Nothin," says the physician, "only your son Willyum's five inches out o'plumb."

"'Then he rigs a contraption made up of guyropes an' stay-laths, an' I has to wear it; an' mebby in three or four weeks he's got me warped back into the perpendic'lar.'

"'But how about this cat hunt?" asks Dan Boggs. 'Which I don't aim to be introosive none, but I'm camped yere through the second drink waitin' for it, an' these procrastinations is makin' me kind o' batty.'

"'That panther hunt is like this,' says the Colonel, turnin' to Dan. 'At the age of seventeen, me an' eight or nine of my intimate brave comrades founds what we-all denom'nates as the "Chevy Chase Huntin' Club." Each of us maintains a passel of odds an' ends of dogs, an' at stated intervals we convenes on hosses, an' with these fourscore curs at our tails goes yellin' an' skally-hootin' up an' down the countryside allowin' we're shore a band of Nimrods.

"'The Chevy Chasers ain't been in bein' as a institootion over long when chance opens a gate to ser'ous work. The deep snows in the Eastern mountains it looks like has done drove a panther into our neighborhood. You could hear of him on all sides. Folks glimpses him now an' then. They allows he's about the size of a yearlin' calf; an' the way he pulls down sech feeble people as sheep or lays desolate some he'pless henroost don't bother him a bit. This panther spreads a horror over the county. Dances, pra'er meetin's, an' even poker parties is broken up, an' the social life of that region begins to bog down. Even a weddin' suffers; the bridesmaids stayin' away lest this ferocious monster should show up in the road an' chaw one of 'em while she's *en route* for the scene of trouble. That's gospel trooth! the pore deserted bride has to heel an' handle herse'f an' never a friend to yoonite her sobs with hers doorin' that weddin' ordeal. The old ladies present shakes their heads a heap solemn.

"'"It's a worse augoory," says one, "than the hoots of a score of squinch owls."

"'When this reign of terror is at its height, the local eye is rolled appealin'ly towards us Chevy Chasers. We rises to

the opportoonity. Day after day we're ridin' the hills an'
vales, readin' the milk white snow for tracks. An' we has
success. One mornin' I comes up on two of the Brackenridge boys an' five more of the Chevy Chasers settin' on
their hosses at the Skinner cross roads. Bob Crittenden's
gone to turn me out, they says. Then they p'ints down to a
handful of close-wove bresh an' stunted timber an' allows
that this maraudin' cat-o-mount is hidin' thar; they sees him
go skulkin' in.

"'Gents, I ain't above admittin' that the news puts my
heart to a canter. I'm brave; but conflicts with wild an' savage beasts is to me a novelty an' while I faces my fate without a flutter, I'm yere to say I'd sooner been in pursoot of
minks or raccoons or some varmint whose grievious
cap'bilities I can more ackerately stack up an' in whose
merry ways I'm better versed. However, the dauntless blood
of my grandsire mounts in my cheek; an' as if the shade of
that old Trojan is thar personal to su'gest it, I searches forth
a flask an' renoos my sperit; thus qualified for perils, come
in what form they may, I resolootly stands my hand.

"'Thar's forty dogs if thar's one in our company as we
pauses to the Skinner cross roads. An' when the Crittenden
youth returns, he brings with him the Rickett boys an' forty
added dogs. Which it's worth a ten-mile ride to get a
glimpse of that outfit of canines! Thar's every sort onder the
canopy: thar's the stolid hound, the alert fice, the sapient
collie; that is thar's individyool beasts wherein the hound,
or fice, or collie seems to preedominate as a strain. The
trooth is thar's not that dog a-whinin' about our hosses' fetlocks who ain't proudly descended from fifteen different
tribes, an' they shorely makes a motley mass meetin'. Still,
they're good, zealous dogs; an' as they're going to go
for'ard an' take most of the resks of that panther, it seems
invidious to criticise 'em.

"'One of the Twitty boys rides down an' puts the eighty
or more dogs into the bresh. The rest of us lays back an'

strains our eyes. Thar he is! A shout goes up as we descries the panther stealin' off by a far corner. He's headin' along a hollow that's full of bresh an' baby timber an' runs parallel with the pike. Big an' yaller he is; we can tell from the slight flash we gets of him as he darts into a second clump of bushes. With a cry—what young Crittenden calls a "view halloo,"—we goes stampedin' down the pike in pursoot.

"'Our dogs is sta'nch; they shore does themse'fs proud. Singin' in twenty keys, reachin, from growls to yelps an' from yelps to shrillest screams, they pushes dauntlessly on the fresh trail of their terrified quarry. Now an' then we gets a squint of the panther as he skulks from one copse to another jest ahead. Which he's goin' like a arrow; no mistake! As for us Chevy Chasers, we parallels the hunt, an' continyoos poundin' the Skinner turnpike abreast of the pack, ever an' anon givin' a encouragin' shout as we briefly sights our game.

"'Gents,' says Colonel Sterett, as he ag'in refreshes him se'f,' its needless to go over that hunt in detail. We hustles the flyin' demon full eighteen miles, our faithful dogs crowdin' close an' breathless at his coward heels. Still, they don't catch up with him; he streaks it like some saffron meteor.

"'Only once does we approach within strikin' distance; that's when he crosses at old Stafford's whiskey still. As he glides into view, Crittenden shouts:

"'"Thar he goes!"

"'For myse'f I'm prepared. I've got one of these misguided cap-an'-ball six shooters that's built doorin' the war; an' I cuts that hardware loose! This weepon seems a born profligate of lead, for the six chambers goes off together. Which you should have seen the Chevy Chasers dodge! An' well they may; that broadside ain't in vain! My aim is so troo that one of the r'armost dogs evolves a howl an' rolls over; then he sets up gnawin' an' lickin' his off hind laig in frantic alternations. That hunt is done for him. We leaves him doctorin' himse'f an' picks him up two hours later on our triumphant return.

"'As I states, we harries that foogitive panther for eighteen miles an' in our hot ardour founders two hosses. Fatigue an' weariness begins to overpower us; also our prey weakens along with the rest. In the half glimpses we now an' ag'in gets of him its plain that both pace an' distance is tellin' fast. Still, he presses on; an' as thar's no spur like fear, that panther holds his distance.

"'But the end comes. We've done run him into a rough, wild stretch of country where settlements is few an' cabins roode. Of a sudden, the panther emerges onto the road an' goes rackin' along the trail. We pushes our spent steeds to the utmost.

"'Thar's a log house ahead; out in the stump-filled lot in front is a frowsy woman an' five small children. The panther leaps the rickety worm-fence an' heads straight as a bullet for the cl'arin'! Horrors! the sight freezes our marrows! Mad an' savage, he's doo to bite a hunk outen that devoted household! Mutooally callin' to each other, we goads our hosses to the utmost. We gain on the panther! He may wound but he won't have time to slay that fam'ly.

"'Gents, it's a soopreme moment! The panther makes for the female squatter an' her litter, we pantin' an' pressin' clost behind. The panther is among 'em; the woman an' the children seems transfixed by the awful spectacle an' stands rooted with open eyes an' mouths. Our emotions shore beggars deescriptions.

"'Now ensooes a scene to smite the hardiest of us with dismay. No sooner does the panther find himse'f in the midst of that he'pless bevy of little ones, than he stops, turns round abrupt, an' sets down on his tail; an' then upliftin' his muzzle he busts into shrieks an' yells an' howls an' cries, a complete case of dog hysterics! That's what he is, a great yeller dog; his reason is now a wrack because we harasses him the eighteen miles.

"'Thar's a ugly outcast of a squatter, mattock in hand, comes tumblin' down the hillside from some'ers out back of the shanty where he's been grubbin':

"'"What be you-all eediots chasin' my dog for?" demands this onkempt party. Then he menaces us with the implement.

"'We makes no retort but stand passive. The great orange brute whose nerves has been torn to rags creeps to the squatter an' with mournful howls explains what we've made him suffer.

"'No, thar's nothin' further to do an' less to be said. That cavalcade, erstwhile so gala an' buoyant, drags itself wearily homeward, the exhausted dogs in the r'ar walkin' stiff an' sore like their laigs is wood. For more'n a mile the complainin' howls of the hysterical yeller dog is wafted to our y'ears. Then they ceases; an' we figgers his sympathizin' master has done took him into the shanty an' shet the door.

"'No one comments on this adventure, not a word is heard. Each is silent ontil we mounts the Big Murray hill. As we collects ourse'fs on this eminence one of the Brackenridge boys holds up his hand for a halt. "Gents," he says, as—hosses, hunters an' dogs—we-all gathers 'round, "gents, I moves you the Chevy Chase Huntin' Club yereby stands adjourned *sine die*." Thar's a moment's pause, an' then as by one impulse every gent, hoss an' dog, says "Ay!" It's yoonanimous, an' from that hour till now the Chevy Chase Huntin' Club ain't been nothin' save tradition. But that panther shore dissappears; it's the end of his vandalage; an' ag'in does quadrilles, pra'rs, an poker resoom their wonted sway. That's the end; an' now, gents, if Black Jack will caper to his dooties we'll uplift our drooped energies with the usual forty drops."

19

How The Raven Died.

"WHICH if you-all is out to hear of Injuns, son," observed the Old Cattleman, doubtfully, "the best I can do is shet my eyes an' push along regyardless, guarantee no facts; none whatever! I never does bend myse'f to severe study of savages an' what notions I packs concernin' 'em is the casual frootes of what I accidental hears an' what I sees. It's only now an' then, as I observes former, that Injuns invades Wolfville; an' when they does, we all scowls 'em outen camp—sort o' makes a sour front, so as to break 'em early of habits of visitin' us. We shore don't hone none to have 'em hankerin' 'round.

"Nacherally, I makes no doubt that if you goes clost to Injuns an' studies their little game you finds some of 'em good an' some bad, some gaudy an' some sedate, some cu'rous an, some indifferent, same as you finds among shore-enough folks. It's so with mules an' broncos; wherefore, then, may not these differences exist among Injuns? come squar' to the turn, you-all finds among shore-enough folks. It's so with mules an' broncos; wherefore, then may not these differences exist among Injuns? Come squar' to the turn, you-all finds white folks separated the same. Some gents follows off one waggon track an' some another; some even makes a new trail.

"Speakin' of what's opposite in folks, I one time an' ag'in sees two white chiefs of scouts who frequent comes pirootin' into Wolfville from the Fort. Each has mebby a score of Injuns at his heels who pertains to him personal. One of these scout chiefs is all buck-skins, fringes, beads an' feathers from y'ears to hocks, while t'other goes garbed in a stiff hat with a little jim crow rim—one of them kind you dee-nom'nates as a darby—an' a diag'nal overcoat; one chief looks like a dime novel on a spree an' t'other as much like the far East as he saveys how. An' yet, son, this voylent person in buckskins is a Second Lootenent—a mere boy, he is—from West P'int; while that outcast in the reedic'lous hat is foaled on the plains an' never does go that clost to the risin' sun as to glimpse the old Missouri. The last form of maverick bursts frequent into Western bloom; it's their am-bition, that a-way, to deloode you into deemin' 'em as fresh from the States as one of them tomatter airtights.

"Thar's old gent Jeffords; he's that sort. Old Jeffords lives for long with the Apaches; he's found among 'em when Gen'ral Crook—the old 'Grey Fox'—an' civilistion and gat-lin' guns comes into Arizona arm in arm. I used to note old Jeffords hibernatin' about the Oriental over in Tucson. I shore reckons he's procrastinatin' about thar yet, if the Great Sperit ain't done called him in. As I says, old Jeffords is that long among the Apaches back in Cochise's time that mem'ry of man don't run none to the contrary. An' yet no gent ever sees old Jeffords wearin' anything more savage than a long-tail black surtoot an' one of them stove pipe hats. Is Jeffords dangerous? No, you-all couldn't call him a distinct peril; still, folks who goes devotin' themse'fs to stir-rin' Jeffords up jest to see if he's alive gets disasterous ac-tion. He has long grey ha'r an' a tangled white beard half-way down his front; an' with that old plug hat an' black coat he's a sight to frighten children or sour milk! Still, Jeffords is all right. As long as towerists an' other inquisitive people don't go pesterin' Jeffords, he shore lets 'em alone. Other-wise, you might as well be up the same saplin' with a cin-namon b'ar; which you'd most likely hear something drop a lot!

"For myse'f, I likes old Jeffords, an' considers him pleasin' conundrum. About tenth drink time he'd take a cha'r an' go camp by himse'f in a far corner, an' thar he'd warble hymns. Many a time as I files away with my nosepaint in the Oriental have been regaled with,

> Jesus, Lover of my soul,
>   Let me to Thy bosom fly,
> While the nearer waters roll,
>   While the tempest still is high,

as emanatin' from Jeffords where he's r'ared back conductin' some personal services. Folks never goes buttin' in interferin' with these concerts' which it's cheaper to let him sing.

"Speakin' of Injuns, as I su'gests, I never does see over-much of 'em in Wolfville. An' my earlier experiences ain't thronged with 'em neither, though while I'm workin' cattle along the Red River I does carom on Injuns more or less. Thar's one old hostile I recalls speshul; he's a fool Injun called Black Feather;—Choctaw, he is. This Black Feather's weakness is fire-water; he thinks more of it than some folks does of children.

"Black Feather used to cross over to where Dick Stocton maintains a store an' licker house on the Upper Hawgthief. Of course, no gent sells these Injuns licker. It's ag'in the law; an' onless you-all is onusual eager to make a trip to Fort Smith with a marshal ridin' herd on you doorin' said visit, impartin' of nosepaint to aborigines is a good thing not to do. But Black Feather, he'd come over to Dick Stocton's an' linger 'round the bar'ls of Valley Tan, an' take a chance on stealin' a snifter or two while Stocton's busy.

"At last Stocton gets tired an' allows he'll lay for Black Feather. This yere Stocton is a mighty reckless sport; he ain't carin' much whatever he does do; he hates Injuns an' shot guns, an' loves licker, seven-up, an' sin in any form; them's Stocton's prime characteristics. an' he gets mighty weary of the whiskey-thievin' Black Feather, an' lays for him.

"One evenin' this aggravatin' Black Feather crosses over an' takes to ha'ntin' about Dick Stocton's licker room as is his wont. It looks like Black Feather has already been buyin' whiskey of one of them boot-laig parties who takes every chance an' goes among the Injuns an' sells 'em nosepaint on the sly. 'Fore ever he shows up on the Upper Hawgthief that time, this Black Feather gets nosepaint some'ers an' puts a whole quart of it away in the shade; an' he shore exhibits symptoms. Which for one thing he feels about four stories tall!

"Stocton sets a trap for Black Feather. He fills up the tin cup into which he draws that Valley Tan with coal-oil—karoseen you-all calls it—an' leaves it, temptin' like, settin' on top a whiskey bar'l. Shore! it's the first thing Black Feather notes. he sees his chance an' grabs an' downs the karoseen; an' Stocton sort o' startin' for him, this Black Feather gulps her down plump swift. The next second he cuts loose the yell of that year, burns up about ten acres of land, and starts for Red River. No, I don't know whether the karoseen hurts him none or not; but he certainly goes squatterin' across the old Red River like a wounded wild duck, an' he never does come back no more.

"But, son, as you sees, I don't know nothin' speshul or much touchin' Injuns, an' if I'm to dodge the disgrace of ramblin' along in this desultory way, I might better shift to a tale I hears Sioux Sam relate to Doc Peets one time in the Red Light. This Sam is a Sioux, an a mighty decent buck, considerin' he's Injun; Sam is servin' the Great Father as a scout with the diag'nal-coat, darby-hat sharp I mentions. Peets gives this saddle-tinted longhorn a 4-bit peice, an' he tells this yarn. It sounds plenty childish; but you oughter b'ar in mind that savages, mental, ain't no bigger nor older than ten year old young-ones among the palefaces.

"'This is the story my mother tells me,' says Sioux Sam, 'to show me the evils of cur'osity. "The Great Sperit allows to every one the right to ask only so many questions," says my mother, "an' when they ask one more than is their right, they die."

"'This is the story of the fate of *Kaw-kaw-chee*, the Raven, a Sioux Chief who died long ago exackly as my mother told me. The Raven died because he asked too many questions an' was too cur'ous. It began when Sublette, who was a trader, came up the *Mitchi-zoor-rah*, the Big-Muddy, an' was robbed by the Raven's people. Sublette was mad at this, an' said next time he would bring the Sioux a present so they would not rob him. So he brought a little cask of fire-water an' left it on the bank of the Big-Muddy. Then Sublette went away, an' twenty of the Raven's young men found the little cask. An' they were greedy an' did not tell the camp; they drank the fire-water where it was found.

"'The Raven missed his twenty young men an' when he went to spy for them, behold! they were dead with their teeth locked tight a' their faces an' bodies writhen an' twisted as the whirlwind twists the cottonwoods. Then the Raven thought an' thought; an' he got very cur'ous to know why his men died so writhen an' twisted. The fire-water had a whirlwind in it, an' the Raven was eager to hear. So he sent for Sublette.

"'Then the Raven an' Sublette had a big talk. They agreed not to hurt each other; an' Sublette was to come an' go an' trade with the Sioux' an' they would never rob him.

"'At this, Sublette gave the Raven some of the whirlwind that so killed an' twisted the twenty young men. It was a powder, white; an' it had no smell. Sublette said the taste was bitter; but the Raven must not taste it or it would lock up his teeth an' twist an' kill him. For to swallow the white powder loosed the whirlwind on the man's heart an' it bent him an' twisted him like the storms among the willows.

"'But the Raven could give the powder to others. So the Raven gave it in some deer's meat to his two squaws; an' they were twisted till they died; an' when they would speak they couldn't, for their teeth were held tight together an' no words came out of their mouths,—only great foam. Then the Raven gave it to others that he did not love; they were twisted an' died. At last there was no more of the powder of the whirlwind; the Raven must wait till Sublette came up the Big-Muddy again an' brought him more.

"'There was a man, the Gray Elk, who was of the Raven's people. The Gray Elk was a *Choo-ayk-eed*, a great prophet. And the Gray Elk had a wife; she was wise an' beautiful, an' her name was Squaw-who-has-dreams. But Gray Elk called her *Kee-nee-moo-sha*, the Sweetheart.

"'While the Raven waited for Sublette to bring him more powder of the whirlwind, a star with a long tail came into the sky. This star with the tail made the Raven heap cur'ous. He asked Gray Elk to tell him about it, for he was a prophet. The Raven asked many questions; they fell from him like leaves from a tree in the month of the first ice. So the Gray Elk called *Che-bee*, the Spirit; an' the Spirit told the Gray Elk. Then the Gray Elk told the Raven.'

"'It was not a tail, it was blood—star blood; an' the star had been bit an' was wounded, but would get well. The Sun was the father of the stars, an' the Moon was their mother. The Sun' *Gheezis*, tried ever to pursue an' capture an' eat his children, the stars. So the stars all ran an' hid when the Sun was about. But the stars loved their mother who was good an' never hurt them; an' when the Sun went to sleep at night an' *Coush-ee-wan*, the Darkness, shut his eyes, the Moon an' her children came together to see each other. But the star that bled had been caught by the Sun; it got out of his mouth but was wounded. Now it was frightened, so it always kept its face to where the Sun was sleeping over in the west. The bleeding star, *Sch-coo-dah*, would get well an' its wound would heal.

"'Then the Raven wanted to know how the Gray Elk knew all this. An' the Gray Elk had the Raven into the medicine lodge that night; an' the Raven heard the spirits come about an' heard their voices; but he could not understand. Also,

the Raven saw a wolf all fire, with wings like the eagle
which flew overhead. Also he heard the Thunder, *Boom-wa-
wa*, talking with the Gray Elk; but the Raven couldn't understand. The Gray Elk told the Raven to draw his knife an'
stab with it in the air outside the medicine lodge. An' when
he did, the Raven's blade an' hand came back covered with
blood. Still, the Raven was cur'ous an' kept askin' to be
told how the Gray Elk knew these things. An' the Gray Elk
at last took the Raven to the Great Bachelor Sycamore that
lived alone, an' asked the Raven if the Bachelor Sycamore
was growing. An' the Raven said it was. Then Gray Elk
asked him how he knew it was growing. An' the Raven said
he didn't know. Then Gray Elk said he did not know how
he knew about *Sch-coo-dah*, the star that was bit. This made
the Raven angry, for he was very cur'ous; an' he thought
the Gray Elk had two tongues.

"'Then it came the month of the first young grass an' Sublette was back for furs. Also he brought many goods; an' he
gave to the Raven more of the powder of the whirlwind in
a little box. At once the Raven made a feast of ducks for
the Gray Elk; an' he gave him of the whirlwind powder; an'
at once his teeth came together an' the Gray Elk was twisted
till he died.

"'Now no one knew that the Raven had the powder of the
whirlwind, so they could not tell why all these people were
twisted and went to the Great Spirit. But the Squaw-who-
has-dreams saw that it was the Raven who killed her husband, the Gray Elk, in a vision. Then the Squaw-who-has-
dreams went into the mountains four days an' talked with
Moh-kwa, the Bear who is the wisest of the beasts. The Bear
said it was the Raven who killed the Gray Elk an' told the
Squaw-who-has-dreams of the powder of the whirlwind.

"'Then the Bear an' the Squaw-who-has-dreams made a
fire an' smoked an' laid a plot. The Bear did not know
where to find the powder of the whirlwind which the Raven
kept always in a secret place. But the Bear told the Squaw-

who-has-dreams that she should marry the Raven an' watch until she found where the powder of the whirlwind was kept in its secret place; an' then she was to give some to the Raven, an' he, too, would be twisted an' die. There was a great danger, though; the Raven would, after the one day when they were wedded, want to kill the Squaw-who-has-dreams. So to protect her, the Bear told her she must begin to tell the Raven the moment she was married to him the Story-that-never-ends. Then, because the Raven was more cur'ous than even he was cruel, he would put off an' put off giving the powder of the whirlwind to the Squaw-who-has-dreams, hoping to hear the end of the Story-that-never-ends. Meanwhile the Squaw-who-has-dreams was to watch the Raven until she found the powder of the whirlwind in its secret place.

"'Then the wise Bear gave the Squaw-who-has-dreams a bowlful of words as seed, so she might plant them an' raise a crop of talk to tell the Story-that-never-ends. An' the Squaw-who-has-dreams planted the seed-words, an' they grew an' grew an' she gathered sixteen bundles of talk an' brought them to her wigwam. After that she put beads in her hair, an' dyed her lips red, an' rubbed red on her cheeks, an' put on a new blanket; an' when the Raven saw her, he asked her to marry him. So they were wedded; an' the Squaw-who-has-dreams went to the teepee of the Raven an' was his wife.

"'But the Raven was old an' cunning like *Yah-mee-kee*, the Beaver, an' he said, "He is not wise who keeps a squaw too long!" An' with that he thought he would kill the Squaw-who-has-dreams the next day with the powder of the whirlwind. But the Squaw-who-has-dreams first told the Raven that she hated *When-dee-goo*, the Giant; an' that she should not love the Raven until he had killed *When-dee-goo*. She knew the Giant was too big an' strong for the Raven to kill with his lance, an' that he must get his powder of the whirlwind; she would watch him an' learn its secret place.

The Raven said he would kill the Giant as the sun went down next day.

"'Then the Squaw-who-has-dreams told the Raven the first of the Story-that-never-ends an' used up one bundle of talk; an' when the story ended for that night, the Squaw-who-has-dreams was saying: "An' so, out of the lake that was red as the sun came a great fish that was green, with yellow wings, an' it walked also with feet, an' it came up to me an' said: "But then she would tell no more that night; nor could the Raven, who was crazy with cur'osity, prevail on her. "I must now sleep an' dream what the green fish with the yellow wings said," was the reply of the Squaw-who-has-dreams, an' she pretended to slumber. So the Raven, because he was cur'ous, put off her death.

"'All night she watched, but the Raven did not go to the secret place where he had hidden the powder of the whirlwind. Nor the next day, when the sun went down, did the Raven kill the Giant. But the Squaw-who-has-dreams took up again the Story-that-never-ends an' told what the green fish with the yellow wings said; an' she used up the second bundle of talk. When she ceased for that time, the Squaw-who-has-dreams was saying: "An' as night fell, *Moh-kwa,* the Bear, called to me from his canyon, an' said for me to come an' he would show me where the great treasure of fire-water was buried for you who are the Raven. So I went into the canyon, an' *Moh-kwa,* the Bear, took me by the hand an' led me to the treasure of fire-water which was greater an' richer than was ever seen by any Sioux."

"'Then the Squaw-who-has-dreams would tell no more that night, while the Raven eat his fingers with cur'osity. But he made up a new plan not to twist the Squaw-who-has-dreams until she showed him the treasure of fire-water an' told him the end of the Story-that-never-ends. On her part, however, the Squaw-who-has-dreams, as she went to sleep, wept an' tore the beads from her hair an' said the Raven did not love her; for he had not killed the Giant as he promised.

She said she would tell no more of the Story-that-never-ends until the Giant was dead; nor would she show to a husband who did not love her the great treasure of fire-water which *Moh-kwa*, the Bear, had found. At this, the Raven who was hot to have the treasure of fire-water an' whose ears rang with cur'osity to hear the end of the Story-that-never-ends saw that he must kill the Giant. Therefore, when the Squaw-who-has-dreams had ceased to sob and revile him, an' was gone as he thought asleep, the Raven went to his secret place where he kept the powder of the whirlwind an' took a little an' wrapped it in a leaf an' hid the leaf in the braids of his long hair. Then the Raven went to sleep.

"'When the Raven was asleep the Squaw-who-has-dreams went also herself to the secret place an' got also a little of the powder of the whirlwind. An' the next morning she arose early an gave the powder of the whirlwind to the Raven on the roast buffalo, the *Pez-hee-kee*, which was his food.

"'When the Raven had eaten, the Squaw-who-has-dreams went out of the teepee among the people an' called all the Sioux to come an' see the Raven die. So the Sioux came gladly, and the Raven was twisted an' writhen with the power of the whirlwind wrenching at his heart; an' his teeth were tight like a trap; an' no words, but only foam, came from his mouth; an' at last the Spirit, the *Chee-bee*, was twisted out of the Raven; an' the Squaw-who-has-dreams was revenged for the death of the Gray Elk whom she loved an' who always called her *Kee-nee-moo-sha*, the Sweetheart, because it made her laugh.

"'When the Raven was dead, the Squaw-who-has-dreams went to the secret place an' threw the powder of the whirlwind into the Big-Muddy; an' after that she distributed her fourteen bundles of talk that were left among all the Sioux so that everybody could tell how glad he felt because the Raven was twisted and died. An' for a week there was nothing but happiness an' big talk among the Sioux; an'

Moh-kwa, the Bear, came laughing out of his canyon with the wonder of listening to it; while the Squaw-who-has-dreams now, when her revenge was done, went with *When-dee-goo*, the Giant, to his teepee and became his squaw. So now everything was ended save the Story-that-never-ends.'

"When Sioux Sam gets this far," concluded the Old Cattleman, "he says, 'an' my mother's words at the end were: "An' boys who ask too many questions will die, as did the Raven whose cur'osity was even greater than his cruelty.""""

Old Man Enright

20

With the Apache's Compliments.

"**O**NDOUBTED," observed the Old Cattleman, during one of our long excursive talks, "ondoubted, the ways an' the motives of Injuns is past the white man's findin' out. He's shore a myst'ry, the Injun is! an' where the paleface forever fails of his s'lootion is that the latter ropes at this problem in copper-colour from the standp'int of the Caucasian. Can a dog onderstand wolf? Which I should remark not!

"It's a heap likely that with Injuns, the white man in his turn is jest as difficult to solve. An' without the Injun findin' onusual fault with 'em, thar's a triangle of things whereof the savage accooses the paleface. The Western Injuns at least—for I ain't posted none on Eastern savages, the same bein happily killed off prior to my time—the Western Injuns lays the bee, the wild turkey, an' that weed folks calls the 'plantain,' at the white man's door. They-all descends upon the Injun hand in hand. No, the Injun don't call the last-named veg'table a 'plantain;' he alloodes to it as 'the White Man's Foot.'

"Thar's traits dominant among Injuns which it wouldn't lower the standin' of a white man if he ups an' imitates a whole lot. I once encounters a savage—one of these blanket Injuns with feathers in his ha'r—an' bein' idle an' careless of what I'm about, I staggers into casyooal talk with him. This buck's been East for the first time in his darkened c'reer an' visited the Great Father in Washin'ton. I asks him

221

what he regyards as the deepest game he in his travels goes ag'inst. At first he allows that pie, that a-way, makes the most profound impression. But I bars pie, an' tells him to su'gest the biggest thing he strikes, not on no bill of fare. Tharupon, abandonin' menoos an' wonders of the table, he roominates a moment an' declar's that the steamboat—now that pie is exclooded—ought to get the nom'nation.

"'The choo-choo boat,' observes this intelligent savage, 'is the paleface's big medicine.'

"'You'll have a list of marvels,' I says, 'to avalanche upon the people when you cuts the trail of your ancestral tribe ag'in?'

"'No,' retorts the savage, shakin' his head ontil the skelp-lock whips his y'ears, an' all mighty decisive; 'no; won't tell Injun nothin'.'

"'Why not?' I demands.

"'If I tell,' he says, 'they no believe. They think it all heap lie.'

"Son, consider what a example to travellers is set by that ontootered savage? That's what makes me say thar be traits possessed of Injuns, personal, which a paleface might improve himse'f by copyin'.

"Bein' white myse'f, I'm born with notions ag'in Injuns. I learns of their deestruction with relief, an' never sees one pirootin' about, full of life an' vivacity, but the spectacle fills me with vain regrets. All the same thar's a load o' lies told East concernin' the Injun. I was wont from time to time to discuss these red folks with Gen'ral Stanton, who for years is stationed about in Arizona, an'—merely for the love he b'ars to fightin'—performs as chief of scouts for Gen'ral Crook.

"'Our divers wars with the Apaches,' says Gen'ral Stanton, 'comes more as the frootes of a misdeal by a locoed marshal than anything else besides. When Crook first shows up in Arizona—this is in the long ago—an' starts to inculcate peace among the Apaches, he gets old Jeffords to bring

Cochise to him to have a pow-pow. Jeffords rounds up
Cochise an' herds him with soft words an' big promises into
the presence of Crook. The Grey Fox—which was the Injun
name for Crook—makes Cochise a talk. Likewise he p'ints
out to the chief the landmarks an' mountain peaks that indi-
cates the Mexican line. An' the Grey Fox explains to Cochise that what cattle is killed an' what skelps is took to the
south'ard of the line ain't goin' to bother him a bit. But
no'th'ard it's different; thar in that sacred region cattle killin' an' skelp collectin' don't go. The Grey Fox shoves the
information on Cochise that every trick turned on the American side of the line has done got to partake of the characteristics of a love affair, or the Grey Fox with his young
men in bloo—his walk-a-heaps an' his hoss-warriors—
noomerous as the grass, they be—will come down on Cochise an' his Apaches like a coyote on a sage hen or a pan of
milk from a top shelf an' make 'em powerful hard to find.

"'Cochise smokes an' smokes, an' after considerin' the
bluff of the Grey Fox plenty profound, allows he won't call
it. Thar shall be peace between the Apache an' the paleface
to the no'th'ard of that line. Then the Grey Fox an' Cochise
shakes hands an' says "How!" an' Cochise, with a bolt or
two of red calico wherewith to embellish his squaws, goes
squanderin' back to his people, permeated to the toes with
friendly intentions.

"'Sech is Cochise's reverence for his work, coupled with
his fear of the Grey Fox, that years float by an' every
deefile an' canyon of the Southwest is as safe as the aisles
of a church to the moccasins of the paleface. Thus it continyoos until thar comes a evenin' when a jimcrow marshal,
with more six-shooters than hoss sense, allows he'll ap-
prehend Cochise's brother a whole lot for some offense that
ain't most likely deuce high in the category of troo crime.
This ediot offeshul reaches for the relative of Cochise; an'
as the latter—bein' a savage an' tharfore plumb afraid of
captivity—leaps back'ard like he's met up with a rattles-

nake, the marshal puts his gun on him an' plugs him so good that he cashes in right thar. The marshal says later in explantion of his game that Cochise's brother turns hostile an' drops his hand on his knife. Most likely he does; a gent's hands—even a Apache's—has done got to be some'ers.

"'But the killin' overturns the peaceful programmes built up between the Grey Fox an' Cochise. When the old chief hears of his brother bein' downed, he paints himse'f black an' red an' sends a bundle of arrows tied with rattlesnake skin to the Grey Fox with a message to count his people an' look out for himse'f. The Grey Fox, who realises that the day of peace has ended an' the sun gone down to rise on a mornin' of trouble, fills the rattlesnake skin with cartridges an' sends 'em back with a word to Cochise to turn himse'f loose. From that moment the war-jig which is to last for years is on. After Cochise comes Geronimo, an' after Geronimo comes Nana; an' one an' all, they adds a heap of spice to life in Arizona. It's no exaggeration to put the number of palefaces who lose their ha'r as the direct result of that fool marshal layin' for Cochise's brother an' that Injun's consequent cuttin' off, at a round ten thousand. Shore! thar's scores an' scores who's been stood up an' killed in the hills whereof we never gets a whisper. I, myse'f, in goin' through the teepees of a Apache outfit, after we done wipes' em off the footstool, sees the long ha'r of seven white women who couldn't have been no time dead.

"'Who be they? Folks onknown who's got shot into while romancin' along among the hills with schemes no doubt of settlement in Californy.

"'With what we saveys of the crooelties of the Apaches, thar's likewise a sperit of what book-sharps calls chivalry goes with 'em; an' albeit on one ha'rhung o'casion I profits mightily tharby, I'm onable to give it a reason. You wouldn't track up on no sim'lar weaknesses among the palefaces an' you-all can put down a stack on that.

"'It's when I'm paymaster,' says the Gen'ral, reachin' for the canteen, 'an' I starts fo'th from Fort Apache on a expedition to pay off the nearby troops. I've got six waggons an' a escort of twenty men. For myse'f, at the r'ar of the procession, I journeys proudly in a amb'lance. Our first camp is goin' to be on top of the mesa out a handful of miles from the Fort.

"'The word goes along the line to observe a heap of caution an' not straggle or go rummagin' about premiscus, for the mountains is alive with hostiles. It's five for one that a frownin' cloud of 'em is hangin' on our flanks from the moment we breaks into the foothills. No. they'd be afoot; the Apaches ain't hoss-back Injuns an' only fond of steeds as food. He never rides on one, a Apache don't, but he'll camp an' build a fire an' eat a corral full of ponies if you'll furnish 'em, an' lick his lips in thankfulness tharfore. But bein' afoot won't hinder 'em for keepin' up with my caravan, for in the mountains the snow is to the waggon beds an' the best we can do, is wriggle along the trail like a hurt snake at a gait which wouldn't tire a papoose.

"'We've been pushin' on our windin' uphill way for mighty likely half a day, an' I'm beginnin'—so dooms slows is our progress—to despair of gettin' out on top the mesa before dark, when to put a coat of paint on the gen'ral trouble the lead waggon breaks down. I turns out in the snow with the rest, an' we-all puts in a heated an' highly profane half-hour restorin' the waggon to health. At last we're onder headway ag'in, an' I wades back through the snow to my amb'lance.

"'As I arrives at the r'ar of my offishul waggon, it occurs to me that I'll fill a pipe an' smoke some by virchoo of my nerves, the same bein' torn and frayed with the many exasperations of the day. I gives my driver the word to wait a bit, an' searchin' forth my tobacco outfit loads an' lights my pipe. I'm planted waist deep in the mountain snows, but havin' on hossman boots the snow ain't no hardship.

"'While I'm fussin' with my pipe, the six waggons an' my twenty men curves 'round a bend in the trail an' is hid by a corner of the canyon. I reflects at the time—though I ain't really expectin' no perils—that I'd better catch up with my escort, if it's only to set the troops a example. As I exhales my first puff of smoke and is on the verge of tellin' my driver to pull out—this yere mule-skinner is settin' so that matters to the r'ar is cut off from his gaze by the canvas cover of my waggon—a slight noise attracts me, an' castin' my eye along the trail we've been climbin', I notes with feelin's of disgust a full dozen Apaches comin'. An' it ain't no hyperbole to say they're shore comin' all spraddled out.

"'In the lead for all the deep snow, an' racin' up on me like the wind, is a big befeathered buck, painted to the eyes; an' in his right fist, raised to hurl it, is a 12-foot lance. As I surveys this pageant, I realises how he'pless, utter, I be, an' with what ca'mness I may, adjusts my mind to the fact that I've come to the end of my trails. He'pless? Shore! I'm stuck as firm in the snow as one of the pines about me; my guns is in the waggon outen immediate reach; thar I stands as certain a prey to that Apache with the lance as he's likely to go up ag'inst doorin' the whole campaign. Why, I'm a pick-up! I remembers my wife an' babies, an' sort o' says "Goodbye!" to 'em, for I'm as certain of my finish as I be of the hills, or the snows beneath my feet. However, since it's all I can do, I continyoos to smoke an' watch my execootioners come on.

"'The big lance Injun is the dominatin' sperit of the bunch. As he draws up to me—he's fifty foot in advance of the others—he makes his lance shiver from p'int to butt. It fairly sings a death song! I can feel it go through an' through me a score of times. But I stands thar facin' him; for, of course, I wants it to go through from the front. I don't allow to be picked up later with anything so onfashionable as a lance wound in my back. That would be mighty onprofessional!

"'You onderstands that what now requires minutes in the recital don't cover seconds as a play. The lance Injun runs up to within a rod of me an' halts. His arm goes back for a mighty cast of the lance; the weapon is vibrant with the very sperit of hate an' malice. His eyes, through a fringe of ha'r that has fallen over 'em, glows out like a cat's eyes in the dark.

"We stands thar—I still puffin my pipe, he with his lance raised—an' we looks on each other—I an' that paint-daubed buck! I can't say whatever is his notion of me, but on my side I never beholds a savage who appeals to me as a more evil an' forbiddin' picture!

"'As I looks him over a change takes place. The fire in his eyes dies out, his face relaxes its f'rocity, an' after standin' for a moment an' as the balance of the band arrives, he turns the lance over his arm an' with the butt presented, surrenders it into my hand. You can gamble I don't lose no time in arguin' the question, but accepts the lance with all that it implies. Bringin' the weapon to a 'Right Shoulder' an' with my mind relieved, I gives the word to my mule-skinner—who's onconscious of the transactions in life an' death goin' on behind his back—an' with that, we-all takes up our march an' soon comes up on the escort where it's ag'in fixed firm in the snow about a furlong to the fore. My savages follows along with me, an' each of 'em as grave as squinch owls an' tame as tabby cats.

"'Joke? no; them Apaches was as hostile as Gila monsters! But beholdin' me, as they regyards it—for they don't in their ontaught simplicity make allowance for me bein' im-planted in the snow, gunless an' he'pless—so brave, await-in' deestruction without a quiver, their admiration mounts to sech heights it drowns within 'em every thought of cancel-lin' me with that lance, an' tharupon they pays me their sav-age compliments in manner an' form deescribed. They don't regyard themse'fs as surrenderin' neither; they esteems pas-sin' me the lance as inauguratin' a armistice an' looks on themse'fs as guests of honor an' onder my safegyard, free to say "How!" an' *vamos* back to the warpath ag'in whenever the sperit of blood begins to stir within their breasts. I knows enough of their ways to be posted as to what they expects; an' bein', I hopes, a gent of integrity, I accedes to 'em that exact status which they believes they enjoys.

"'They travels with me that day, eats with me that evenin' when we makes our camp, has a drink with me all 'round, sings savage hymns to me throughout the night, loads up with chuck in the mornin', offers me no end of flattery as a dead game agent whom they respects, says *adios;* an' then they scatters like a flock of quail. Also, havin' resoomed business on old-time lines, they takes divers shots at us with their Winchesters doorin' the next two days, an' kills a hoss an' creases my sergeant. Why don't I corral an' hold 'em when they're in my clutch? It would have been breakin' the trooce as Injuns an' I onderstands sech things; moreover, they let me go free without conditions when I was loser by every roole of the game.'"

21

The Mills of
Savage Gods.

"THAR might, of course, be romances in the West," observed the Old Cattleman, reflectively, in response to my question, "but the folks ain't got no time. Romance that a-way demands leesure, an' a party has to be more or less idlin' about to get what you-all might style romantic action. Take that warjig whereof I recently relates an' wherein this yere Wild Bill Hickox wipes out the McCandlas gang—six to his Colt's, four to his bowie, an' one to his Hawkins rifle; eleven in all—I asks him myse'f later when he's able to talk, don' he regyard the eepisode as some romantic. An' Bill says, 'No, I don't notice no romance tharin; what impresses me most is that she's shore a zealous fight—also, mighty busy.'

"Injuns would be romantic, only they're so plumb ignorant they never once saveys. Thar's no Injun word for 'romantic'; them benighted savages never tumblin' to sech a thing as romance bein' possible. An' yet said aborigines engages in plays which eddicated Eastern taste with leesure on its hands an' gropin' about for entertainment would pass on as romantic.

"When I'm pesterin' among the Osages on that one o'casion that I'm tryin' to make a round-up of my health, the old buck Strike Axe relates to me a tale which I allers looks on as a possessin' elements. Shore; an' it's as simple an' straight as the sights of a gun. It's about a squaw an' three bucks, an' thar's enough blood in it to paint a waggon.

Which I reckons now I'll relate it plain an' easy an' free of them frills wherewith a professional racontoor is so prone to overload his narratives.

"The Black Cloud is a Osage medicine man an' has high repoote about Greyhoss where he's pitched his teepee an' abides. He's got a squaw, Sunbright, an' he's plenty jealous of this yere little Sunbright. The Black Cloud has three squaws, an' Sunbright is the youngest. The others is Sunbright's sisters, for a Osages weds all the sisters of a fam'ly at once, the oldest sister goin' to the front at the nuptials to deal the weddin' game for the entire outfit.

"Now this Sunbright ain't over-enamoured of Black Cloud; he's only a half-blood Injun for one thing, his father bein' a buffalo-man (negro) who's j'ined the Osages, an' Sunbright don't take kindly to his nose which is some flatter than the best rools of Osage beauty demands; an' likewise thar's kinks in his ha'r. Still, Sunbright sort o' keeps her aversions to herse'f, an' if it ain't for what follows she most likely would have travelled to her death-blankets an' been given a seat on hill with a house of rocks built 'round her— the same bein' the usual burial play of a Osage—without Black Cloud ever saveyin' that so far from interestin' Sunbright, he only makes her tired.

"Over south from Black Cloud's Greyhoss camp an' across the Arkansaw an' some'ers between the Polecat an' the Cimmaron thar's livin' a young Creek buck called the Lance. He's straight an' slim an' strong as the weepon he's named for; an' he like Black Cloud is a medicine sharp of cel'bration an' stands' way up in the papers. The Creeks is never weary of talkin' about the Lance an' what a marvel as a medicine man he is; also, by way of insultin' the Osages, they declar's onhesitatin' that the Lance lays over Black Cloud like four tens, an' offers to bet hosses an' blankets an' go as far as the Osages likes that this is troo.

"By what Strike Axe informs me,—an' he ain't none likely to overplay in his statements—by what Strike Axe tells me, I says, the Lance must shore have been the high kyard as a medicine man. Let it get dark with the night an' no moon in the skies, an' the Lance could take you-all into his medicine lodge, an' you'd hear the sperits flappin' their pinions like some one flappin' a blanket, an' thar'd be whisperin's an' goin's on outside the lodge an' in, while fire-eyes would show an' burn an' glower up in the peak of the teepee; an' all plenty skeary an' mystifyin'. Besides these yere accomplishments the Lance is one of them mesmerism sports who can set anamiles to dreamin'. He could call a coyote or a fox, or even so fitful an' nervous a prop'sition as a antelope; an' little by little, snuffin' an' snortin', or if it's a coyote, whinin', them beasts would approach the Lance ontil they're that clost he'd tickle their heads with his fingers while they stands shiverin' an' sweatin' with apprehensions. You can put a bet on it, son, that accordin' to this onbiassed buck, Strike Axe, the Lance is ondoubted the big medicine throughout the Injun range.

"As might be assoomed, the Black Cloud is some heated ag'in the Lance an' looks on him with baleful eye as a rival. Still, Black Cloud has his nerve with him constant, an' tharfore one day when the Osages an' Creeks has been dispootin' touchin' the reespective powers of him an' the Lance, an' this latter Injun offers to come over to Greyhoss an' make medicine ag'in him, Black Cloud never hesitates or hangs back like a dog tied onder a waggon, but calls the bluff a heap prompt an' tells the Lance to come.

"Which the day is set an' the Lance shows in the door, as monte sharps would say. Black Cloud an' the Lance tharupon expands themse'fs an' delights the assembled Creeks an' Osages with their whole box of tricks, an' each side is braggin' an' boastin' an' puttin' it up that their gent is most likely the soonest medicine man who ever buys black paint. It's about hoss an' hoss between the two.

"Black Cloud accompanies himse'f to this contest with a pure white pony which has eyes red as roobies—a kind o' albino pony—an' he gives it forth that this milk-coloured bronco is his 'big medicine' or familiar sperit. The Lance observes that the little red-eyed hoss is mighty impressive to the savages, be they Creeks or Osages. At last he says to Black Cloud:

"'To show how my medicine is stronger than yours, tomorry I'll make your red-eyed big medicine bronco go lame in his off hind laig.''

"Black Cloud grins scornful at this; he allows that no sport can make his white pony go lame.

"He's plumb wrong; the next mornin' the white pony is limpin' an' draggin' his off hind hoof, an' when he's standin' still he p'ints the toe down like something's fetched loose. Black Cloud is sore; but he can't find no cactus thorn nor nothin' to bring about the lameness an' he don't know what to make of the racket. Black Cloud's up ag'inst it, an' the audience begins to figger that the Lance's medicine is too strong for Black Cloud.

"What's the trouble with the red-eyed pony? That's simple enough, son. The Lance done creeps over in the night an' ties a hossha'r tight about the pony's laig jest above the fetlock. Black Cloud ain't up to no sech move, the same bein' a trade secret of the Lance's an' bein' the hossha'r is hid in the ha'r on the pony's laig, no one notes its presence.

"After Black Cloud looks his red-eyed big medicine pony all over an' can't onderstand its lameness, the Lance asks him will he cure it. Black Cloud, who's scowlin' like midnight by now, retorts that he will. So he gets his pipe an' fills it with medicine tobacco an' blows a mouthful of smoke in the red-eyed pony's nose. Sech remedies don't work; that pony still limps on three laigs, draggin' the afflicted member mighty pensive.

"At last the Lance gives Black Cloud a patronisin' smile an' says that his medicine'll cure the pony sound an' well while you're crackin' off a gun. He walks up to the pony an' looks long in its red eyes; the pony's y'ears an' tail droops, its head hangs down, an' it goes mighty near to sleep. Then the Lance rubs his hand two or three times up an' down the lame laig above the fetlock an' elim'nates that hossha'r ligature an' no one the wiser. A moment after, he wakes up the red-eyed pony an' to the amazement of the Osages an' the onbounded delight of the Creeks, the pony is no longer lame, an' the laig so late afficted is as solid an' healthy as a sod house. What's bigger medicine still, the red-eyed pony begins to follow the Lance about like a dog an' as if it's charmed; an' it likewise turns in to bite an' r'ar an' pitch an' jump sideways if Black Cloud seeks to put his paw on him. Then all the Injuns yell with one voice: 'The Lance has won the Black Cloud's big medicine red-eyed pony away from him.'

"The Lance is shore the fashion, an' Black Cloud discovers he ain't a four-spot by compar'son. His repootation is gone, an' the Lance is regyarded as the great medicine along the Arkansaw.

"Sunbright is lookin' on at these manoovers an' her heart goes out to the Lance; she falls more deeply in love with him than even the red-eyed bronco does. That evenin' as the Lance is goin' to his camp onder the cottonwoods, he meets up with Sunbright standin' still as a tree in his path with her head bowed like a flower that's gone to sleep. The Lance saveys; he knows Sunbright; likewise he knows what her plantin' herse'f in his way an' droopin' attitoode explains. He looks at her, an' says:

"'I am a guest of the Osages, an' to-night is not the night. Wait ontil the Lance is in his own teepee on the Polecat; then come.'

"'Sunbright never moves, never looks up; but she hears an' she knows this is right. No buck should steal a squaw while he's a guest. The Lance walks on an' leaves her standin', head bowed an' motionless.

"Two days later the Lance is ag'in in his own teepee. Sunbright counts the time an' knows that he must be thar.

She skulks from the camp of Black Cloud an' starts on her journey to be a new wife to a new husband.

"Sunbright is a mile from camp when she's interrupted. It's Black Cloud who heads her off. Black Cloud may not be the boss medicine man, but he's no fool, an' his eyes is like a wolf's eyes an' can see in the dark. He guesses the new love which has stampeded Sunbright.

"Injuns is a mighty cur'ous outfit. Now if Sunbright had succeeded in gettin' to the lodge of her new husband, the divorce between her an' Black Cloud would have been complete. Moreover, if on the day followin' or at any time Black Cloud had found her thar, he wouldn't so much as have wagged a y'ear or batted a eye in recognition. He wouldn't have let on he ever hears of a squaw called 'Sunbright.' This ca'mness would be born of two causes. It would be ag'in Injun etiquette to go trackin' about makin' a onseemly uproar an' disturbin' the gen'ral peace for purely private causes. Then ag'in it would be beneath the dignity of a high grade savage an' a big medicine sharp to conduct himse'f like he'd miss so trivial a thing as a squaw.

"'But ontil Sunbright fulfils her elopement projects an' establishes herse'f onder the protectin' wing of her new love, she's runnin' resks. She's still the Black Cloud's squaw; an' after she pulls her marital picket pin an' while she's gettin' away, if the bereaved Black Cloud crosses up with her he's free, onder the license permitted to Injun husbands, to kill her an' skelp her an' dispose of her as consists best with his moods.

"Sunbright knows this; an' when she runs ag'in the Black Cloud in her flight, she seats herse'f in the long prairie grass an' covers her head with her blanket an' speaks never a word.

"'Does Sunbright so love me,' says Black Cloud, turnin' a heap ugly, 'that she comes to meet me? Is it for me she has combed her h'ar an' put on a new feather an' beads? Does she wear her new blanket an' paint her face bright for

Black Cloud? Or does she dress herse'f like the sun for that Creek coyote, the Lance?' Sunbright makes no reply. Black Cloud looks at her a moment an' then goes on: "It's for the Lance! Good! I will fix the Sunbright so she will be a good squaw to my friend, the Lance, an' never run from his lodge as she does now from Black Cloud's.' With that he stoops down, an' a slash of his knife cuts the heel-tendons of Sunbright's right foot. She groans, and writhes about the prairie, while Black Cloud puts his knife back in his belt, gets into his saddle ag'in an' rides away.

"The next day a Creek boy finds the body of Sunbright where she rolls herse'f into the Greyhoss an' is drowned.

"When the Lance hears the story an' sees the knife slash on Sunbright's heel, he reads the trooth. It gives him a bad heart; he paints his face red an' black an thinks how he'll be revenged. Next day he sends a runner to Black Cloud with word that Black Cloud has stole his hoss. This is to arrange a fight on virtuous grounds. The Lance says that in two days when the sun is overhead Black Cloud must come to the three cottonwoods near the mouth of the Cimmaron an' fight, or the Lance on the third day an' each day after will hunt for him as he'd hunt a wolf ontil Black Cloud is dead. The Black Cloud's game, an' sends word that on the second day he'll be thar by the three cottonwoods when the sun is overhead; also, that he will fight with four arrows.

"Then Black Cloud goes at once, for he has no time to lose, an' kills a dog near his lodge. He cuts its heart an' carries it to the rocky canyon where the rattlesnakes have a village. Black Cloud throws the dog's heart among them an' teases them with it; an' the rattlesnakes bite the dog's heart ag'in an' ag'in ontil it's as full of p'isen as a bottle is of rum. After that, Black Cloud puts the p'isened heart in the hot sun an' lets it fret an' fester ontil jest before he goes to his dooel with the Lance. As he's about to start, Black Cloud dips the four steel arrowheads over an' over in the p'isened heart, bein' careful to dry the p'isen on the arrowheads; an' now whoever is touched with these arrows so that the blood comes is shore to die. The biggest medicine in the nation couldn't save him.

"Thar's forty Osage and forty Creek bucks at the three cottonwoods to see that the dooelists get a squar' deal. The Lance an' Black Cloud is thar; each has a bow an' four arrows; each has made medicine all night that he may kill his man.

"But the dooel strikes a obstacle.

"Thar's a sombre, sullen sport among the Osages who's troo name is the 'Bob-cat,' but who's called the 'Knife Thrower.' The Bob-cat is one of the Osage forty. Onknown to the others, this yere Bob-cat—who it looks like is a mighty impressionable savage—is himse'f in love with the dead Sunbright. An' he's hot an' cold because he's fearful that in this battle of the bows the Lance'll down Black Cloud an' cheat him, the Bob-cat, of his own revenge. The chance is too much; the Bob-cat can't stand it an' resolves to get his stack down first. An' so it happens that as Black Cloud an' the Lance, painted in their war colours, is walkin' to their places, a nine-inch knife flickers like a gleam of light from the hand of the Bob-cat, an' merely to show that he ain't called the 'Knife Thrower' for fun, catches Black Cloud flush in the throat, an' goes through an' up to the gyard at the knife-haft, Black Cloud dies standin', for the knife p'int bites his spine.

"No, son, no one gets arrested; Injuns don't have jails, for the mighty excellent reason that no Injun culprit ever vamoses an' runs away. Injun crim'nals, that a-way, allers stands their hands an' takes their hemlock. The Osages, who for Injuns is some shocked at the Bob-cat's interruption of the dooel—it bein' mighty onparliamentary from their standp'ints—tries the Bob-cat in their triboonals for killin' Black Cloud an' he's decided on as guilty accordin' to their law. They app'ints a day for the Bob-cat to be shot; an' as he ain't present at the trial none, leavin' his end of the game to be looked after by his reelatives, they orders a kettle-tender or tribe crier to notify the Bob-cat when an' where he's to come an' have said sentence execooted upon him. When he's notified, the Bob-cat don't say nothin'; which is satisfactory enough, as thar's nothin' to be said, an' every Osage knows the Bob-cat'll be thar at the drop of the handkerchief if he's alive.

"It so turns out; the Bob-cat's thar as cool as wild plums. He's dressed in his best blankets an' leggin's; an' his feathers an' gay colours makes him a overwhelmin' match for peacocks. Thar's a white spot painted over his heart.

"The chief of the Osages, who's present to see jestice done, motions to the Bob-cat, an' that gent steps to a red blanket an' stands on its edge with all the blanket spread in front of him on the grass. The Bob-cat stands on the edge, as he saveys when he's plugged that he'll fall for'ard on his face. When a gent gets the gaff for shore, he falls for'ard. If a party is hit an' falls back'ards, you needn't get excited none; he's only creased an' 'll get over it.

"Wherefore, as I states, the Bob-cat stands on the edge of the blanket so it's spread out in front to catch him as he drops. Thar's not a word spoke by either the Bob-cat or the onlookers, the latter openin' out into a lane behind so the lead can go through. When the Bob-cat's ready, his cousin, a buck whose name is Little Feather, walks to the front of the blanket an' comes down careful with his Winchester on the white mark over the Bob-cat's heart. Thar's a moment's silence as the Bob-cat's cousin runs his eye through the sights; thar's a flash an' a hatful of gray smoke; the white spot turns red with blood; an' then the Bob-cat falls along on his face as soft as a sack of corn.

"What becomes of the Lance? It's two weeks later when that scientist is waited on by a delegation of Osages. They reminds him that Sunbright has two sisters, the same bein' now widows by virchoo of the demise of the egreegious Black Cloud. Also, the Black Cloud was rich; his teepee was sumptuous, an' he's left a buckskin coat with ivory elk teeth sewed onto it plenty as stars at night. The coat is big medicine; moreover thar's the milkwhite big medicine bronco with red eyes. The Osage delegation puts forth these trooths while the Lance sets cross-laiged on a b'arskin an' smokes willow bark with much dignity. In the finish, the Osage outfit p'ints up to the fact that their tribe is shy a medicine man, an' a gent of the Lance's accomplishments who can charm anamiles an' lame broncos will be a mighty welcome addition to the Osage body politic. The Lance lays down his pipe at this an' says, 'It is enough!' An' the next day he sallies over an' weds them two relicts of Black Cloud an' succeeds to that dead necromancer's estate an' both at one fell swoop. The two widows chuckles an' grins after the manner of ladies, to get a new husband so swift; an' abandonin' his lodge on the Polecat the Lance sets up his game at Greyhoss, an' onless he's petered, he's thar dealin' it yet."

22

Tom and Jerry;
Wheelers.

"**O**BSTINACY or love, that a-way, when folks pushes 'em to excess, is shore bad medicine. Which I'd be a heap loath to count the numbers them two attribootes harries to the tomb. Why, son, it's them sentiments that kills off my two wheel mules, Tom an' Jerry."

The Old Cattleman appeared to be on the verge of abstract discussion. As a metaphysician, he was not to be borne with. There was one method of escape; I interfered to coax the currents of his volubility into other and what were to me, more interesting channels.

"Tell me of the trail; or a story about animals," I urged. " You were saying recently that perfect systems of oral if not verbal communication existed among mules, and that you had listened for hours to their gossip. Give me the history of one of your freighting trips and what befell along the trail; and don't forget the comment thereon—wise, doubtless, it was—of your long-eared, servants of the rein and trace-chain."

"Tell you what chances along the trail? Son, you-all opens a wide-flung range for my mem'ry to graze over. I might tell you how I'm lost once, freightin' from Vegas into the Panhandle, an' am two days without water—blazin' Jooly days so hot you couldn't touch tire, chain, or bolt-head without fryin' your fingers. An' how at the close of the second day when I hauls in at Cabra Springs, I lays down by that cold an' blessed fountain an' drinks till I aches. Which them two days of thirst terrorises me to sech degrees that for one plumb year tharafter, I never meets up with water when I don't drink a quart, an' act like I'm layin' in ag'in another parched spell.

"Or I might relate how I stops over one night from Springer on my way to the Canadian at a Triangle-dot camp called Kingman. This yere is a one-room stone house, stark an' sullen an' alone on the desolate plains, an' no scenery worth namin' but a half-grown feeble spring. This Kingman ain't got no windows; its door is four-inch thick of oak; an' thar's loopholes for rifles in each side which shows the sports who builds that edifice in the stormy long-ago is lookin' for more trouble than comfort an' prepares themse'fs. The two cow-punchers I finds in charge is scared to a standstill; they allows this Kingman's ha'nted. They tells me how two parties who once abides thar—father an' son they be—gets downed by a hold-up whose aim is pillage, an' who comes cavortin' along an' butchers said fam'ly in their sleep. The cow-punchers declar's they hears the spooks go scatterin' about the room as late as the night before I trails in. I ca'ms 'em—not bein' subject to nerve stampedes myse'f, an' that same midnight when the sperits comes ha'ntin' about ag'in, I turns outen my blankets an' lays said spectres with the butt of my mule whip—the same when we strikes a light an' counts 'em up for a mighty thrillin' tale if I throws myse'f loose with its reecital an' daubs in the colour plenty vivid an' free.

"Then thar's the time I swings over to the K-bar-8 ranch for corn—bein' I'm out of said cereal—an' runs up on a cow gent, spurs, gun-belt, big hat an' the full regalia, hangin' to the limb of a cottonwood dead as George the Third, an' not a hundred foot from the ranch door. An' how inside I finds a half-dozen more cow folks, lookin' grave an' sayin' nothin'; an' the ranch manager has a bloody bandage about his for'ead an' another holdin' up his left arm, half bandage an' half sling, the toot ensemble, as Colonel Sterett calls it, showin' sech recent war that the blood's still wet on the cloths an' drops on the floor as we talks. An' how none of us says a word about the dead gent in the cottonwood or of the manager who's shot up; an' how that same manager outfits me with ten sacks of mule-food an' I goes p'intin' out for the Southeast an' forgets all I sees an' never mentions it ag'in.

"Then thar's Sim Booth of the Fryin' Pan outfit, who's one evenin' camped with me at Antelope Springs; an' who saddles up an' ropes onto the laigs of a dead Injun where they're stickin' forth—bein' washed free by the rains—an' pulls an' rolls that copper-coloured departed outen his sepulchre a lot, an' then starts his pony off at a canter an' sort o' fritters the remains about the landscape. Sim does this on the argyment that the obsequies, former, takes place too near the spring. This yere Sim's pony two months later steps in a dog hole when him an' Sim's goin' along full swing with some cattle on a stampede, an' the cayouse falls on Sim an' breaks everything about him incloosive of his neck. The other cow-punchers allers allow it's because Sim turns out that aborigine over by Antelope Springs. Now sech a eepisode, properly elab'rated, might feed your atention an' hold it spellbound some.

"Son, if I was to turn myse'f loose on, great an' little, the divers incidents of the trail, it would consoome days in the relation. I could tell of cactus flowers, blazin' an' brilliant as a eye of red fire ag'in the brown dusk of the deserts; or of mile-long fields of Spanish bayonet in bloom; or of some Mexican's doby shinin' like a rooby in the sunlight a day's journey ahead, the same one onbroken mass from roof to the ground of the peppers they calls *chili*, all reddenin' in the hot glare of the day.

"Or, if you has a fancy for stirrin' incident an' lively scenes, thar's a time when the rains has raised the old Canadian ontil that quicksand ford at Tascosa—which has done eat a hundred teams if ever it swallows one!—is torn up complete an' the bottom of the river nothin' save b'ilin' sand with a shallow yere an' a hole deep enough to drown a house scooped out jest beyond. An' how since I can't pause a week or two for the river to run down an' the ford to settle, I goes spraddlin' an' tumblin' an' swimmin' across on Tom, my nigh wheeler, opens negotiations with the LIT ranch, an' Bob Roberson, has his riders round-up the pasture, an' comes chargin' down to the ford with a bunch of one thousand ponies, all of 'em dancin' an' buckin' an' prancin' like chil'en outen school. Roberson an' the LIT boys throws the thousand broncos across an' across the ford for mighty likely it's fifty times. They'd flash 'em through—the whole band together—on the run; an' then round 'em up on the opp'site bank, turn 'em an' jam 'em through ag'in. When they ceases, the bottom of the river is tramped an' beat out as hard an' as flat as a floor, as' I hooks up an' brings the waggons over like the ford—bottomless quicksand a hour prior—is one of these yere asphalt streets.

"Or I might relate about a cowboy tournament that's held over in the flat green bottom of Parker's arroya; an' how Jack Coombs throws a rope an' fastens at one hundred an' four foot, while Waco Simpson rides at the herd of cattle one hundred foot away, ropes, throws an' ties down a partic'lar steer, frees his lariat an' is back with the jedges ag'in in forty-eight seconds. Waco wins the prize, a Mexican saddle—stamp-leather an' solid gold she is—worth four hundred dollars, by them onpreecedented alacrities.

"Or, I might impart about a Mexican fooneral where the hearse is a blanket with two poles along the aige, the same as one of these battle litters; of the awful songs the mournful Mexicans sings about departed; of the candles they burns an' the dozens of baby white-pine crosses they sets up on little jim-crow stone-heaps along the trail to the tomb; meanwhiles, howlin' dirges constant.

"Now I thinks of it I might bresh up the recollections of

a mornin' when I rolls over, blankets an' all, onto something that feels as big as a boot-laig an' plenty squirmy; an' how I shows zeal a-gettin' to my feet, knowin' I'm reposin' on a rattlesnake who's bunked in ag'in my back all sociable to warm himse'f. It's worth any gent's while to see how heated an' indignant that serpent takes it because of me turnin' out so early and so swift.

"Then thar's a mornin' when I finds myse'f not five miles down the wind from a prairie fire; an' it crackin' an' roarin' in flame-sheets twenty foot high an' makin' for'ard jumps of fifty foot. What do I do? Go for'ard down the wind, set fire to the grass myse'f, an' let her burn ahead of me. In two minutes I'm over on a burned deestrict of my own, an' by the time the orig'nal flames works down to my fire line, my own speshul fire is three miles ahead an' I myse'f am ramblin' along cool an' saloobrious with a safe, shore area of burnt prairie to my r'ar.

"An' thar's a night on the Serrita la Cruz doorin' a storm, when the lightnin' melts the tire on the wheel of my trail-waggon, an' me layin' onder it at the time. An' it don't even wake me up. Thar's the time, too, when I crosses up at Chico Springs with eighty Injuns who's been buffalo huntin' over to the South Paloduro, an' has with 'em four hundred odd ponies loaded with hides an' buffalo beef an' all headed for their home-camps over back of Taos. The bucks is restin' up a day or two when I rides in; later me an' a half dozen jumps a band of antelopes jest 'round a p'int of rocks. Son, you-all would have admired to see them savages shoot their arrows. I observes one young buck a heap clost. He holds the bow flat down with his left hand while his arrows in their cow-skin quiver sticks over his right shoulder. The way he would flash his right hand back, yank forth a arrow, slam it on his bow, pull it to the head an' cut it loose, is shore a heap earnest. Them missiles would go sailin' off for over three hundred yards, an' I sees him get seven started before ever the first one strikes the ground. The Injuns acquires four antelope by this archery an' shoots mebby some forty arrows; all of which they carefully reclaims when the excitement subsides. She's trooly a sperited exhibition an' I finds it mighty entertainin'.

"I throws these hints loose to show what might be allooded by way of stories, grave and gay, of sights pecooliar to the trail if only some gent of experience ups an' devotes himse'f to the relations. As it is, however, an' recurrin' to Tom an' Jerry—the same bein' as I informs you, my two wheel mules—I reckons now I might better set forth as to how they comes to die that time. It's his obstinacy that downs Jerry; while pore, tender Tom perishes the victim—volunteer at that—of the love he b'ars his contrary mate.

"Them mules, Tom an' Jerry, is obtained by me orig'nal in Vegas. They're the wheelers of a eight-mule team; an' I gives Frosty—who's a gambler an' wins 'em at monte of some locoed sport from Chaparita—twelve hundred dollars for the outfit. Which the same is cheap an' easy at double the *dinero*.

"These mules evident has been part an' passel of the estates of some Mexican, for I finds a cross marked on each harness an' likewise on both waggons. Mexicans employs this formal'ty to run a bluff on any evil sperit who may come projectin' round. Your American mule skinner never makes them tokens. As a roole he's defiant of sperits; and even when he ain't he don't see no refooge in a cross. Mexicans, on the other hand, is plenty strong on said symbol. Every mornin' you holds a Mexican with a dab of white on his fore'erd an' on each cheek bone, an' also on his chin where he crosses himse'f with flour; shore, the custom is yooniversal an' it takes a quart of flour to fully fortify a full-blown Greaser household ag'inst the antic'pated perils of the day.

"No sooner am I cl'ar of Vegas—I'm camped near the Plaza de la Concepcion at the time—when I rounds up the eight mules an' looks 'em over with reference to their characters.

This is jest after I acquires 'em. It's allers well for a gent to know what he's ag'inst; an' you can put down a stack the disp'sitions of eight mules is a important problem.

"The review is plenty satisfactory. The nigh leader is a steady practical person as a lead mule oughter be, an' I notes by his ca'm jedgmatical eye that he's goin' to give himse'f the benefit of every doubt, an' ain't out to go stampedin' off none without knowin' the reason why. His mate at the other end of the jockey-stick is nervous an' hysterical; she never trys to solve no riddles of existence herse'f, this Jane mule don't, but relies on her mate Peter an' plays Peter's system blind. The nigh p'inter is a deecorous form of mule with no bad habits; while his mate over the chain is one of these yere hard, se'fish, wary parties an' his little game is to get as much of everything except work an' trouble as the lay of the kyards permits. My nigh swing mule is a wit like I tell you the other day. Which this jocose anamile is the life of the team an' allers lettin' fly some dry, quaint observation. This mule wag is partic'lar excellent at a bad ford or a hard crossin', an his gay remarks, full of p'int as a bowie knife, shorely cheers an' uplifts the sperits of the rest. The off swing is a heedless creature who regyards his facetious mate as the very parent of fun, an' he goes about with his y'ear cocked an' his mouth ajar, ready to laugh them 'hah, hah!' laughs of his'n at every word his pard turns loose.

"Tom an' Jerry is different from the others. Bein' bigger an' havin' besides the respons'bilities of the hour piled onto them as wheel mules must, they cultivates a sooperior air an' is distant an' reserved in their attitoods towards the other six. As to each other their pose needs more deescription. Tom, the nigh wheeler—the one I rides when drivin'—is infatyooated with Jerry. I hears a sky-sharp aforetime preach about Johathan an' David. Yet I'm yere to assert, son, that them sacred people ain't on speakin' terms compared to the way that pore old lovin' Tom mule feels towards Jerry.

"This affection of Tom's is partic'lar amazin' when you-all recalls the fashion in which the sullen Jerry receives it. Doorin' the several years I spends in their s'ciety I never once detects Jerry in any look or word of kindness to Tom. Jerry bites him an' kicks him an' cusses him out constant; he never tol'rates Tom closter than twenty foot onless at times when he orders Tom to curry him. Shore, the imbecile Tom submits. On sech o'casions when Jerry issues a summons to go over him, usin' his upper teeth for a comb an' bresh, Tom is never so happy. Which he digs an' delves at Jerry's ribs that a-way like it's a honour; after a half hour, mebby, when Jerry feels refreshed s'fficient, he w'irls on Tom an' dismisses him with both heels.

"'I track up on folks who's jest the same,' says Dan Boggs, one time when I mentions this onaccountable in-fatyooation of Tom. 'This Jerry loves that Tom mule mate of his, only he ain't lettin' on. I knows a lady whose treatment of her husband is a dooplicate of Jerry's. She metes out the worst of it to that long-sufferin' shorthorn at every bend in the trail; it looks like he never wins a good word or a soft look from her once. An' yet when that party cashes in, whatever does the lady do? Takes a hooker of whiskey, puts in p'isen enough to down a dozen wolves, an' drinks off every drop. "Far'well, vain world, I'm goin' home," says the lady; "which I prefers death to sep'ration, an' I'm out to jine my beloved husband in the promised land." I knows, for I attends the fooneral of that family—said fooneral is a double-header as the lady, bein' prompt, trails out after her husband before ever he's pitched his first camp—an' later assists old Chandler in deevisin' a epitaph, the same occurin' in these yere familiar words:

> "She sort o got the drop on him,
>   In the dooel of earthly love;
> Let's hope he gets an even break
>   When they meets in heaven above."

"'Thar, 'concloods Dan, 'is what I regyards as a parallel experience to this Tom an' Jerry. The lady plays Jerry's system from soda to hock, an' yet you-all can see in the lights of that thar sooicide how deep she loves him.'

"'That's all humbug, Dan,' says Enright; 'the lady you relates of isn't lovin', she's only locoed that a-way.'

"'Whyever if she's locoed, then,' argues Dan, 'don't they up an' have her in one of their madhouse camps? She goes chargin' about as free an' fearless as a cyclone.'

"'All the same,' says Texas Thompson, 'her cashin' in don't prove no lovin' heart. Mebby she does it so's to chase him up an' continyoo onbroken them hectorin's of her's. I could onfold a fact or two about that wife of mine who cuts out the divorce from me in Laredo that would lead you to concloosions sim'lar. But she wasn't your wife; an' I don't aim to impose my domestic afflictions on this innocent camp, which bein' troo I mootely stands my hand.'

"This Jerry's got one weakness; however, I don't never take advantage of it. He's scared to frenzy if you pulls a gun. I reckons, with all them crimes of his'n preyin' on his mind, that he allows you're out, to shoot him up. Jerry is ca'm so long as your gun's in the belt, deemin' it as so much onmeanin' ornament. But the instant you pulls it like you're goin' to put it in play, he onbuckles into piercin' screams. I reaches for my six-shooter one evenin' by virchoo of antelopes, an' that's the time I discovers this foible of Jerry's. I never gets a shot. At the sight of the gun Jerry evolves a howl an' the antelopes tharupon hits two or three high places an' is miles away. Shore, they thinks Jerry is some new breed of demon.

"When I turns to note the cause of Jerry's clamours he's loppin' his fore-laigs over Tom's back an' sobbin' an' sheddin' tears into his mane. Tom sympathises with Jerry an' says all he can to teach him that the avenger ain't on his trail. Nothin' can peacify Jerry, however, except jam-

min' that awful six-shooter back into its holster. I goes
over Jerry that evenin' patiently explorin' for bullet marks,
but thar ain't none. No one's ever creased him; an' I figgers final by way of a s'lootion some killin' between
hoomans, inadvertent, an' has the teeth of his apprehesions
set on aige.

"Jerry is that high an' haughty he won't come up for corn
in the mornin onless I petitions him partic'lar an' calls him
by name. To jest whoop 'Mules!' he holds don't incloode
him. Usual I humours Jerry an' shouts his title speshul, the
others bein' called in a bunch. When Jerry hears his name
he walks into camp, delib'rate an' dignified, an' kicks every
mule to pieces who tries to shove in ahead.

"Once, feelin' some malignant myse'f, I tries Jerry's patience out. I don't call 'Jerry,' merely shouts 'Mules' once
or twice an' lets it go at that. Jerry, when he notices I don't
refer to him partic'lar lays his y'ears back; an' although his
r'ar elevation is towards me I can see he's hotter than a hornet. The faithful Tom abides with Jerry; though he tells him
it's feed time an' that the others with a nosebag on each of
'em is already at their repasts. Jerry only gets madder an'
lays for Tom an' tries to bite him. After ten minutes, sullen
an' sulky, hunger beats Jerry an' he comes bumpin' into
camp like a bar'l down hill an' eases his mind by wallopin'
both hind hoofs into them other blameless mules, peacefully
munchin' their rations. Also, after Jerry's let me put the
nosebag onto him he reeverses his p'sition an' swiftly lets
fly at me. But I ain't in no trance an' Jerry misses. I don't
frale him; I saveys it's because he feels hoomiliated with me
not callin' him by name.

"As a roole me an' Jerry gets through our dooties harmonious. He can pull like a lion an' never flinches or flickers at a pinch. It's shore a vict'ry to witness the heroic way
Jerry goes into the collar at a hard steep hill or some swirl-
in', rushin' ford. Sech bein' Jerry's work habits I'm prepared to overlook a heap of moral deeficiencies an' never

lays it up ag'in Jerry that he's morose an' repellant when I flings him any kindnesses.

"But while I don't resent 'em none by voylence, still Jerry has habits ag'inst which I has to gyard. You-all recalls how long ago I tells you of Jerry's bein' a thief. Shore, he can't he'p it; he's a born kleptomaniac. Leastwise 'kleptomaniac' is what Colonel Sterett calls it when he's tellin' me of a party who's afflicted sim'lar.

"'Otherwise this gent's a heap respectable,' says the Colonel. 'Morally speakin' thar's plenty who's worse. Of course, seein' he's crowdin' forty years, he ain't so shamefully innocent neither. He ain't no debyootanty; still, he ain't no crime-wrung debauchee. I should say he grades midway in between. But deep down in his system this person's a kleptomaniac, an' at last his weakness gets its hobbles off an' he turns himse'f loose, an' begins to jest nacherally take things right an' left. No, he don't get put away in Huntsville; they sees he's locoed an' he's corraled instead in one of the asylums where thar's nothin' loose an' little kickin' 'round, an' tharfore no temptations.'

"Takin' the word then from Colonel Sterett, Jerry is a kleptomaniac. I used former to hobble Jerry but one mornin' I'm astounded to see what looks like snow all about my camp. Bein' she's in Joone that snow theery don't go. An' it ain't snow, it's flour; this kleptomaniac Jerry creeps to the waggons while I sleeps an' gets away, one after the other, with fifteen fifty-pound sacks of flour. Then he entertains himse'f an' Tom by p'radin' about with the sacks in his teeth, shakin' an' tossin' his head an' powderin' my 'Pride of Denver' all over the plains. Which Jerry shore frosts that scenery plumb lib'ral.

"It's the next night an' I don't hobble Jerry; I pegs him out on a lariat. What do you-all reckon now that miscreant does? Corrupts pore Tom who you may be certain is sympathisin' 'round, an' makes Tom go to the waggons, steal the flour an' pack it out to him where he's pegged. The soopine Tom, who otherwise is the soul of integrity, abstracts six sacks for his mate an' at daybreak the wretched Jerry's standin' thar, white as milk himse'f, an' flour a foot deep in a cirkle whereof the radius is his rope Tom's gazin' on Jerry in a besotted way like he allows he's certainly the greatest sport on earth.

"Which this last is too much an' I ropes up Jerry for punishment. I throws an' hawgties Jerry, an' he's layin' thar on his side. His eye is obdoorate an' thar's neither shame nor repentance in his heart. Tom is sort o' sobbin' onder his breath; Tom would have swapped places with Jerry too quick an' I sees he has it in his mind to make the offer, only he knows I'll turn it down."

"The other six mules comes up an' loafs about observant an' respectful. They jestifies my arrangements; besides Jerry is mighty onpop'lar with 'em by reason of his heels. I can hear Peter the little lead mule sayin' to Jane, his mate: "The boss is goin' to lam Jerry a lot with a trace-chain. Which it's shore comin' to him!"

"I w'irls the chain on high an' lays it along Jerry's evil ribs, *kerwhillup*! Every other link bites through the hide an' the chain plows a most excellent an' wholesome furrow. As the chain descends, the sympathetic Tom jumps an' gives a groan. Tom feels a mighty sight worse than his *compañero*. At the sixth wallop Tom can't b'ar no more, but with tears an' protests come an' stands over Jerry an' puts it up he'll take the rest himse'f. This evidence of brotherly love stands me off, an' for Tom's sake I desists an' throws Jerry loose. That old scoundrel—while I sees he's onforgivin' an' a-harbourin' of hatreds ag'in me—don't forget the trace-chain an' comports himse'f like a law-abidin' mule for months. He even quits bitin' an' kickin' Tom, an' that lovin' beast seems like he's goin' to break his heart over it, 'cause he looks on it as a sign that Jerry's gettin' cold.

"But thar comes a day when I loses both Tom an' Jerry. It's about second drink time one August mornin' an' me an' my eight mules goes scamperin' through a little Mexican plaza called Tramperos on our way to the Canadian. Over by a'doby stands a old fleabitten gray mare; she's shore hideous.

"Now if mules has one overmasterin' deloosion it's a gray mare; she's the religion an' the goddess of the mules. This knowledge is common; if you-all is ever out to create a upheaval in the bosom of a mule the handiest, quickest lever is a old gray mare. The gov'ment takes advantage of this aberration of the mules. Thar's trains of pack mules freightin' to the gov'ment posts in the Rockies. They figgers on three hundred pounds to the mule an' the freight is packed in panniers. The gov'ment freighters not bein' equal to the manifold mysteries of a diamond-hitch, don't use no reg'lar shore-enough pack saddle but takes refooge with their ignorance in panniers.

"Speakin' gen'ral, thar's mebby two hundred mules in one of these gov'ment pack trains. An' in the lead, followed, waited on an' worshipped by the mules, is a aged gray mare. She don't pack nothin' but her virchoo an' a little bell, which last is hung 'round her neck. This old mare, with nothin' but her character an' that bell to encumber her, goes fa'rly flyin' light. But go as fast an' as far as she pleases, them long-y'eared locoed worshippers of her's won't let her outen their raptured sight. The last one of 'em, panniers, freight an' all, would go surgin' to the topmost pinnacle of the Rockies if she leads the way.

"An' at that this gray mare don't like mules none; she abhors their company an' kicks an' abooses' em to a standstill whenever they draws near. But the fool mules don't care; it's ecstacy to simply know she's livin' an' that mule's cup of joy is runnin' over who finds himse'f permitted to crop grass within forty foot of his old, gray bellbedecked idol.

"We travels all day, followin' glimpsin' that fleabitten cayouse at Tramperos. But the mules can't think or talk of nothin' else. It arouses their religious enthoosiasm to highest pitch; even the cynic Jerry gets half-way keyed up over it. I looks for trouble that night; an' partic'lar I pegs out Jerry plenty deep and strong. The rest is hobbled, all except Tom. Gray mare or not, I'll gamble the outfit Tom wouldn't abandon Jerry, let the indoocement be ever so alloorin'.

"Every well-organised mule team that a-way aller carries along a bronco. This little steed, saddled an' bridled, trots throughout the day by the side of the off-wheeler, his bridle-rein caught over the wheeler's hame. The bronco is used to round up the mules in event they strays or declines in the mornin' to come when called. Sech bein' the idee, the cayous is allers kept strictly in camp.

"'James' is my bronco's name; an' the evenin', followin' the vision of that Tramperos gray mare I makes onusual shore that James stays with me. Not that gray mares impresses James—him bein a hoss an' hosses havin' religious convictions different from mules—or is doo to prove temptations to him; but he might conceal other plans an' get strayed prosecootin' of 'em to a finish. I ties James to the trail-waggon, an' following' bacon, biscuits, airtights an' sech, the same bein' my froogal fare when on the trail, I rolls in onder the lead-waggon an' gives myse'f up to sleep.

"Exactly as I surmises, when I turns out at sunup thar's never a mule in sight. Every one of them idolaters goes poundin' back, as fast as ever he can with hobbles on, to confess his sins an' say his pray'rs at the shrine of that old gray mare. Even Jerry, whose cynicism shoud have saved him, pulls his picket-pin with the rest an', takin' Tom along, goes curvin' off. It ain't more than ten minutes, you can gamble! when James an' me is on their trails.

"One by one, I overtakes the team strung all along between my camp an' Tramperos. Peter, the little lead mule, bein' plumb agile an' a sharp on hobbles, gets cl'ar thar; an' I finds him devourin' the goddess gray mare with heart an'

soul an' eyes, an' singin' to himse'f the while in low, satis-
fied tones.

"As one after the other I passes the pilgrim mules I turns
an' lifts about a squar' inch of hide off each with the
blacksnake whip I'm carryin', by way of p'intin' out their
heresies an' arousin' in 'em a eagerness to get back to their
waggon an' a upright, pure career. They takes the chastise-
ment humble an' dootiful, an' relinquishes the thought of
reachin' the goddess gray mare.

"When I overtakes old Jerry I pours the leather into him
speshul, an' the way him an' his pard Tom goes scatterin'
for camp refreshes me a heap. An' yet after I rescoos Peter
from the demoralisin' inflooences of the gray mare, an' begins to pick up the other members of the team on the journey back, I'm some deepressed when I don't see Tom or
Jerry. Nor is either of them mules by the waggons when
I arrives.

"It's onadulterated cussedness! Jerry, with no hobbles an'
merely draggin' a rope, can lope about free an' permiscus.
Tom, with nothin' to hamper him but his love for Jerry, is
even more lightsome an' loose. That Jerry mule, hatin' me
an' allowin' to make me all the grief he can, sneakingly
leaves the trail some'ers after I turns him an' touches him
up with the lash. An' now Tom an' Jerry is shorely hid out
an' lost a whole lot. It's nothin' but Jerry's notion of revenge on me.

"I camps two days where I'm at, an' rounds up the region
for the trooants. I goes over it like a fine-tooth comb an'
rides James to a show-down. That bronco never is so long
onder the saddle since he's foaled; I don't reckon he knows
before thar's so much hard work in the world as falls to him
when we goes ransackin' in quest of Tom an' Jerry.

"It's no use; the ground is hard an' dry an' I can't even
see their hoof-marks. The country's so rollin', too, it's no
trouble for 'em to hide. At last I quits an' throws my hand
in the diskyard. Tom an' Jerry is shore departed an' I'm

deeficient my two best mules. I hooks up the others, an' seein' it's down hill an' a easy trail I makes Tascosa an' refits.

"I never crosses up on Tom an' Jerry in this yere life no more, but one day I learns their fate. It's a month later on my next trip back, an' I'm camped about a half day's drive of that same locoed plaza of Tramperos. As I'm settin' in camp with the sun still plenty high—I'm compilin' flapjacks at the time—I sees eight or ten ravens wheelin' an' cirklin' over beyond a swell about three miles to the left.

"'Tom an' Jerry for a bloo stack!' I says to myse'f; an' with that I cinches the saddle onto James precip'tate.

"Shore enough; I'm on the scene of the tragedy. Half way down a rocky slope where thar ain't grass enough to cover the brown nakedness of the ground lies the bones of Tom an' Jerry. This latter, who's that obstinate an' resentful he won't go back to camp when I wallops him on that gray mare mornin', allows he'll secrete himse'f an' Tom off to one side an' worrit me up. While he's manooverin' about he gets the half-inch rope he's draggin' tangled good an' fast in a mesquite bush. It shorely holds him; that bush is old Jerry's last picket—his last camp. Which he'd a mighty sight better played his hand out with me, even if I does ring in a trace-chain on him at needed intervals. Jerry jest nacherally starves to death for grass an' water. An' what's doubly hard the lovin' Tom, troo to the last, starves with him. Thar's water within two miles; but Tom declines it, stays an' starves with Jerry, an' the ravens an' the coyotes picks their frames."

23

Bill Connors of the Osages.

"NACHERALLY, if you-all is frettin' to hear about Injuns," observed the Old Cattleman in reply to my latest request, "I better onfold how Osage Bill Connors gets his wife. Not that thar's trouble in roundin' up this squaw; none whatever. She comes easy; all the same said tale elab'rates some of them savage customs you're so cur'ous concernin'."

My companion arose and kicked together the logs in the fireplace. This fireplace was one of the great room's comforts as well as ornaments. The logs leaped into much accession of flame, and crackled into sparks, and these went gossiping up the mighty chimney, their little fiery voices making a low, soft roaring like the talk of bees.

"This chimley draws plenty successful," commented my friend. "Which it almost breaks even with a chimley I constructs once in my log camp on the Upper Red. That Red River floo is a wonder! Draw? Son, it could draw four kyards an' make a flush. But that camp of mine on the Upper Red is over eight thousand foot above the sea as I'm informed by a passel of surveyor sports who comes romancin' through the hills with a spyglass on three pegs; an' high altitoods allers proves a heap exileratin' to a fire.

"But speakin' of Bill Connors: In Wolfville—which them days is the only part of my c'reer whereof I'm proud an' reviews with onmixed satisfaction—Doc Peets is, like you, inquis'tive touchin' Injuns. Peets puts it up that some day he's doo to write books about 'em. Which in off hours, an' when we-all is more or less at leesure over our Valley Tan, Peets frequent comes explorin' 'round for details. Shore, I imparts all I saveys about Bill Connors, an' likewise sech other aborigines as lives in mem'ry; still, it shakes my estimates of Peets to find him eager over Injuns, they bein' low an' debasin' as topics. I says as much to Peets.

"'Never you-all mind about me,' says Peets. 'I knows so much about white folks it comes mighty clost to makin' me sick. I seeks tales of Injuns as a relief an' to promote a average in favor of the species.'

"This Bill Connors is a good-lookin' young buck when I cuts his trail; straight as a pine an' strong an' tireless as a bronco. It's about six years after the philanthrofists ropes onto Bill an' drags him off to a school. You-all onderstands about a philanthrofist—one of these sports who's allers improvin' some party's condition in a way the party who's improved don't like.

"'A philanthrofist,' says Colonel Sterett, one time when Dan Boggs demands the explanation at his hands; 'a philanthrofist is a gent who insists on you givin' some other gent your money.'

"For myse'f, however, I regyards the Colonel's definition as too narrow. Troo philanthrofy has a heap of things to it that's jest as onreasonable an' which does not incloode the fiscal feachers mentioned by the Colonel.

"As I'm sayin'; these well-meanin' though darkened sports, the philanthrofists, runs Bill down—it's mebby when he's fourteen, only Injuns don't keep tab on their years none—an' immures him in one of the gov'ment schools. It's thar Bill gets his name, 'Bill Connors.' Before that he cavorts about, free an' wild an' happy onder the Injun app'lation of the 'Jack Rabbit.'

"Shore! Bill's sire—a savage who's way up in the picture kyards an' who's called 'Crooked Claw' because of his left hand bein' out of line with a Ute arrow through it long ago—gives his consent to Bill j'inin' that sem'nary. Crooked Claw can't he'p himse'f; he's powerless; the Great Father in Washin'ton is backin' the play of the philanthrofists.

"'Which the Great Father is too many for Crooked Claw,' says this parent, commentin' on his he'plessness. Bill's gone canterin' to his old gent to remonstrate, not hungerin' for learnin', an' Crooked Claw says this to Bill: 'The Great Father is too many for Crooked Claw; an' too strong. You must go to school as the Great Father orders; it is right.The longest spear is right.'

"Bill is re-branded, 'Bill Connors,' an then he's done bound down to them books. After four years Bill grad-yooates; he's got the limit an' the philanthrofists takes Bill's hobbles off an' throws him loose with the idee that Bill will go back to his tribe folks an' teach 'em to read. Bill comes back, shore, an' is at once the Osage laughin'-stock for wearin' pale-face clothes. Also, the medicine men tells Bill he'll die for talkin' paleface talk an' sportin' a paleface shirt, an' these prophecies preys on Bill who's eager to live a heap an' ain't ready to cash in. Bill gets back to blankets an' feathers in about a month.

"Old Black Dog, a leadin' sharp among the Osages, is goin' about with a dab of clay in his ha'r, and wearin' his most ornery blanket. That's because Black Dog is in mournin' for a squaw who stampedes over the Big Divide, mebby it's two months prior. Black Dog's mournin' has got dealt down to the turn like; a' windin' up his grief an' tears, Osage fashion, he out to give a war-dance. Shore; the savages rings in a war-dance on all sorts of cer'monies. It don't allers mean that they're hostile, an' about to spraddle forth on missions of blood. Like I states, Black Dog, who's gone to the end of his mournful lariat about the departed squaw, turns himse'f on for a war-dance; an' he nacherally invites the Osage nation to paint an' get in on the festiv'ties.

"Accordin' to the rooles, pore Bill, jest back from school, has got to cut in. Or he has his choice between bein' fined a pony or takin' a lickin' with mule whips in the hands of a brace of kettle-tenders whose delight as well as dooty it is to mete out the punishment. Bill can't afford to go shy a pony, an' as he's loth to accept the larrupin's, he wistfully makes ready to shake a moccasin at the *baile*. An' as nothin' but feathers, blankets, an' breech-clouts goes at a war-dance—the same bein' Osage dress-clothes—Bill shucks his paleface garments an' arrays himse'f after the breezy fashion of his ancestors. Bill attends the war dance an' shines. Also, bein' praised by the medicine men an' older bucks for quit-tin' his paleface duds' an' findin' likewise the old-time blan-ket an' breech-clout healthful an' saloobrious—which Bill forgets their feel in his four years at that sem'nary—he adheres to 'em. This lapse into aboriginal ways brews trouble for Bill; he gets up ag'inst the agent.

"It's the third day after Black Dog's war-dance, an' Bill, all paint an' blankets an' feathers, is sa'nterin' about Pawhusky, takin' life easy an' Injun fashion. It's then the agent connects with Bill an' sizes him up. The agent asks Bill does he stand in on this yere Black Dog war-dance.

"'Don't they have no roast dog at that warjig?' asks Dan Boggs, when I'm relatin' these reminiscences in the Red Light.

"'No,' I says; 'Osages don't eat no dogs.'

"'It's different with Utes a lot,' says Dan. 'Which Utes regyards dogs fav'rable, deemin' 'em a mighty sucyoolent an' nootritious dish. The time I'm with the Utes they pulls off a shindig, "tea dance" it is, an', as what Huggins would call "a star feacher" they ups an' roasts a white dog. That canine is mighty plethoric an' fat, an' they lays him in his broad, he'pless back an' shets off his wind with a stick cross-wise of his neck, an' two bucks pressin' on the ends. When he's good an' dead an' all without no suffoosion of blood, the Utes singes his fur off in a fire an' bakes him as he is. I partakes of that dog—some. I don't nacherally lay for said repast wide-jawed, full-toothed an' reemorseless, like it's flapjacks—I don't gorge myse'f none; but when I'm in Rome, I strings my chips with the Romans like the good book says, an' so I sort o' eats baked dog with the Utes. Otherwise, I'd hurt their sens'bilities; an' I ain't out to harrow up no entire tribe an' me playin' a lone hand.'

"That agent questions Bill as to the war-dance carryin's on of old Black Dog. Then he p'ints at Bill's blankets an' feathers an' shakes his head a heap dissapprobative.

"'Shuck them blankets an' feathers,' says the agent, 'an' get back into your trousers a whole lot; an' be sudden about it, too. I puts up with the divers an' sundry rannikabooisms of old an' case-hardened Injuns who's savage an' ontaught. But you're different; you've been to school an' learned the virchoos of pants; wherefore, I looks for you to set examples.'

"It's then Bill gets high an' allows he'll wear clothes to suit himse'f. Bill denounces trousers as foolish in their construction an' fallacious in their plan. Bill declar's they're a bad scheme, trousers is; an' so sayin' he defies the agent to do his worst. Bill stands pat on blankets an' feathers.

"'Which you will, will you!' remarks this agent.

"Then he claps Bill in irons mighty decisive, an' plants him up ag'in the high face of a rock bluff which has been frownin' down on Bird River since Adam makes his first camp. Havin' got Bill posed to his notion, this earnest agent, puttin' a hammer into Bill's rebellious hand, starts him to breakin' rock.

"'Which the issue is pants,' says the obdurate agent sport; 'an' I'll keep you-all whackin' away at them boulders while the cliff lasts onless you yields. Thar's none of you young bucks goin' to bluff me, an' that's whatever!'

"Bill breaks rocks two days. The other Osages comes an' perches about, sympathetic, an' surveys Bill. They exhorts him to be firm; they gives it out in Osage he's a patriot.

"Bill's willin' to be a patriot as the game is commonly dealt, but when his love of country takes the form of poundin' rocks, the noble sentiments which yeretofore bubbles in Bill's breast commences to pall on Bill an' he becomes none too shore but what trousers is right. By second drink time— only savages don't drink, a pateranl gov'ment barrin' nosepaint on account of it makin' 'em too fitfully exyooberant—by second drink time the second evenin' Bill lays down his hand—pitches his hammer into the diskyard as it were— an' when I crosses up with him, Bill's that abject he wears a necktie. When Bill yields, the agent meets him half way, an' him an' Bill rigs a deal whereby Bill arrays himse'f Osage fashion whenever his hand's crowded by tribal customs. Other times, Bill inhabits trousers; an' blankets an' feathers is rooled out.

"Shore, I talks with Bill's father, old Crooked Claw. This yere savage is the ace-kyard of Osageland as a fighter. No, that outfit ain't been on the warpath for twenty years when I sees 'em; then it's with Boggs' old pards, the Utes. I asks Crooked Claw if he likes war. He tells me that he dotes on carnage like a jaybird, an' goes forth to battle as joobilant as a drunkard to a shootin' match. That is, Crooked Claw used to go curvin' off to war, joyful, at first. Later his glee is subdooed because of the big chances he's takin'. Then he lugs out 'leven skelps, all Ute, an' eloocidates.

"'This first maverick,' says Crooked Claw—of course, I gives him in the American tongue, not bein' equal to the reedic'lous broken Osage he talks'—this yere first maverick,' an' he strokes the braided ha'r of a old an' smoke-dried skelp, 'is easy. The chances, that a-way, is even. Number two is twice as hard; an' when I snags onto number three—I downs that hold-up over by the foot of Fisher's Peak—the chances

has done mounted it be three to one ag'in me. So it goes gettin' higher an' higher, ontil when I corrals my 'leventh, it's
'leven to one he wins onless he's got killin's of his own to
stand off mine. I don't reckon none he has though,' says
Crooked Claw, curlin' his nose contemptuous. 'He's heap big
squaw—a coward; an' would hide from me like a quail. He
looks big an' brave an' strong, but his heart is bad—he is a
poor knife in a good sheath. So I don't waste a bullet on him,
seein' his fear, but kills him with my war-axe. Still, he raises
the chances ag'inst me to twelve to one, an' after that I goes
careful an' slow. I sends in my young men; but for mysc'f I
sort o' hungers about the suburbs of the racket, takin' no resks
an' on the prowl for a cinch, —some sech pick-up as a
sleeper, mebby. But my 'leventh is my last; the Great Father
in Washin'ton gets tired with us an' he sends his walk-a-heaps
an' buffalo soldiers'—these savages calls niggers 'buffalo soldiers,' bein' they're that woolly'—an makes us love peace.
Which we'd a-had the Utes too dead to skin if it ain't for the
walk-a-heaps an' buffalo soldiers.'

"An' at this Crooked Claw tosses the bunch of Ute top-
knots to one of his squaws, fills up his red-stone pipe with
kinnikinick an' begins to smoke, lookin' as complacent as a
catfish doorin' a Joone rise.

"Bill Connors has now been wanderin' through this vale
of tears for mebby she's twenty odd years, an' accordin' to
Osage tenets, Bill's doo to get wedded. No, Bill don't make
no move; he comports himse'f lethargic; the reesponsibilities
of the nuptials devolves on Bill's fam'ly.

"It's one of the excellentest things about a Injun that he
don't pick out no wife personal, deemin' himse'f as too
locoed to beat so difficult a game.

"Or mebby, as I observes to Texas Thompson one time in
the Red Light when him an' me's discussin', or mebby it's
because he's that callous he don't care, or that shiftless he
won't take trouble.

"'Whatever's the reason,' says Texas, on that o'casion, heavin' a sigh, 'thar's much to be said in praise of the custom. If it only obtains among the whites thar's one sport not onknown to me who would have shore passed up some heart aches. You can be a hoss, no fam'ly of mine would pick out the lady who beats me for that divorce back in Laredo to be the spouse of Texas Thompson. Said household's got too much savey to make sech a break.'

"While a Osage don't select that squaw of his, still I allers entertains a theery that he sort o' saveys what he's ag'inst an' no he'pmeet gets sawed off on him objectionable an' blind. I figgers, for all he don't let on, that sech is the sityooation in the marital adventures of Bill. His fam'ly picks the Saucy Willow out; but it's mighty likely he signs up the lady to some discreet member of his outfit before they goes in to make the play.

"Saucy Willow for a savage is pretty—pretty as a pinto hoss. Her parent, Old Strike Axe, is a morose but common form of Osage, strong financial, with a big bunch of cattle an' more' two hundred ponies. Bill gets his first glimpse, after he comes back from school, of the lovely Saucy Willow at a dance. This ain't no war-dance nor any other cer'monious splurge; it's a informal merrymakin', innocent an' free, same as is usual with us at the Wolfville dance hall. Shore, Osages, lacks guitars an' fiddles, an' thar's no barkeep nor nosepaint—none, in trooth, of the fav'rable adjuncts wherewith we makes a evenin' in Hamilton's hurdygurdy a season of social elevation, an' yet they pulls off their fandangoes with a heap of verve, an' I've no doubt they shore enjoys themse'fs.

"For two hours before sundown the kettletenders is howlin' an' callin' the dance throughout the Osage camp. thar's to be a full moon, an' the dance—the *Ingraska* it is; a dance the Osages buys from the Poncas for eight ponies—is to come off in a big, high-board corral called the 'Round House.'

"Followin' the first yell of the kettletenders, the young bucks begins to paint up for the hilarity. You might see 'em all over camp, for it's August weather an' the walls of the tents an' teepee is looped up to let in the cool, daubin' the ocher on their faces an' braidin' the feathers into their ha'r. This organisin' for a *baile* ain't no bagetelle, an' two hours is the least wherein any se'f-respectin' buck who's out to make a centre shot on the admiration of the squaws an' wake the envy of rival bucks, can lay on the pigments, so he paints away at his face, careful an' acc'rate, sizin'up results meanwhile in a jimcrow lookin' glass. At last he's as radiant as a rainbow, an' after garterin' each laig with a belt of sleighbells jest below the knee, he regyards himse'f with a fav'rable eye an' allows he's ondoubted the wildest wag in his set.

"Each buck arrives at the Round House with his blanket wropped over his head so as not to blind the onwary with his splendours. It's mebby second drink time after sundown an' the full moon is swingin' above effulgent. The bucks who's doo to dance sets about one side of the Round House on a board bench; the squaws—not bein' in on the proposed activities—occupies the other half, squattin' on the ground. Some of 'em backs their papooses tied on to a fancy-ribboned, highly beaded board, an' this they makes a cradle of by restin' one end on the ground an' the other on their toe, rockin' the same meanwhile with a motion of the foot. Thar's a half hoop over the head-end of these papoose boards, hung with bells for the papoose to get infantile action on an' amoose his leesure.

"The bucks settin' about their side of the round House, still wrops themse'fs in their blankets so as not to dazzle the squaws to death preematoor. At last the music peals forth. The music confines itse'f to a bass drum—paleface drum it is—which is staked out hor'zontal about a foot high from the grass over in the centre. The orchestra is a decrepit buck with a rag-wropped stick; with this weepon he beats the drum, chantin' at the same time a pensive refrain.

"Mebby a half-dozen squaws, with no papooses yet to distract 'em, camps 'round this virchuoso with the rag-stick, **an' yoonites their girlish howls** with his. You-all can put down a bet it don't remind you none of nightingales or mockin' birds; but the Injuns likes it. Which their simple sperits wallows in said warblin's! But to my notion they're more calc'lated to loco a henhawk than furnish inspiration for a dance.

"'Tunk! tunk! tunk! tunk!' goes this rag-stick buck, while the squaws chorus along with, 'Hy-yah! hy-yah! hy-yah-yah-yah! Hy-yah! hy-yah! hy-yah-yah-yah!' an' grievous, an' make no mistake!

"At first 'tunk!' the bucks stiffen to their feet and cast off the blankets. Feathers, paint, an' bells! they blaze an' tinkle in the moonlight with a subdooed but savage elegance.They skates out onto the grass, stilt-laig, an' each buck for hims'f. They go skootin' about, an' weave an' turn an' twist like these yere water-bugs jiggin' it on the surface of some pond. Sometimes a buck'll lay his nose along the ground **while he dances**—light bells jinglin', feathers tossin'! Then he'll straighten up ontil he looks like he's eight foot tall; an' they shore throws themse'fs with a heap of heart an' sperit.

"It's as well they does. If you looks clost you observes a brace of bucks, and each packin' a blacksnake whip. Them's kettle-tenders, —floor managin' the *baile* they be; an' if a buck who's dancin' gets preeoccupied with thinkin' of somethin' else an' takes to prancin' and' dancin' listless, the way the kettle-tenders pours the leather into him to remind him his fits of abstraction is bad form, is like a religious ceremony. An' it ain't no bad idee; said kettle-tenders shore promotes **what Colonel Sterett** calls the *elan* of the dancin' bucks no end.

"After your eyes gets used to this whirlin' an' skatin' an' skootin' an' weavin' in an' out, you notes two bucks, painted to a finish an' feathered to the stars! who out-skoots an' out-whirls an' out'skated their fellow bucks like four to one. They gets their nose a little lower one time an' then stands higher in the air another, than is possible to the next best buck. Them enthoosiasts ain't Osages at all; which they're niggers—full-blood Senegambians they be, who's done j'ined the tribe. These Round House festivals with the paint, the feathers, an' forgettin' all about the white folks an' their gyarded ways, they're the biggest Injuns to warm a heel that night.

"Saucy Willow is up by the damaged rag-stick buck lendin' a mouthful or two of cl'ar, bell-like alto yelps to the harmony of the evenin'. Bill who's a wonder in feathers an' bells, an' whose colour-scheme would drive a temp'rance lecturer to drink, while zippin' about the moonlight gets his eye on her. Mighty likely Bill's smitten; but he don't let on, the fam'ly like I relates, allers ropin' up a gent's bride. It's good bettin' this yere Saucy Willow counts up Bill. If she does, however, —no more than Bill, —she never tips her hand. The Saucy Willow yelps on onconcerned, like her only dream of bliss is to show the coyotes what vocal failures they be.

"It's a week after the *Ingraska*, an' Bill's fam'ly holds a round-up to pick Bill out a squaw. He ain't present, havin' the savey to go squanderin' off to play Injun poker with some Creek sports he hears has money over on the Polecat. Bill's fam'ly makes quite a herd, bucks an' squaws buttin' in on the discussion permiscus an' indiscrim'nate. Shore! the squaws has as much to say as the bucks among Injuns. They owns their own ponies an' backs their own play an' is as big a Injun as anybody, allowin' for that nacheral difference between squaw dooties an' buck dooties—one keeps camp while the other hunts, or doorin' war times when one protects the herds an' plunder while the other faces the foe. You hears that squaws is slaves? However is anybody goin' to be a slave where thar's as near nothin' to do in the way of work as is possible an' let a hooman live? Son, thar ain't as much hard labour done in a Injun camp in a week—ain't as much to do as gets transacted at one of them rooral oyster suppers to raise money for the preacher!

"Bill's fam'ly comes trailin' in to this powwow about pickin' out a squaw for Bill. Besides Crooked Claw, thar's Bill's widow aunt, the Wild Cat—she's plumb cunnin', the Wild Cat is, an' jest then bein' cel'brated among the Osages for smokin' ponies with Black B'ar, a old buck, an' smokin' Black B'ar out of his two best cayouses. Besides these two, thar's The-man-who-bleeds, The-man-who-sleeps, Tom Six-killer, The-man-who-steps-high, an' a dozen other squaws an' bucks, incloosive of Bill's mother who's called the Silent Comanche, an' is takin' the play a heap steady an' livin' up to her name.

"The folks sets 'round an' smokes Crooked Claw's kinnikinick. Then the Wild Cat starts in to deal the game. She says it's time Bill's married, as a onmarried buck is a menace; at this the others grunts agreement. Then they all turns in to overhaul the el'gible young squaws. Which they shore shows up them belles! One after the other they're drug over the coals. At last the Wild Cat mentions the Saucy Willow jest as every savage present knows will be done soon or late from the jump. The Saucy Willow obtains a speshul an' onusual run for her money. But it's settled final that while the Saucy Willow ain't none too good, she's the best they can do. The Saucy Willow belongs to the Elk clan, while Bill belongs to the B'ar clan, an' that at least is c'rrect. Injuns don't believe in inbreedin' so they allers marries out of their clan.

"As soon as they settles on the Saucy Willow as Bill's squaw, they turns in to make up the 'price.' The Wild Cat, who's rich, donates a kettle, a side of beef, an' the two cayouses she smokes outen she besotted Black B'ar. The rest

chucks in accordin' to their means, Crooked Claw comin' up
strong with ten ponies; an' Bill's mother, the Silent Comanche, showin' down with a bolt of calico, two buffalo
robes, a sack of flour an' a lookin' glass. This plunder is to
go to the Saucy Willow's folks as a 'price' for the squaw.
No, they don't win on the play; the Saucy Willow's parents
is out *dinero* on the nuptials when all is done. They has to
give Bill their wickeyup.

"When Bill's outfit's fully ready to deal for blood they
picks out some bright afternoon. The Saucy Willow's fam'ly
is goin' about lookin' partic'lar harmless an' innocent; but
they're coony enough to be in camp that day. A procession
starts from the Crooked Claw camp. Thar's The-man-who-
steps-high at the head b'arin' a flag, union down, an' riotin'
along behind is Tom Six-killer, The-man-who-sleeps, the
Wild Cat and others leadin' five ponies an' packin' kettles,
flour, beef, an' sim'lar pillage. They lays it all down an'
stakes out the broncos about fifty yards from Strike Axe's
camp an' withdraws.

"Then some old squaw of the Strike Axe outfit issues
forth an' throws the broncos loose. That's to show that the
Saucy Willow is a onusual excellent young squaw an'
pop'lar with her folks, an' they don't aim to shake her social
standin' by acceptin' sech niggard terms.

"But the Crooked Claw outfit ain't dismayed, an' takes
this rebuff phlegmatic. It's only so much etyquette; an' now
it's disposed of they reorganise to lead ag'in to win. This
time they goes the limit, an' brings up fifteen ponies an'
stacks in besides with blankets, robes, beef, flour, calico,
kettles, skillets, and looking-glasses enough to fill eight
waggons. This trip the old Strike Axe squaw onties the fifteen ponies an' takin' 'em by their ropes brings 'em in clost
to the Strike Axe camp, tharby notifyin' the Crooked Claw
band that their bluff for the Saucy Willow is regyarded as
feasible an' the nuptials goes. With this sign, the Crooked

Claws comes caperin' up to the Strike Axes an' the latter fam'ly proceeds to rustle a profoosion of grub; an' with that they all turns in an' eats old Strike Axe outen house an' home. The 'price' is split up among the Strike Axe bunch, shares goin' even to second an' third cousins.

"Mebby she's a week later when dawns the weddin' day. Bill, who's been lookin' a heap numb ever since these rites becomes acoote, goes projectin' off alone onto the prairie. The Saucy Willow is hid in the deepest corner of Strike Axe's teepee; which if she's visible, however, you'd be shore amazed at the foolish expression she wears, but all as shy an' artless as a yearlin' antelope.

"But it grows time to wind it up, an' one of the Strike Axe bucks climbs into the saddle an' rides half way towards the camp of Crooked Claw. Strike Axe an' Crooked Claw in antic'pation of these entanglements has done pitched their camps about half a mile apart so as to give the pageant spread an' distances. When he's half way, the Strike Axe buck fronts up an' slams loose with his Winchester; it's a signal the *baile* is on.

"At the rifle crack, mounted on a pony that's the flower of the Strike Axe herd, the Saucy Willow comes chargin' for the Crooked Claws like a shootin' star. The Saucy Willow is a sunburst of Osage richness! an' is packin' about five hundred dollars' worth of blankets, feathers, beads, calicoes, ribbons, an' buckskins, not to mention six pounds of brass an' silver jewelry. Straight an' troo comes the Saucy Willow; skimmin' like a arrow an' as rapid as the wind!

"As Saucy Willow embarks on this expedition, thar starts to meet her—afoot they be but on the run—Tom Six-killer an' a brace of squaw cousins of Bill's. Nacherally, bein' he out-lopes the cousins, Tom Six-killer runs up on the Saucy Willow first an' grabs her bronco by the bridle. The two young squaw cousins ain't far behind the Six-killer, for they can run like rabbits, an' they arrives all laughter an' cries, an' with one move searches the Saucy Willow outen the saddle. In less time than it takes to get action on a drink of licker the two young squaws has done stripped the Saucy Willow of every feather, bead an' rag, an' naked as when she's foaled they wrops her up, precious an' safe in a blanket an' packs her gleefully into the camp of Crooked Claw. Here they re-dresses the Saucy Willow an' piles on the gewgaws an' adornments, ontil if anything she's more gorgeous than former. The pony which the Saucy Willow rides goes to the Six-killer, while the two she-cousins, as to the balance of her apparel that a-way, divides the pot.

"An' now like a landslide upon the Crooked Claws comes the Strike Axe household. Which they're thar to the forty-'leventh cousin; savages keepin' exact cases on relatives a mighty sight further than white folks. The Crooked Claw fam'ly is ready. It's Crooked Claw's turn to make the feast, an' that eminent Osage goes the distance. Crooked Claw shorely does himse'f proud, while Bill's mother, the Silent Comanche, is hospitable, but dignified. It's a great weddin'. The Wild Cat is pirootin' about, makin' mean an' onfeelin' remarks, as becomes a widow lady with a knowledge of the world an' a bundle the size an' shape of a roll of blankets. The two fam'lies goes squanderin' about among each other, free an' fraternal, an' thar's never a cloud in the sky.

"At last the big feed begins. Son, you should have beheld them fool Osages throw themse'fs upon the Crooked Claw's good cheer. It's a p'int of honour to eat as much as you can; an' b'arin' that in mind the revellers mows away about twenty pounds of beef to a buck—the squaws, not being' so ardent, quits out on might likely it's the thirteenth pound. Tom Six-killer comes plenty clost to sacrificin' himse'f utter.

"This last I knows, for the next day I sees the medicine men givin' some sufferer one of their aboriginal steam baths. They're on the bank of Bird River. They've bent

down three or four small saplin's for the framework of a
tent, like, an' thar's piled on 'em blankets an' robes a foot
deep so she's plumb airtight. Thar's a fire goin' an' they're
heatin' rocks, same as Colonel Sterett tells about when they
baptises his grandfather into the church. When the rocks is
red-hot they takes 'em, one by one, an' drops 'em into a
bucket of water to make her steam. Then they shoves this
impromptoo cauldron inside the little robe house where as
I'm aware—for I onderstands the signs from the start—
thar's a sick buck quiled up awaitin' relief. This yere invalid
buck stays in thar twenty minutes. The water boils an' bubbles an' the steam gets that abundant not to say urgent she
half lifts the robes an' blankets at the aiges to escape. The
ailin' buck in the sweat tent stays ontil he can't stay no
more, an' then with a yowl, he comes burstin' forth, a reek
of sweat an' goes splashin' into the coolin' waters of Bird
River. It's the Six-killer; that weddin' feast comes mighty
near to downin' him—gives him a 'bad heart,' an' he onder-
goes the steam bath for relief.

"But we're strayed from the weddin'. Bein' now re-ar-
rayed in fullest feather the Saucy Willow is fetched into the
ring an' receives a platter with the rest. Then one of the
bucks, lookin' about like he's amazed, says: 'Wherever is
the Jack Rabbit?' that bein' Bill's Osage title. Crooked Claw
shakes his head an' reckons most likely the Jack Rabbit's
rummagin' about loose some'ers, not knowin' enough to
come in an' eat. A brace of bucks an' a young squaw starts
up an' figgers they'll search about an' see if they can't
round him up. They goes out an' thar's Bill settin' off on a
rock a quarter of a mile with his back to the camp an' the
footure.

"The two sharps an' the squaw herds Bill into camp an'
stakes him out, shoulder to shoulder, with the little Saucy
Willow. Neither Bill nor the little Saucy Willow su'gests by
word, screech or glance that they saveys either the game or

the stakes, an' eats on, takin' no notice of themse'fs or any of the gluttons who surrounds 'em. Both Bill an' the little Saucy Willow looks that witless you-all would yearn to bat 'em one with the butt of a mule whip if onfortoonately you're present to be exasperated by sech exhibitions. At last, however, jest as the patience of the audience is plumb played, both Bill an' the little Saucy Willow gives a start of surprise. Which they're pretendin' to be startled to find they're feedin' off the same dish. Thar you be; that makes 'em 'buck an' squaw'—'man an wife;' an' yereafter, in Osage circles they can print their kyards 'Mister an' Missis Bill Connors,' while Bill draws an' spends the little Saucy Willow's annooty on payment day instead of Strike Axe."

24

Colonel Coyote Clubbs.

"**W**HICH as a roole," said the Old Cattleman, "I speaks with deference an yields respects to whatever finds its source in nacher, but this yere weather simply makes sech attitoode reedic'lous, an' any encomiums passed tharon would sound sarkastic." Here my friend waved a disgusted hand towards the rain-whipped panes and shook his head. "Thar's but one way to meet an' cope successful with a day like this," he ran on, "an' that is to put yourse'f in the hands of a joodicious barkeep—put yourse'f in his hands an' let him pull you through. Actin' on the idee I jest despatches my black boy Tom for a pitcher of peach an' honey, an', onless you-all has better plans afoot, you might as well camp an' wait deevelopments, same as old man Wasson does when he's treed by the b'ar."

Promptly came the peach and honey, and with its appearance the pelting storm outside lost power to annoy. My companion beamingly did me honour in a full glass. After a moment fraught of silence and peach and honey, and possibly, too, from some notion of pleasing my host with a compliment, I said: "That gentleman with whom you were in converse last evening told me he never passed a more delightful hour than he spent listening to you. You recall whom I mean?"

"Recall him? Shore," retorted my friend as he recurred to the pitcher for a second comforter. "You-all alloodes to the little gent who's lame in the nigh hind laig. He appeals to me, speshul, as he puts me in mind of old Colonel Coyote

Clubbs who scares up Doc Peets that time. Old Coyote is lame same as this yere person."

"Frightens Peets!" I exclaimed, with a great air; "you amaze me! Give me the particulars."

"Why, of course," he replied, "I wouldn't be onderstood that Peets is terrorised outright. Still, old Colonel Coyote shore stampedes him an' forces Peets to fly. It's either *vamos* or shoot up pore Coyote; an' as Peets couldn't do the latter, his only alternative is to go scatterin' as I states.

"This yere Coyote has a camp some ten miles to the no'th an' off to one side of the trail to Tucson. Old Coyote lives alone an' has built himse'f a dugout—sort o' log hut that's half in an' half outen the ground. His mission on earth is to slay coyotes—'Wolfin' 'he calls it—for their pelts; which Coyote gets a dollar each for the furs, an' the New York store which buys 'em tells Coyote to go as far as he likes. They stands eager to purchase all he can peel off them anamiles.

"No; Coyote don't shoot these yere little wolves; he p'isens 'em. Coyote would take about twelve foot, say, of a pine tree he's cut down—this yere timber is mebby eight inches through—an' he'll bore in it a two-inch auger hole every two foot. These holes is some deep; about four inches it's likely. Old Coyote mixes his p'isen with beef tallow, biles them ingredients up together a lot, an' then, while she's melted that a-way, he pours it into these yere auger holes an' lets it cool. It gets good an' hard, this arsenic-tallow does, an' then Coyote drags the timber thus reg'lated out onto the plains to what he regyards as a elegible local'ty an' leaves it for the wolves to come an' batten on. Old Coyote will have as many as a dozen of these sticks of timber, all bored an' framed up with arsenic-tallow, scattered about. Each mornin' while he's wolfin', Coyote makes a round-up an' skins an' counts up his prey. An' son, you hear me! he does a flourishin' trade.

"Why don't Coyote p'isen hunks of meat you asks? For obvious reasons. In sech events the victim bolts the piece of beef an' lopes off mebby five miles before ever he succumbs. With this yere augur hole play it's different. The wolf has to lick the arsenic-tallow out with his tongue an' the p'isen has time an' gets in its work. That wolf sort o' withers right thar in his tracks. At the most he ain't further away than the nearest water;   arsenic makin' 'em plenty thirsty, as you-all most likely knows.

"Old Coyote shows up in Wolfville about once a month, packin' in his pelts an' freightin' over to his wickeyup whatever in the way of grub he reckons he needs. Which, if you was ever to see Coyote once, you would remember him. He's shore the most egreegious person, an' in appearance is a cross between a joke, a disaster an' a cur'osity. I don't reckon now pore Coyote ever sees the time when he weighs a hundred pound; an' he's grizzled an' dried an' lame of one laig, while his face is like a squinch owl's face—kind o' wide-eyed an' with a expression of ignorant wonder, as if life is a never-endin' surprise party.

"Most likely now what fixes him firmest in your mind is, he don't drink none. He declines nosepaint in every form; an' this yere abstinence, the same bein' yoonique in Wolfville, together with Coyote conductin' himse'f as the p'litest an' best-mannered gent to be met with in all of Arizona, is apt to introode on your attention. Colonel Sterett once mentions Coyote's manners.

"'Which he could give Chesterfield, Coyote could, kyards an' spades,' observes the Colonel. I don't, myse'f, know this Chesterfield none, but I can see by the fashion in which Colonel Sterett alloodes to him that he's a Kaintuckian an' a jodarter on manners an' etiquette.

"As I says, a pecooliar trait of Coyote is that he won't drink nothin' but water. Despite this blemish, however, when the camp gets so it knows him it can't he'p but like

him a heap. He's so quiet an' honest an' ignorant an' little
an' lame, an' so plumb p'lite besides, he grows on you. I
can almost see the weasened old outlaw now as he comes
rockin' into town with his six or seven burros packed to
their y'ears with pelts!

"This time when Coyote puts Doc Peets in a toomult is
when he's first pitched his dug-out camp an' begins to honour Wolfville with his visits. As yet none of us appreciates
pore Coyote at his troo worth, an' on account of them guileless looks of his sech humourists as Dan Boggs an' Texas
Thompson seizes on him as a source of merriment.

"It's Coyote's third expedition into town, an' he's hoverin' about the New York store waitin' for 'em to figger up
his wolf pelts an' cut out his plunder so he freights it back
to his dug-out. Dan an' Texas is also procrastinatin' 'round,
an' they sidles up allowin' to have their little jest. Old
Coyote don't know none of 'em—quiet an' sober an' p'lite
like I relates, he's slow gettin' acquainted—an' Dan an'
Texas, as well as Doc Peets, is like so many onopened
books to him. For that matter, while none of them pards of
mine knows Coyote, they manages to gain a sidelight on
some of his characteristics before ever they gets through.
Doc Peets later grows ashamed of the part he plays, an' two
months afterwards when Coyote is chewed an' clawed to a
standstill by a infooriated badger which he mixes himse'f up
with, Peets binds him up an' straightens out his game, an'
declines all talk of recompense complete.

"'It's merely payin' for that outrage I attempts on your
feelin's when you rebookes me so handsome,' says Peets, as
he turns aside Coyote's *dinero* an' tells him to replace the
same in his war-bags.

"However does Coyote get wrastled by that badger? It's
another yarn, but at least she's brief an' so I'll let you have
it. Badgers, you saveys, is sour, sullen, an' lonesome. An'
a badger's feelin's is allers hurt about something; you never

meets up with him when he ain't hostile an' half-way bent
for war. Which it's the habit of these yere morose badgers
to spend a heap of their time settin' half in an' half outen
their holes, considerin' the scenery in a dissatisfied way like
they has some grudge ag'inst it. An' if you approaches a
badger while thus employed he tries to run a blazer on you;
he'll show his teeth an' stand pat like he meditates trouble.
When you've come up within thirty feet he changes his mind
an' dissappears back'ard into his hole; but all malignant an'
reluctant.

"Now, while Coyote saveys wolves, he's a heap dark on
badgers that a-way. An' also thar's a badger who lives clost
to Coyote's dug-out. One day while this yere ill-tempered
anamile is cocked up in the mouth of his hole, a blinkin'
hatefully at surroundin' objects, Coyote cuts down on him
with a Sharp's rifle he's got kickin' about his camp an' turns
that weepon loose.

"He misses the badger utter, but he don't know it none.
Comin' to the hold, Coyote sees the badger kind o' quiled
up at the first bend in the burrow, an' he exultin'ly allows
he's plugged him an' tharupon reaches in to retrieve his
game. That's where Coyote makes the mistake of his c'reer;
that's where he drops his watermelon!

"That badger's alive an' onhurt an' as hot as a lady who's
lost money. Which he's simply retired a few foot into his
house to reconsider Coyote an' that Sharp rifle of his.
Nacherally when the ontaught Coyote lays down on his face
an' goes to gropin' about to fetch that badger forth the latter
never hes'tates. He grabs coyote's hand with tooth and claw,
braces his back ag'in the ceilin' of his burrow an' stands
pat.

"Badgers is big people an' strong as ponies too. An' obdurate! Son, a badger is that decided an' set in his way that
sech feather-blown things as hills is excitable an' vacillatin'
by comparison. This yere partic'lar badger has the fam'ly

weaknesses fully deeveloped, an' the moment he cinches
onto Coyote, he shore makes up his mind never to let go
ag'in in this world nor the next.

"As I tells you, Coyote is little an' weak, an' he can no
more move that hardened badger, nor yet fetch himse'f
loose, than he can sprout wings an' soar. That badger's got
Coyote; thar he holds him prone an' flat ag'in the ground
for hours. An' at last Coyote swoons away.

"Which he'd shore petered right thar, a prey to badgers,
if it ain't for a cowpuncher—he's one of Old Man Enright's
riders—who comes romancin' along an' is attracted to the
spot by some cattle who's prancin' an' waltzin' an' curvin'
their tails in wonder at the spectacle. Which the visitin' cow
sharp, seein' how matters is headed, shoves his six-shooter
in alongside of Coyote's arm, drills this besotted badger, an'
Coyote is saved. It's a case of touch an' go at that. But to
caper back to where we leaves Dan an' Texas on the verge
of them jocyoolarities.

"'No, gentlemen,' Coyote is sayin', in response to some
queries of Dan an' Texas; 'I've wandered hither an' yon a
heap in my time, an' now I has my dug-out done, an' seein'
wolves is oncommon plenty, I allows I puts in what few de-
clinin' days remains to me right where I be. I must say, too,
I'm pleased with Wolfville an' regyards myse'f as fortu-
nate an' proud to be a neighbour to sech excellent folks as
you-all.'

"'Which I'm shore sorry a lot,' says Dan, 'to hear you
speak as you does. Thar's a rapacious sport about yere who
the instant he finds how you makes them dug-out improvements sends on an' wins out a gov'ment patent an' takes
title to that identical quarter-section which embraces your
camp. Now he's allowin' to go squanderin' over to Tucson
an' get a docyment or two from the jedge an' run you out.'

"Son, this pore innocent Coyote takes in Dan's fictions
like so much spring water; he believes 'em utter. But the

wonder is to see how he changes. He don't say nothin', but his eyes sort o' sparks up an' his face gets as gray as his ha'r. It's now that Doc Peets comes along.

"'Yere is this devourin' scoundrel now,' says Texas Thompson, p'intin' to Peets. 'You-all had better talk to him some about it.' Then turnin' to Peets with a wink, Texas goes on: 'Me an' Mister Boggs is tellin' our friend how you gets a title to that land he's camped on, an' that you allows you'll take possession mebby next week.'

"'Why shore,' says Peets, enterin' into the sperit of the hoax, an' deemin' it a splendid joke; 'be you-all the maverick who's on that quarter-section of mine?'

"'Which I'm Colonel Coyote Clubbs,' says Coyote, bowin' low while his lips trembles, 'an' I'm at your service.'

"'Well,' says Peets, 'it don't make much difference about your name, all you has to do is hit the trail. I needs that location you've done squatted on because of the water.

"'An' do I onderstand, sir,' says Coyote some agitated, 'that you'll come with off'cers to put me outen my dug-out?'

"'Shore,' says Peets, in a case-hardened, pitiless tone, 'an' why not? Am I to be debarred of my rights by some coyote-slaughterin' invader an' on-murmurin'ly accede tharto? Which I should shore say otherwise.'

"'Then I yereby warns you, sir,' says Coyote, gettin' pale as paper. 'I advises you to bring your coffin when you comes for that land, for I'll down you the moment you're in range.'

"'In which case,' says Peets, assoomin' airs of bloodthirsty trucyoolence, 'thar's scant use to wait. If thar's goin' to be any powder burnin' we might better burn it now.'

"'I've no weepon, sir,' says Coyote, limpin' about in a circle, 'but if ary of these gentlemen will favour me with a gun I'll admire to put myse'f in your way.'

"'Which the appearance of Coyote when he utters this, an' him showin' on the surface about as warlike as a prairie-dog, convulses Dan an' Texas, It's all they can do to keep a grave front while pore Coyote in his ignorance calls the bluff of one of the most deadly an' gamest gents who ever crosses the Missouri—one who for nerve an' finish is a even break with Cherokee Hall.

"'Follow me,' says Peets, frowinin' on Coyote like a thunder cloud; 'I'll equip you with a weepon myse'f. I reckons now that your death an' deestruction that a-way is after all the best trail out.

"'Peets moves off a heap haughty, an' Coyote limps after him. Peets goes over where his rooms is at. 'Take a cha'r,' says Peets, as they walks in, an' Coyote camps down stiffly in a seat. Peets crosses to a rack an' searches down a 8-inch Colt's. Then he turns to Coyote. 'This yere discovery annoys me,' says Peets, an' his words comes cold as ice, 'but now we're assembled, I finds that I've only got one gun.'

"'Well, sir,' says Coyote, gettin' up an' limpin' about in his nervous way, his face workin' an' the sparks in his eyes beginnin' to leap into flames; 'well, sir, may I ask what you aims to propose?'

"'I proposes to beef you right yere,' says Peets, as f'rocious as a grizzly. 'Die, you miscreant!' An' Peets throws the gun on Coyote, the big muzzle not a foot from his heart.

"'Peets, as well as Dan an' Texas, who's enjoyin' the comedy through a window, ondoubted looks for Coyote to wilt without a sigh. An' if he had done so, the joke would have been both excellent an' complete. But Coyote never wilts. He moves so quick no one ever does locate the darkened recess of his garments from which he lugs out that knife; the first p'inter any of 'em gets is that with the same breath wherein Peets puts the six-shooter on him, Coyote's organised in full with a bowie.

"'Make a centre shot, you villyun!' roars Coyote, an' straight as adders he la'nches himse'f at Peets's neck.

"Son, it's the first an' last time that Doc Peets ever runs.

An' he don't run now, he flies. Peets comes pourin' through the door an' into the street, with Coyote frothin' after him not a yard to spar'. The best thing about the whole play is that Coyote's a cripple; it's this yere element of lameness that lets Peets out. He can run thirty foot to Coyote's one, an' the result occurs in safety by the breadth of a ha'r.

"It takes two hours to explain to Coyote that this eepisode is humour, an' to ca'm him an' get his emotions bedded down. At last, yoonited Wolfville succeeds in beatin' the trooth into him, an' he permits Peets to approach an' apol'gise.

"'An' you can gamble all the wolves you'll ever kill an' skin,' says Doc Peets, as he asks Coyote to forgive an' forget, 'that this yere is the last time I embarks in jests of a practical character or gives way to humour other than the strickly oral kind. Barkeep, my venerated friend, yere will have a glass of water; but you give me Valley Tan.'"

25

The Widow Dangerous.

"WHICH I've told you," observed the Old Cattleman, puffing at his briar pipe—"which I've already told you how Missis Rucker goes on surroundin' old Rucker with connoobial joy to sech a degree that, one mornin' when her wifely back is turned, he ups an' stampedes off into the hills, an' takes refutch with the Apaches. But I never reelates how he gets aroused to his dooty as a husband, an' returns. That mir'cle comes to pass in this wise." Following a reminiscent, smoke-filled pause, the old gentleman continued: "When Rucker is guilty of this yere desertion, Wolfville says nothin' an' does nothin'. It is no part of Wolfville's commoonal respons'bility, as it sees the same, to go pirootin' off on the trail of Rucker, with a purpose of draggin' him back that a-way to his domestic happiness. His elopment is wholly a private play, an' one wharin we ain't entitled to ask for kyards. Shorely not, wantin' speesific requests from Missis Rucker so to do; an' sech don't come.

"On the imme'jit heels of Rucker's plunge into savagery, Missis Rucker never alloods to him—never lets on she so much as notices his absence. She continyoos to deal her game at the O. K. Restauraw onmoved; she fries our daily salthoss, an' compiles our daily flap-jacks—six to the stack—an' neither bats an eye nor wags a y'ear concernin' that vanished husband.

"Nacherally, thar ain't no one so prodded of a morbid

283

cur'osity as to go askin' Missis Rucker. With her views as to what's comin' to her as a lady, an' her bein' allers in the kitchen, surrounded by sech weepons as flatirons an' griddles an' stove-lifters, any sech impolite break might result disasterous. Old Man Enright puts it right, an' his views gains endorsement by Doc Peets, an' others among the best intellects of the camp.

"'To go pesterin' around Missis Rucker,' says he, 'in her bereavements, would be ongentlemanly to the verge of bein' rash, an' the gent don't live in Wolfville who's that foolishly oncooth.'

"If mem'ry is sittin' squar'ly in the saddle, I reckon now it's mebby a year before Missis Rucker mentions her loss. It's one time when we-all shows up for chuck, an' finds her in a dress as black as a spade flush.

"'The same bein' mournin',' she explains, in answer to a remark by Doc Peets complimentin' her looks—which Peets was the genteelest sharp, an' the best edicated, that ever dwells in Arizona. 'I'm mournin' for my departed he'pmeet. I hears about it in Tucson. Pore Rucker is deceased; an' of course I dons black, as markin' his cashin' in.'

"'Yere Missis Rucker snuffles a little, an' gouges into one corner of her eye with her handkerchief, like she's roundin' up a tear. After which, she sort o' runs a calk'latin' glance over us gents, then an' thar assembled, like she's sizin' up as to what you-all might call our domestic p'ints.

"Thar's a heap of silence follows that look. Not bein' gifted none as a mind reader, I can't say how it affects the balance of the outfit; but, speakin' for myse'f personal, a chill like ice creeps up an' down my back. Also, I observes a appreehensive look on the faces of Enright an' Boggs, as though they smell a peril. As to Texas Thompson, who is camped next to me at the table, an' has had marital experiences which culminates in a divorce down Laredo Way, I overhears him grind his teeth, plenty determined, an' mutter:

"'By the Lone Star of my natif state, I won't be took!'

"We're all some eager to ask about them tidings which Missis Rucker ropes onto in Tucson, but none has the nerve. It's Faro Nell who comes headin' to the general rescoo. She's perched next to Cherokee Hall, an' looks gently up from a piece of pie she's backin' off the board, and says:

"'Good sakes, Missis Rucker! An' whatever do you-all track up ag'inst about pore Mister Rucker?'

"'That onforchoonate pard o' my bos'm has departed this life,' responds the widow, moppin' away her grief. 'I crosses up with a Tucson party, who asshores me that, when them Apaches goes all spraddled out last spring, they nacherally begins them hostilities by pronouncin' on Rucker, an' leavin' him on both sides of the canyon.'

"'That's right!' chimes in Dave Tutt, who, bein' married a whole lot to Tucson Jennie, feels immune from further wedlock. "Whenever them savages digs up the waraxe, they yoosually inaugurated negotiations by layin' out what pale-faces is weak-minded enough to be among 'em, too dead to skin. No; it ain't crooelty, it's caution. Which they figgers them squaw-men, if spared will be off to the nearest army post, with preematoor word of the uprisin'. Wharfore, they descends on 'em like a fallin' star, an' blots 'em out. After which, they proceeds with their reg'lar killin' an' skelpin' more at leesure.'

"It's over in the Red Light, to which we reepairs when feed is through, that the subject comes up in form. Black Jack, the barkeep, is so impressed by the gravity on our faces as we files in, that he announces the drinks is on the house. We refooses; it bein' too close on the hocks of that salthoss an' them flapjacks for nose-paint, an' we takes seegyars instead. When we're smokin' sociable, an' in spite of them alarmin' fulminations of Missis Rucker, has become somewhat onbuckled an' confident ag'in, Enright brings the topic for'ard.

"'About her bein' a widow that a-way, Doc?' he says, addressin' Peets. 'What do you-all, as a scientist, think yourse'f?'

"'Which it seems feasable enough,' responds Peets, bitin' thoughtful at his seegyar. 'You know what Injuns be? Startin' out to slay that a-way, they ain't apt to overlook no sech bet as Rucker. They'd be onto him, first flash out o' the box, like a mink onto a settin' hen.'

"'Yes,' returns Enright, some oneasy as to tone; 'I reckon you calls the turn, Doc. They'd about bump off old Rucker by way of curtain raiser, as they calls it over to the Bird Cage Op'ry House.'

"'Don't you allow now,' breaks in Boggs, some agitated on' appealin' to Enright an' Peets together—'don't you allow now, that old Rucker bein' wiped out that a-way, sort o' leaves the camp ongyarded?'

"'As how?' returns Peets.

"'As how?' repeats Boggs, his excitement risin'. 'What's to prevent her deescendin' onto one of us, like a pan of milk from a top shelf, an' weddin' him a heap? She's a mighty resoloote female, is Missis Rucker, an' it's only last week she ups an' saws it off on me, all casyooal, that she's jest thirty-eight years old last grass. I sees her drift now! That lady's makin' ready for a spring. Which she's aimin' to snatch a husband from our shrinkin' midst; an' nothin' short!'

"'After what I passes through with that Laredo wife of mine,' says Texas Thompson, grim as tombstones, 'you can gamble a bloo stack I'll never be wedded alive!'

"'As to myse'f,' remarks Peets, imitatin' a cheerful countenance, 'I'm barred. Drug sharps, onder the rooles, cannot be claimed in private matrimony—belongin' as they do to the whole commoonity. Enright, yere, is likewise out, bein' too old.'

"'That's right!' coincides Enright, relief stealin' into his eyes; 'I'm too far gone in years to become raw material for nuptials. Speakin' what I feel, however, I looks on the sityooation as a heap extreme. As Dan says, it's plain she has intentions. Then thar's that black frock: Which widows is dangerous in preecise proportion as they sheds tears an'

piles on mournin'. It's my onbiased jedgement that she's
fixin' her sights for Dan or Texas thar.'

"'Gents,' interrupts Texas Thompson ag'in, his manner
iron, 'you hears what I says a moment back! Wolfville may
follow me to the tomb, but never to no altar.'

"'If I thought this yere widow was that imminent,' says
Boggs, pacin' to an' fro like a startled wildcat, 'I'd line out
for Tucson ontil the footure's more guaranteed. I'm nacherally plumb nervous; I can't camp down in the shadow of a
great threat onmoved. We was shoore locoed to ever let
Rucker get away that time. We might have knowed it would
end in some sech bluff as this. If I had foreseen the trap he
was settin' for us, I'd have reestored that old profligate to
Missis Rucker's arms, or got downed by the Apaches tryin'.
Whatever's your advice, Sam?' he concloods, gazin' anx-
ious-eyed at Enright. 'If it was nothin' worse that a hostile
sheriff on my trail, I'd stand by hand; but this yere is when
I reequires counsel.'

"Seein' Boggs so keyed up, Enright goes off on a soothin'
angle, Peets chippin' in. They both suggests to Boggs that
thar's no call to be preecipitate. It'll most likely be weeks
before Missis Rucker really declar's herse'f, an' sinks them
widowed talons into her seelected prey. Meanwhile, as pre-
parin' for the worst, all Boggs has to do, they agrees, is
keep his mind on his number, an' sing out 'No' to everything she says. Likewise, it might be as well to hold a pony
saddled in the corral, in case of sudden swoops.

"'In which event,' says Enright, 'if it turns out we on-
derestimates her activities an' she wheels on you abrupt,
thar's the pony; an' you plays the same—quirt an' heel—as
a last resort. Still, it's possible we're seein' onnecessary
ghosts. She may have it in her heart to make happy some
other gent entire.'

"'Thar's one thing,' observes Peets; 'I wants it onderstood, in case this conference comes to Missis Rucker's
notice later, that I say she is an esteemable lady, an'

cal'klated to raise the gent, so forchoonate as to become her husband, to pinnacles of bliss.'

"'Also,' declar's Enright, some hasty, 'let it be onderstood that I'm in on them observations. As the preesidin' inflooence of the O. K. Restauraw, Missis Rucker is onapproached an' onapproachable—her pies is poems an' her beans a dream, as I've said former.'

It happens, as it frequent does, that these yere preemonitions of the camp is onsustained. Not that I blames Boggs an' the rest for entertainin' 'em. After he crosses to the sunset side of the Missouri, a gent can't be too proodent, 'speshully in the matter of widows. When one of them forlorn ladies spreads her pinions, an' takes to sailin' an' soarin' an' soarin' an' sailin' that a-way, it's time for every single gent to break for cover.

"No; as I states, the timidities of Boggs an' the balance ain't upheld. Not that Missis Rucker don't frame it up none to come flutterin' from her lonely perch; only it ain't Boggs or Texas or any of the boys proper, it's old Colonel Coyote Clubbs on whom she's closin' down.

"You recalls how, yeretofore, I onfurls to you concernin' the little Colonel?—how he's grizzled, an' harmless, an' dried, an' lame of the nigh hind laig?—how he's got a face like a squinch owl?—innocent an' wide-eyed an' full of ignorant wonder, like life is an onendin' s'prise party? As I then explains, he's p'isenin' coyotes—a dollar a pelt—an' at first has a camp an hour's ride over towards Tucson. Mebby it's two months prior to when Missis Rucker gives it out she's alone in the world, an' goes to ghost dancin', he's done give up his dugout, an' took to boardin' at the O. K. Restauraw. Bein' gregar'ous, the Colonel likes company; an' as for them little wolves, they're as prolific an' as apt to find his arsenic in the subbubs of Wolfville, itse'f, as farther out on the plains. So, as I observes, he's now gettin' his *chili-con-carne* at Missis Rucker's, an' workin' out from camp instead of into it.

"Which it's plenty likely we-all would have seen it was the Colonel's personal trouble from the jump, only the day Missis Rucker goes into black an' scares us up that a-way, the old cimarron is across to Red Dog, dealin' for a train of burros to pack his wolf pelts to Tucson. As it is, it ain't a day after he gets back before we identifies him as the gent in interest. Missis Rucker, as though concealment is now at an end an' the hour ripe for throwin' off disguises, takes to hoverin' over him at chuck time, with a terrifyin' solicitood that comes mighty clost to bein' tenderness. She takes to heapin' his plate with viands, to a degree that's enough of itse'f to set any sport of thoughtfulness to jumpin' sideways. It shore rattles the Colonel, you bet! an' his appetite gets less the more she lavishes them delicacies upon him.

"'Which you ain't eatin' more than sparrer birds, Colonel!' she says, givin' him a most onmistakable grin. 'Yere; let me get you some plum preeserves—which they ought to tempt a angel!'

"With that she totes forth one of her partic'ler airtights, which even Enright don't get a glimpse of only Fo'th of Jooly an' Christmas, an' onloads the same on the Colonel. He grows white at this; for, jest as the good book says that it's vain for the fowler to spread his nets in the sight of any bird, so also is it footile for a widow to go inondatin' any speshul gent with plum preeserves, an' hope to have them sweetmeats misconstrooed.

"Shore, the Colonel—for all he's the guilelessest party that ever makes a moccasin track in Arizona—realizes she's put him in nom'nation to be Rucker's successor. Likewise the whole outfit grasps this trooth; an', while the Colonel is turin' gray about the gills, Boggs is breathin' freer, an' the desparate look in the eyes of Texas Thompson begins to fade away. Which the same shows how, at bottom, man is a anamile utterly selfish. Once Boggs an' Texas an' them others feels safe, the knowledge that the pore old Colonel must go cavortin' across the red-hot plow shares, don't bother 'em a bit. But sech is life! They coldly leaves him to tread the wine press alone; an' all as onfeelin' as a band of prairie dogs. Which I don't scroople later, to reeproach Boggs with this yere lack of sympathy.

"'What can we-all do?' he replies. 'I'm a friend of the Colonel's; but what then? This is a case whar every gent must kill his own snakes. Besides I see now she's doo to make him happy. Do you note how free she plays them plum air-tights on him? An' no more holdin' back than if they're canned tomatters! Rightly looked at, the Colonel's in a heap of luck.'

"'Luck or no luck,' says Enright, 'the hands of Wolfville is tied. The camp has an onbroken record of backin' every matrimonial venture as soon as seen. Don't we put down the Washwoman's War, by weddin' French to one of the contendin' females? Ain't we thar with the goods on the occasion of Tucson Jennie takin' Dave for better or for worse? An', ag'in when that pinfeather person, Toad Allen, comes squanderin' along with old Gleggs' girl, Abby? Also, ain't said course resulted in sech onmixed triumphs as that blessed infant Enright Peets Tutt? No; it's Wolfville's system to play wedlock to win. An', while I won't go so far as to say that, in the present instance, we remains inert in case it's Dan or Texas—said gents bein' entitled to partic'ler consid'ration—now it turns out to be the Colonel who's to draw the prize, Wolfville stands nootral. Barkeep, bring on the nose-paint. Inasmuch as I trusts that all will regyard these yere words of mine as final, it is meet we should yoonite in drinkin' onbridled victory to Missis Rucker, an' the gent she's honored with her preferences.'

"'Thar's one syllable I'd like to edge in,' says Boggs, when he's emptied his glass. 'Don't you-all reckon, Sam, that some of us oughter ride herd on the Colonel till she's tied him down? He's a gent of honor, an' as clean strain as hornets; but thar's fates before which even the gamest spirit breaks ground. An' you sees yourse'f that, if the Colonel should *vamos*, it onkivers others to attack.'

"'Which them cautionary moves,' says Enright, 'might not be thrown away. Although, I'm frank to say, it's four for one the Colonel meets his happiness onflinchin'ly. He's too p'lite, that a-way however much he may distrust his merits, to fly from the affections of a lady an' take to hidin' out.'"

Texas Thompson

26

Cherokee Hall, Gambler.

"WHICH you-all," the Old Cattleman, continued, with a look both confidential and confident, "don't have to be told by now that Cherokee Hall's a gambler. An' while a gent might do better than gamble, leastwise better for himse'f, I allers allows Cherokee can't he'p it none. You see he's gaited congen'tal to take chances—a sort o' preedestined kyard-sharp from the jump.

"Shore, I don't find no fault with gamblers. For that matter I don't find no fault with no gent, onless he's connivin' ag'in me pers'nal; in which eevent I nacherally adopts measures. Moreover, speakin' of gamblers, they're a might guileless bevy of folks. Which if the onexpected ever happens, an' I'm took sudden with the notion of sallyin' forth on the trail of mankind, to deplete it of its wealth neefarious, I'll shore adhere to gamblers as my reg'lar prey. As to business men proper, tharby meanin' store-keeps an' sim'lar commercial chiefs of scouts, I'll pass up all sech chilled steel tarrapins complete.

"No; this yere preference as to victims ain't doo to the sooperior savey of business folks; for mere wisdom, them stoodents to trade ain't got nothin' on your kyard-sharps. But where it comes to standin' pat concernin' money, they've got mere gamblers that a-way left standin' sideways. Business men an' gamblers is onlike each other utter. Their money attitoods is as wide apart as poetry an' prose. An' for this yere essenshul reason: At his game, when a gambler gives, he don't get; an' when he gets, he don't give. Your business gent goes squanderin' through the chute of existence the other way about. He never gives without gettin'; an' he never gets without givin'—assoomin' he's on the level, which he freequent ain't.

"Gamblers an' business men runs opp'site from soda to hock. One takes nothin' but chances; the other takes everything except. A business man never lets go one hold till he's got another; a gambler lets go all holds, an' trusts to outluck you for a fresh one. Also, thar's other p'ints of sep'ration: For example, a gambler never thinks of lendin' you money ontil you're busted. Which is the preecise eepock a business gent won't let you have a splinter.

"Go weavin' forth an' try it, if you nurses doubts. Approach a kyard-sharp for a stake, an' you with a bundle: That indignant sport'll onbosom hims'f in language to take the nap off your coat. What he says, you bet! will be more decisive than encouragin'—hot, an' plenty explicit. Come around when you're broke, an' he'll revive your faintin' fortunes with half his bankroll. As opposed to this, whenever you goes troopin' up ag'inst a business gent to neegotiate a borry, you'll have to back the play with a bale of secoorities as big as a roll of kyarpet. He'll want to have 'em in his hand, too, before ever he permits you to so much as lay b'ar your errand.

"Wharfore's this yere difference? You don't have to dig none deep for causes: Gamblers by nacher are romantic; a business gent roosts close to the ground. One is 'motional; the other's as hard an' pulseless as a iron wedge. The former's a bird, an' gaily spends his onthinkin' time among the clouds; the latter never soars higher than he can lift hims'f on wings of bricks an' mortar.

"Likewise gamblers is more excellent as company. When I'm onbuckled, an' romancin' 'round for sociability onp'isened of ulterior designs, I shore searches out your kyard-sharp every time. Gettin' sociable with a business gent, is about as likely a enterprise as winnin' the affections of a burglar-proof safe. Thar's a timelock goes with his friendship, an' even he himse'f can't break into it none outside of business hours.

"Re-tracin' our trail to the orig'nal prop'sition, I'm yere to say that of all in Wolfville it's likely Cherokee's the most onwary, an' him whose blind side lies openest to the world. Which he's certainly the most ongyarded sport! Plumb honest hims'f, with a dealbox as straight as if laid out in its angles by one of them civil engineer mavericks, the last he's expectin' is the double cross.

"An' at that, if some evil-minded party's out to skin Cherokee, to go settin' traps an' diggin' pitfalls ag'in him would be a waste of time. All that plotter has to do to start Cherokee's *dinero* comin' his way, is set 'round an' look pensive a whole lot. Cherokee's so sympathetic, an' carelessly soft of heart, that to pull on a expression of gloom means, for the cunnin' wolf who dons it, a tenth of all Cherokee's got. Which if he was to track up on ten people in succession, all of 'em down an' out, it's a cinch he'd have to begin life anew.

"While not exyooberant like Boggs, Cherokee's at heart a optimist in a ondeemonstrative way. Likewise, as I says, he's onable to bear other people's sorrows, an' constrooes 'em, when vis'ble, to indicate a utter lack of coin. Once he embraces the latter idee, the end is on its way; life'll be a failure ontil he's reestored the affairs of that busted prairie dog to a cash basis.

"An' if Cherokee can't stake said bankrupt direct, the latter bein' too sens'tive to accept, he'll go jumpin' sideways at him. Some folks grows haughty exactly as they grows poor; they're humble only when they're rich, an' refooses favors onless they can get along without 'em. Whenever Cherokee crosses up with one of these yere high-strung parties, he'plessly in the hole, he goes pirootin', mighty cautious, round the flanks of his pride, inveigles him into some shore-thing racket, an' lets him win himse'f out. Shore, I sees him do it more'n once.

"Gamblers ain't respectable, you says? Well I don't say they be. Which I will remark, however, that when we're all gathered together in the misty beyond, if some gent who's been lined up for eternal jedgement, can't say nothin' for himse'f except he's respectable, the best thing he can do is pass an' offer to make it a jack.

"As I casts the eye of mem'ry r'arward, thar's no figger more pleasin' than that of Cherokee. Planted over back of his faro-box, Nell up ag'inst his right shoulder lookin' out the play, he's shore a benignant influence. As I onder-stands, he's foaled orig'nal in Indiana. I once hears some jaundiced trant'ler—which I quotes this verbal pig-nut prior—declar' that Indiana is settled by folks who started for the West but lost their nerve. Sech bluffs don't incloode Cherokee a little bit. He's weak only with the weak, afraid only of the timid. While he's buffaloed by babes an' sucklin's easy, the war-song of the bad man huntin' trouble is as the music of a bridal to his y'ears.

"Likewise Cherokee has views, an' when he's got confi-dence in his aujience he voices 'em. Once over to the O. K. House at chuck time, some one—Texas I reckons, or mebby now it's Boggs—starts oratin' about ladies; an' lets on that, while they're plumb excellent in a heap of entrancin' re-especks, you-all can't put a bet on 'em, they bein' fitful not to say difoosive in their fancies, an' prone to shift camp on a gent when least looked for.

"Cherokee combats these yere doctrines. 'The same not bein' my experience, none whatever!' says he. Then glancin' at Nell who, pretty as a stack of bloos, is mowin' away her flapjacks an' salt-hoss with the rest of us, he continyoos. 'Ladies is a heap likelier to run troo then gents. Which I've seen a lady hock her frock for the gent she loves. Also, if they ever does quit you, they quits you only in prosperity. Whoever hears of a lady abandonin' a party, an' him down?

The same bein' the time, speakin' gen'ral, your he-friends
seelects to murmur *adios.'*

"'Well,' breaks in Texas, 'every sport to his own notion!
But I certainly does find myse'f in wrong, when I weds that
Laredo wife of mine! Which the toomultuous hours I passes
in my capac'ty as a husband, leaves me girl-shy ever since.'

"'Jest the same,' remarks Boggs, 'ladies is mighty alloorin'. The Doc thar—lookin' over to Peets—'recites some
stanzas, about seventh drink-time last evenin' that shore
matches my feelin's exact:

"'Oh woman in our hour of ease,
Oncertain, coy an' hard to please;
But seen too oft, familiar with her face,
We first endure, then pity, then embrace.

"'Yes, sir-ee!' concloodes Boggs, dippin' into a can of
air-tights, 'you can gamble all you're worth that them's my
sent'ments.'

"'Another thing about ladies,' resoomes Cherokee, 'they
shore don't go 'round draggin' their verbal lariats an' tellin'
things. Ladies is plenty reticent an' moote about what they
knows.'

"'Some of 'em, however,' grumbles Texas, 'is plenty
commoonicative touchin' what they don't know. It ain't her
tellin' things of which she's aware, wharby my Laredo wife
drives me locoed; it's by reelatin' things of which she's ignorant complete. Which if that lady only confines hers'f to
facts them times, I'd have done stayed an' give her a battle;
but the gent don't live who's able to keep his feet ag'in tor-
rents of invidious fictions. That's where my former he'pmeet
puts me on the run. I freely confesses that, whenever she
starts excercisin' her fancy an' her tongue at one an' the
same time, I begins hittin' the high places in the scenery,
plenty frantic, in efforts at a get-away.'

"'Speakin' of Cherokee possessin' the deep-sea wisdom of
a cinnamon b'ar that a-way, why he'll even tackle religion,

get him started once. It's what he tosses off all casyooal one evenin', that more or less serves in framin' up what you-all might call my theeol'gy. Peets is sayin' that, while he's eager to accept the idee of a footure life, his argyooment breaks down every time he seeks to convince himse'f tharof.

"'I don't seem to connect none,' says Peets; 'an' so, while sech theeries don't make no hit with me, I'm constrained to regyard Boot Hill as the final finish.'

"'It's yere Cherokee sets in a reemonstrative stack. 'Doc,' says he, 'that's because you faces the wrong way. Now, startin' from the ondeniable fact that you're livin' a whole lot, instead of tryin' to prove thar is a yereafter, s'ppose you tries to prove thar ain't. It's my notion you'll find yourse'f more up ag'inst it even than you are before.' Then, appearin' like he's some ashamed, an' turnin' to Nell—who's keepin' tabs, as well as lookin' out the deal—he shifts the subject by askin', 'Whatever does that last jack do?'"

27

The Looking Out
Of Faro Nell.

F ARO NELL'S full partner with Cherokee in his bank, an' he not only believes in her jedgment but in her luck. Let the game go rompin' along ag'inst him for three or four deals, an' he never fails to call Nell in behind the box. Likewise, the change is freequent ben'ficial. Many a time an' oft she brings home to the checkrack them hundreds Cherokee's lost out. Yoosual, however, he does the dealin', while Nell holds down her offishul p'sition on the lookout stool.

"Cherokee sets a heap of store by little Nell. Nothin' 'll cloud him up so quick as ontoward or sultry utterances where she is. Nacherally, no se'f respectin' gent'll say what shocks a lady, an' the lady thar. Shorely, no one who's a citizen of Wolfville, in good standin', 'll go lettin' his conversation get stampeded that a-way, no matter what's took place. With chance-blown sports, the case is sometimes otherwise. But they soon learns from the way Cherokee looks as well as what he does—for from time to time he's forced to buffalo a few—that, with Nell in the picture, it's a heap discreet to do their talkin' with the hobbles on. Not that these yere reestrictions works a hardship neither. In emergencies that's still the street, an' any gent whose fate is more'n he can b'ar is free to go outside an' cuss.

"For myse'f, I attaches no valyoo to that street franchise, bein' ag'in bad language at all times, whatever the indooce-ments. Profanity is never a advantage, an' sometimes works a loss; which last is shown in the business of the English Dooke. It's the verbal short-comin's of that peer which sets Nell's s'picions to millin'. Cherokee? He's no more expectin' that titled Briton to turn himse'f loose fraudyoolent, than for Black Jack to ask a blessin' or break forth into the doxology. Also, the affair's a heap to Nell's credit; an' it shows that, when she's lookin' out, she's a adjunct not wisely to be deespised.

"Old Monte brings news of that patrician first. 'An' that nobleman,' says he, 'is threatenin' Wolfville with a call. He's pesterin' about Tucson now; an', you hear your Uncle Monte! what he's doin' to farobank in that meetrop'lis would fill a book! Dookes, that a-way, is certainly high-rollers.'

"The Dooke it looks like exhausts Tucson, an' then he comes bulgin' into Wolfville per schedyool. Thar bein' no reason in partic'lar to have it in for dookes, the camp meets him plenty cordial. Enright an' Peets both drinks with him, an' tells him to browse 'round in the same onmuzzled way he would in England.

"In the beginnin', the Dooke gives gims'f up to askin' questions concernin' the 'Resources of Arizona.' An' you can gamble he don't ask in vain. Which if he keeps tabs on them 'Resources,' as Texas an' Boogs an' Tutt enoomerates the same, the complete round-up's shore calk'lated to make him dizzy. Accordin' to them statisticians, Arizona, as a land flowin' with milk an' honey, has Canaan backed plumb off the map. Canaan ain't got a look-in! The Dooke, however, lets on he likes it, an' goes rummagin' about, buyin' licker an' droppin' 'Hs,' an' all mighty aff'ble an' permiscus.

"He's a big, good-lookin' sport, the Dooke is; an' among other *impedimenta*, as the Mexicans say, he's got a valet. Whatever a gent needs of a valet in a cow country is too many for me, but the camp figgers it's a way dookes has, an' lets it go at that. This yere valet puts in his servile time standin' 'round, an' never opens his clamshell. In case the Dooke makes signals, however, he jumps to the fervent front like a jackrabbit.

"It's the second afternoon when the Dooke decides to give Cherokee's game a whirl. He don't make no bones about it, but pulls up a cha'r as condescendin' as any other hoss thief, buys a couple of stacks of reds, an' stands blandly in. Nothin' much happens for mebby it's a hour. The luck swings to an' fro, like the pendyoolum of one of these yere Dutch clocks; now the Dooke's ahead, now he's behind, but on the whole he's loser.

"Through divers an' sundry vicissitoods, the Dooke keeps his temper, an' it ain't ontil his swell bet's swept in his language begins to get hectic. He's in for the limit, two hundred simoleons, on the big squar', coppered. The king falls to win, an' nacherally the specyoolation goes ag'inst him. Wharat the Dooke onburdens in a mouthful of mighty dire oaths.

"Cherokee halts the deal, his thumb on the face of the winnin' king.

"'Excoose me,' says Cherokee, eyein' the Dooke a heap icy an' implac'ble. 'Let me remark in passin' that, while I don't aim to lay down no lingual rooles for the British nobility, if you-all is ag'in guilty of sech oral malefactions in the presence of this yere young lady, you'll get all kyarved up. The last offender has to sw'ar in his vote 'lection day, his feachures bein' altered to that degree he loses his identity. He looks so plumb strange an' new that even his acquaintances don't know him none.'

"The Dooke breaks into p-rofoose 'pologies. His feelin's, he explains, gets their bridle off inadvertent, an' it ain't goin' to happen no more.

"''Pon me word, it woan't! says the Dooke.

"'All right!' returns Cherokee, proceedin' with the turn. 'Which I'd have sliced you into half-apples at once, only I remembers how you're English, an' a Dooke besides, an' makes allowances for a nacheral ignorance. But don't do it no more. Seven lose, nine win!'

"The Dooke keeps on goin' behind, an' when the next deal's down to the turn his last red chip finds its way back into the rack.

"'James,' says he, motionin' to his valet who's hoverin' in the background, 'give me me check-book.'

"The valet capers for'ard with the check-book, an' one of them new-fangled pens which has ink up its sleeve. The Dooke gets busy an' indites a check. He pauses about the middle, an' remarks to Cherokee in that tired way which is the indoobitable mark of bloo blood, 'Me dear sir, this game is trivial to the verge of fatiguin'. Would you mind advaun-cin' the limit to a thousand on doubles an' five hundred on a case? Reelly, I don't know but I might take some interest in it then.'

"'No sech appeal,' replies Cherokee, 'is ever made to me in vain. In order that Wofville may seem in all respecks like London to you, I yereby authorizes you to bet 'em higher'n a cat's back.'

"'Thanks, aw'fly! says the Dooke.

"The Dooke signs the check, an' starts to pass it over to Cherokee. Then he draws it back.

"'No,' says he, smilin' like a p'lite bob-cat, 'it would be too presumptuous to ask a stranger to accept me signachoor for so large a sum. This is for one thousand pounds—I should say five thousand dollars; I'll send it down to the ex-press company.' Then to the valet:—'James, take this to the Wells-Fargo office. They've had instructions, an' will give you gold for it.'

"The valet bows to the floor as he ropes onto the check. 'Very good sir!' he says, an' ambles off.

"'An' now,' observes the Dooke to Cherokee, 'if you'll be so kind as to oblige me with five thousand dollars in chips, pendin' me valet's return, I think we may continyoo. The cash to pay for them will be here presently—not a doubt of it! Or, if by any accident—an' that's hardly to be thought of as possible—a mistake has occurred in the express company's instructions, an' the check is not honored, the play need bind no one. Win or lose, it's onderstood that onless James returns with the five thousand, the play don't go.'

"Cherokee never dreams of hesitatin', but shoves over five thousand in yellow chips—a hundred dollars a chip. The Dooke sweeps 'em towards him, an' the deal begins.

"It's yere an' now that luck shifts; the Dooke commences to win. He's pilin' up the yellow boys in of stacks ten, too—a cool thousand on a kyard! Likewise, since he's placin' each bet so it's down four ways at once, he's gettin' veheement action. Everything's the Dooke's like a avalanche, an' by the time the deal's half out, he's ten thousand to the good an' still a-goin'. Also, he ain't so thoroughbred but what his eyes is blazin' with avarice. Cherokee's face is as deevoid of expression as the wrong side of a tombstone. The deal goes on, the stream of the Dooke's winnin's flowin' in onchecked.

"When that valet goes weavin' off to the Wells-Fargo folks, packin' the Dooke's five thousand-dollar check, Nell slides off her perch, an' motions Boggs to take her place. No one minds; she does the same thing often when she's tired. The deal proceeds, Boggs actin' as lookout, an' Nell sa'nters forth into the street.

"The Wells-Fargo office is at the far end of camp, an' onless the valet's a antelope it'll be twenty minutes before he's doo to show up. The Dooke's skirmishin' with his eye watchin', an', when at last he does get back, sees him the moment he steps in the door. Black Jack, who's faced so he can tell, avers that the Dooke signs up to the valet with a pecooliar wink, an' tharupon the valet, like the wink means the Dooke's on knee-deep velvet that a-way, pulls a roll of money from his jeans.

"'I beg pardon, sir,' says the valet; ''ere's the money, sir. They didn't 'ave the gold, sir; I 'opes the bills'll do.'

"'Certainly!' says the Dooke, takin' the roll plenty lofty; 'bills or gold, it's all the same.'

"The Dooke runs through the bundle—ten five-hundred-dollar notes, an' passes it over to Cherokee.

"'That makes good.' says he.

"'Not yet it don't!'

"It's Nell who interferes—Nell who, comin' in on the heels of the valet, now rounds herse'f up at Cherokee's shoulder. As she takes charge of the sityooation, she pushes the money back to the Dooke.

"'Beg pardon, Miss!' observes the Dooke; an', for all his bluff front, a frightened look drifts across his face. 'Beg pardon; but I reely don't onderstand!'

"'You don't!' repeats Nell, her eye some scornful. then to Cherokee: 'That tin-horn bandit of a valet never offers no check to the Wells-Fargo folks. He goes to the office, an' asks a fool question or two; but, so far from cashin' any check, that worthless docyooment's in his clothes right now. I'll bet a new bonnet this titled horned-toad ain't got a *centouse* with the express people. He's been handin' you an' me the old-thing.'

"'Oh, I see!' says Cherokee, an' the glance he bestows upon the Dooke is the kind that frequent ushers in a fooneral. 'The notion ain't so bad, neither! This yere noble hold-up writes a no-account check, an' sends it out by his partner; who strolls about, goes as far as the express offices for the looks of the thing an' to kill time proper, an' returns. An' the idee's this: If you wins'—turnin' to the Dooke direct—'you gives him the office, an' he reports the check cashed. If you're behind, you signs him up to that effect. Perceivin' which, he's sorry, but is obleeged to say the express people ain't received no instructions none as yet, an' turns the check down. Thar bein' no money forth-comin', accordin' to the onderstandin' win or lose, the play don't go. It's a beautiful scheme—a scheme where my only chance is to lose, an' your only chance is to win!'

"'Me dear sir,' shatters the Dooke, 'this is Greek to me!
I don't onderstand it at all! James!'

"Thar's no 'James'; the valet's faded.

"'An' shows his sense!' remarks Boggs.

"'You don't savey?' repeats Cherokee. 'All you needs is
a five thousand dollar roll, a English accent, a imitation
valet, an' a blinded come-on like me, an' your fortune's
made! I've been imposed upon a heap of ways, but this yere
wrinkle's new complete. Come; set in those chips! While
you can't have my money, as a lesson to myse'f, seein' how
close you comes to landin' me, I'm goin' to let you deepart
with the honors of war—your life and your bank-roll.'

"Cherokee counts the Dooke's chips back into the check-
rack, an the count shows he has the game beat for clost onto
fifteen thousand dollars.

"'You come mighty near makin' a killin', Dooke!' remarks
Boggs, who's listenin' an' lookin' on a heap interested.

"The Dooke is murmurin' onder his breath about how he
'don't onderstand,' when Cherokee cuts him short.

"'Yere!' exclaims Cherokee; 'go with Jack Moore to the
Wells-Fargo people; an', if they cashes your check, I'll
make good this yere fifteen thousand dollars worth of chips
twice over. But thar's this proviso: If the Wells-Fargoes
don't come down, you'll shore find some one shootin' at
you with two guns at once.'

"Not bein' locoed, the Dooke don't take Cherokee's prof-
fer, but makes a gesture like he's the victim of misonderstandin's.

"'You better hit the trail a lot!' says Enright to the Dooke,
as that member of the House of Lords hesitates about the
Red Light door. 'For while this yere's a idle sort o' afternoon, an' I don't feel much like goin' through the labors of
lynchin', the idee of swingin' off a nobleman is far from
bein' reepellant. It's my opinion, should some member of the
stranglers make a motion to that effect, it'd carry yoonanimous. As I su'ggests, Dooke, you'd better hit the trail!'

"'An' havin' hit it, don't stop goin, neither!' warns Jack Moore. 'Keep forgin' right ahead ontil you're miles beyond the confines of this camp. The game law's out on dookes, an' if you stays loiterin' round, some gent who's makin' a collection'll take to bombardin' you up by way of addin' you to his mooseyum.'

"'But where can I go!' pleads the Dooke, castin' a despairin' glance about, like he's seekin' to locate that vanished valet.

"'Go to Red Dog,' breaks in Boggs; 'they'll be tickled to death to see you over thar. If you beats that gang of drunkards out of anything, you can keep it. However, I don't much reckon you will, for as shorething artists they're cap'ble of goin' some themselves. Also, if you starts anything, an' them veterans in crime ketches you at it, you're a gone fawnskin. Them Red Dog outcasts ain't so leenient as Cherokee yere.'

"'However do you come to think of it, Nell?' asks Cherokee later 'That wily stranger, with his little check book, would have got by me like runnin' water!'

"'In my experience,' returns Nell, with the air of bein' a hundred years old, 'bad checks an' bad manners goes hand in hand. I knows what I thinks of this yere Dooke's language, an' it strikes me I'll trail out after that valet an' see what the express people thinks of his signachoor.'

"'Well,' says Cherokee, snappin' the deck in the box for another deal, 'I ain't as a roole in favor of encouragin' habits of s'picion in the very young; but in the present instance, Nell, since it leaves you an' me them sev'ral thousand kopecs to the good, it would shore seem farfetched in me to go formyoolatin' any reproofs. In short, I regyards it rather as a season for congratyoolations; in which sperit I yereby apprises our honored bar-keep that the camp's honin' to yoonite in a libation to your health. Jack,' concloods Cherokee, motionin' to Black Jack, 'as the Ganymede of the establishment the rest reemains with you.'"

28

The Off-Wheeler
Offends.

"**S**PEAKIN' of Cherokee holdin' them views as to a footure life," observed the Old Cattleman, feeling for the lemon peel in his glass, "I'm bound to say that personal I ain't religious none; leastwise in the church sense, ownin' no talents tharfor. Also, as a roole, I prefers doin' good to doin' right. The gent who does right is thinkin' of himse'f; the gent who does good is thinkin' of others—which is a heap better for hoomanity. No, I'm not religious; an' yet, if ever I'm inclined to doubt the eff'cacy of religion, them changes wrought in the Off-Wheeler makes said doubts reedic'lous.

"Is Wolfville religious? you asks. While its religious feelin' is some latent, you can bet your pony an' throw the saddle in, Wolfville is a Christian commoonity. I makes this announcement confident; because, when a obtroosive proflagate comes weavin' over from Red Dog, allowin' he's a atheist, Boggs is thar with all four hoofs to call his bluff.

"We're playin' poker at the time, Boggs jugglin' the deck. 'An' so,' says Boggs, pausin' in mid-deal, as this pagan person decl'res himse'f as sech, 'you're one of them cunnin' tarrapins who don't believe in nothin'?'

"'That's whatever!' retorts the Red Dog pagan, mighty sprightly. 'Go on with the deal, I ain't got but three kyards.'

"'The same bein' all you're goin' to get,' returns Boggs, tossin' the deck onto the table an' shovin' back his cha'r. 'Do you-all reckon I'd set across from an outcast who denies the trooths of Holy Writ? Not if I holds four kings an' a ace perpetyooal.'

"The balance of the outfit follows Boggs' smoke; Cherokee Hall bars the onbeliever at faro-bank, the Red Light refooses him licker, an' Missis Rucker gives it out cold that, if she only receives word in time, she'd have shore pinched down on his grub. In less space then it takes to rope an' hawgtie a steer, he's 'ostracised,' as Doc Peets calls it. Which that ostracism works, too; an' it so deepresses the Red Dog pagan thet, next mornin' at sun-up, he pulls his subdooed an' ondeemonstrative freight. Shore, he goes back to Red dog; where, surrounded by that passel of Ishmaels which is its citizens, he ondoubted feels as much at home as a drunkard at a barbecue.

"It's as well he makes that get-away plenty prompt; for the idee of him bein' a atheist, gets so proned into Boggs that, by third drink time, the sight of him would have brought on a religious war. Boggs goes so far as to tell Old Man Enright, that, in his pore, sinful estimation, it's our dooty as a camp to paint up for a croosade ag'in Red Dog, her harborin' sech heathen. Enright, however, allows they're protected by the constitootion, an' so Boggs simmers down.

"An' I'm yere to remark that the subsequent doin's of this pagan person jestifies the elevation of Wolfville's attitoode. It ain't more'n months when he sticks up the stage over by the Whetstone Springs, an' prounces on the mail-bag an' the Wells-Fargo box felonious.

"'You-all takes it from me,' says Boggs, when he's told of the coach bein' rustled, 'them atheists is all hold-ups in their hearts. Which they'd every man jack of 'em be out workin' the trail right now, only thar ain't mail-bags an' express boxes to go 'round.'

"'From the stand we takes in the case of this yere Red Dog pagan, you-all sees that, onderneath the surface like a streak of ore, Wolfville is rich in religious feelin'. It's dor-

mant, merely, because none of them evangelical engineers
has come pirootin' along, to sink a shaft an' work it.

"For one brief moment, an' one only, is the gospel torch
set blazin' in our midst. An' of all folks, it's the Off-
Wheeler who lights it up! That it's him proves as amazin'
as a cow on a front proch. Doc Peets himse'f speaks of it
as a 'pheenomenon:' an' when it comes to readin' the brands
on a pheenomenon, an' readin' 'em right, I'll back Peets
ag'in entire Arizona. I've said freequent that he's the best
eddicated scientist in the Territory, an' I only desires to add
at this eepock that the statement goes for the limit, with any
gent who feels inclined.

"This yere Off-Wheeler has been hankerin' 'round Wolfville, mebby it's six months, before he takes to jumpin'
sideways religious that a-way. His days is spent vibratin' between the Red Light an' the O.K. Restauraw, with now an'
then a evenin' at the dance hall. Not that he ever shakes a
festive laig at the latter 'Temple of Harmonious Mirth,' as
Hamilton is fond of callin' the same; not that he becomes
gala in any polkas, or waxes circooitous in any walses, or
loosens the floor boards in any quadrilles. Is he too old? I
don't reckon now he's overtook thirty years as yet; but,
commonly, he's too seedated to dance, which is to say he's
too drunk. Inebriated gents is plenty out o' place in a quadrille, though some of 'em frequent holds contrary views. As
to the Off-Wheeler; he never falls into no sech error. His
licker, instead of renderin' him vivacious, sort o' bogs him
down; realizin' which, he ain't that fool-minded as to go
lapsin' into the dizzy whirl as a performer.

"It's from Black Jack, with whom he's more or less free
across the Red Light counter, that I gleans what little I
saveys concernin' the Off-Wheeler. It looks like his folks
don't want him East none; an', I must say, no gent who
makes a study of the quantity of Old Jordan he consoomes,
is obleeged to ask the reasons why. Old Monte, for years,
is the offishul drunkard of Wolfville; an' yet the Off-

Wheeler boy comes rollickin' along, an' wrests the bac-
chanalian laurels from Old Monte's brow, as easy as if that
dipsomaniac has only learned the taste of licker yesterday!

"Of course, the latter sot is thar with his yoosual excuses,
an' p'ints out that his deebauches is neccessarily interrupted,
him havin' to sober up s'fficient to take out the stage. The
Off-Wheeler, he says, with no stage to drive, an' no mail-
bag an' express box reespons'bilities, has the advantage.
Still it's the expert Wolfville view, beginnin' with Dave Tutt
an' goin' to Enright, that with the stage coach left out entire
Old Monte never stands a chance. That pore old profligate
wouldn't be ace high ag'in the Off-Wheeler in nose-paint
competitions. Which the Mohave desert is a swamp compared to the latter artist, he's that onslaked.

"While none of us deems ill of the Off-Wheeler," continued the old gentleman, pouring a reflective three fingers
of his favorite refreshment, "the only party about the camp
who reely loves him is Black Jack. The trooth is—him bein'
commonly dulled by drink that a-way—none of the rest of
us gets much acquainted with him. Also, from a bashful
habit he deevelops, of hoppin' out the door every time a
gent starts some triflin' gun-play, the belief gains ground
that he's 'most too timid for Arizona. This nacherally don't
he'p his standin' none, in a camp where the only aristocracy
is the aristocracy of nerve.

"'The trouble with him, gents,' explains Jack, attemptin'
the Off-Wheeler's rescoo as to that question of nerve, 'is
he's gun-shy. It's because he's over-bred, him comin' from
a bloo-blood family. You notices the same thing in dogs
that's bred too fine.'

"None of us regyards this theery of Jack's as possessin'
signif'cance, or provin' anything except he's so foolish fond
of the Off-Wheeler it obscoores his jedgement.

"You see Jack has a moosical ear, an' the Off-Wheeler
can shore sing a whole lot. It's his singin' which biases
Jack. Evenin's, when trade is slack at the Red Light, Jack

an' the Off-Wheeler frequent finds themselves alone. Jack'll be lightin' up the karosene lamps, or mebby teeterin' 'round turnin' down them that smokes. Feelin' lonesome, he'll request the Off-Wheeler to sing *Home, Sweet Home.* Which that victim of rum never refooses, but, cl'arin' his valves with another hooker, allers cuts loose.

"The strange thing, considerin' how Jack himse'f goes honin' for said madrigal, is it's shore to make that drink-mixer weep. He's a mighty sentimental barkeep, Jack is, an', every time the Off-Wheeler hands him *Home, Sweet Home,* he shorely does shed tears profoose.

"An' yet I regyards them lamentations as to Jack's credit; the more, when I finds out he never has no home—as he, himse'f, confesses to me private. I'm sayin' how them childhood's scenes which surrounds his yooth must have been hotbeds of affectionate peace, to make him feel like he does.

"'That's it!' he returns, gulpin' down a sob, an' swabbin' off the bar hysterical; 'my yooth goes onnursed of any home outside a cow camp. Which is why I howls when I hears that ballad! You sports, who've had homes, of course don't mind.'

"It's in Tucson the Off-Wheeler is took religious that time; an' the very way he comes to shift his blankets to said meetropolis, looks of itse'f like the movin' of the hand of Providence. He slides over to Tucson by request of Hamilton, who is that maddened about business troubles—of which the Off-Wheeler is the onintentional bug onder the chip—he says he's afraid of what may ensoo if the Off-Wheeler stays in sight.

"'It's not, I confess, for me,' says Hamilton, 'to go forcin' a gent to migrate, wharfore I puts this on personal grounds entire. I requests you, merely as gent to gent, to *vamos* for Tucson, ontil sech times as I gets my feelin's bedded down. It's odds on, if you-all remains where I can see you, an' me aggravated the way I be it'll bring on 'motional insanity, onder the inflooence of which I'll jest about shoot you up a lot. Tharfore, I begs as a favor that you jump over to Tucson, ontil my wounds is healed an' this yere fit wears off.'

"No one blames Hamilton partic'lar for makin' these su'-gestions, for he's shore suffered a heap. Besides, he's by nacher as nervous a party as Boggs, an' as much a slave to the emotions. On the other hand, we don't exactly go trac-kin' 'round condemnin' the Off-Wheeler neither. It's askin' too much of a gent, an' him a tender-foot, to expect him to stay planted where most likely he'll get all shot up, over is-sues wharin he has no interest.

"At that, as Texas Thompson, who sort o' leans to the Hamilton side, says, thar's right ways an' wrong ways to go eelim'natin' of yourse'f from other gents' wars; an', when the Off-Wheeler, in gettin' out from between Doc Holiday—who's payin' us a friendly visit—an' an offensive sport from Prescott, almost t'ars the side out o' the dance hall, he somewhat oversteps.

"Whatever is the trouble? It's this a-way: It begins by the Prescott party, in a mood of roode exyooberance, tanglin' up his spurs in the trooseau of Holiday's partner, who's floatin' by in a Pocatello reel. Holiday, with that, starts in to teach the Prescott party what's due a lady with his six-shooter. Shore; Holiday is right! the first dooty of a gent is to re-booke vulgarity.

"Now the Off-Wheeler, inadvertent, is in the line of fire; an', when the lead begins to sing, he takes it on the run. But he don't make for the front door—which is the public's; he heads for the orchestra's private door.

"Moosicians in Arizona is some sparse. The Dutchman with the big fiddle, Hamilton freights in from twelve hundred miles away, an' pays five hundred dollars for. In a sperit of proodence, Hamilton plants his high-priced troo-badours by a side door, so they can skip out safe in case of gun-playin' an' war-dancin' on the floor. His arrangements would have been perfect, only it befalls that when Holiday

an' the Prescott boor hooks up, the Off-Wheeler, in his frenzied rush for the orchestra's private door, mounts an' walks
down the virchuoso with the big fiddle, an' leaves 'em both
a wreck. That invalyooable big fiddle is redooced to toothpicks! No wonder it locoes Hamilton!.

"'It's not the Dutchman I bewails,' says Hamilton, 'but
wherever am I to get another doghouse voylin?'

"While the Off-Wheeler comes in for a modicum of disre-
poote because of this eepisode, opinion as stated don't all
run one way. The day the Off-Wheeler leaves, as Texas
Thompson goes to criticisin' him over the layout to
Cherokee, Faro Nell who's the lookout stool where she belongs, cuts in for the Off-Wheeler.

"'Which I don't think,' says Nell, takin' the words out o'
Cherokee's mouth, 'that that Off-Wheeler boy is none to
blame. The Prescott person is actin' like he's out to down
everybody in the room—he's shootin' so difoose. Jim
Hamilton's no business to go to ghost-dancin'.'

"'Straighten up them chips on the eight,' observes
Cherokee, across to Texas.

"Cherokee aims to change the subject, but Nell don't heed
him more'n if he's the wind that blows.

"'You bet, I'll shore tell Jim Hamilton what I thinks,' she
goes on, pickin' up a stack Texas has jest lost on the trey; 'an'
so'll Missis Rucker. The idee of him trackin' 'round permiscus, about a measly old fiddle!'

"'Texas an' Cherokee says nothin'; it ain't lucky to go
contradictin' Nell.

"'The Off-Wheeler's been in Tucson two weeks, an' none
of us is thinkin' of him partic'lar, when of a sudden Old
Monte brings the word. Which we-all sees thar's something
in the wind, long before the stage reaches town, from the
fuss the old reprobate is raisin'. He's pourin' the leather into
the six horses, an' sendin' 'em to beat four of a kind.

"'Mebby it's a lady,' says Boggs, watchin' the nearin'
dust-cloud, an givin' extra cock to his Chihuahua hat. 'That

bond slave of alcohol allers keeps his team up ag'inst the bit, when thar's a lady aboard.'

"But it ain't no lady; thar's nobody in the stage save sev'ral pale he-towerists, who seems pleased to get shet of sech drivin'.

"It's in the Red Light, where he goes to rinse the thirst out o' his mouth, Old Monte onfurls what's happened. Also, he's most onfeelin' slow gettin' started. Now he's with us, his headlong dust-raisin' haste disappears; he measures out his forty drops that deeliberate, thar ain't one of us don't eetch to beat in his head with a gun. Boggs, who's as inquisitive as a pet b'ar, at last can no longer reestrain his cur'osity.

"'Smoke up thar, you old prairie dog!' he roars. 'Is it a killin'? Does any of them Tucson horned toads get beefed?'

"'Beefed?' repeats Old Monte, contempchoous, settin' down his glass; 'it's a mighty sight awfuller than that! The Off-Wheeler's j'ined the church.'

"'What!' shouts Boggs.

"'Moreover,' goes on Old Monte, after the information trickles into us, 'he's plottin' to come down on this devoted outfit all spraddled out, my next trip back from Tucson, an' preach a heap. He allows he'll show us our sins as in a lookin'-glass; which them's his words, gents!' "Wolfville experiences me at my worst; she shall now behold me at my best!" says he.'

"'So he's goin' out to preach!' exclaims Texas Thompson. 'Well, if that don't beat a royal flush! Whatever is this yere Off-Wheeler party thinkin' of? Does he reckon he's goin' to tree the camp in this onlicensed manner, an' go promulgatin' doctrines?'

"'An' why not?' demands Boggs, who's pleased by excitement. 'Ain't the Off-Wheeler a free immoral agent? Which if this sheep that was lost an' is found ag'in—as parson Cartwright back in Missouri used to say—desired to be heard theological, it's up to us, instead of obstructin' the play, to sort o' cosset it along. I'm yere to say I'm with him for them services.'

"'It's mighty likely Texas would have locked horns with Boggs; but seein' that Enright an' Peets, with Dave Tutt trailin', expresses themselves sim'lar he waives it.

"'Black Jack, when he hears, is that delighted he forgets his dooties as barkeep. Bein' reeproved by Peets, he slams all his bottles on the bar, utterly reckless

"'It's on the house, gents!' he says. 'He'p yourselves hearty! Which I knowed the Off-Wheeler would make you-all coyotes set up, once he struck his gait!'

"'Old Monte, who don't propose to get lost in the shuffle, takes up in deetail how the Off-Wheeler becomes religious.

"'This is how it falls in, gents,' he explains. 'Thar's a gospel sharp got a tent over thar, an' the way he's holdin' forth is shore prodigious. Not that I goes maraudin' 'round his game none myse'f, fearin' he might get his runnin' iron onto me. Religion is ondoubted all right; but it wouldn't blend happ'ly with stage drivin'. Bein' younger, an' I might add drunker, this Off-Wheeler ain't so discreet as me; an' he takes to idlin' 'round the meetin's, till, bang! one evenin' when he's off his gyard, he's roped an, throwed an' branded into life everlastin' like crackin' off a Colt's-45.'

"'Does he tell you this himse'f?' asks Enright.

"'It's the barkeep at the Oriental. He puts it up I ought to ride over to that gospel herd, an' cut the Off-Wheeler out a lot. I'm yere to say I don't see eevents in that light. Some of the biggest hostiles in Tucson is at them meetin's on their knees, an' at the least sign of me tamperin' with the Off-Wheeler, or tryin' to snake the game, they'd have took enough of my ha'r to stuff a cushion for the pulpit.'

"'Still, you converses with the Off-Wheeler?' interrogates Peets.

"'Nothin' shorer!' says Old Monte. 'But, say! I can tell they his him cinched with the first word! He does all the talkin', calls me a lost soul personal, gives it out that he

himse'f is a brand snatched from the burnin', an' final defies
every gent, not of his way of thinkin', as a emissary of evil.
Seein' he's plumb beyond control, I goes to the diskyard.
Reply was useless, gents,' continyoos Old Monte, thinkin'
mebby he needs defence. 'It would have been like talkin' to
a sand storm—the Off-Wheeler's took that bad! Besides he
ain't so tame as he was. His air is grown brash an' cocky;
an' he might resent me tryin' to play his hand. Which I've
seen these yere reevivals in the state; an' thar's no foretellin'
what a gent will do, once he's filled with grace.'

"'Whatever,' says Dave Tutt, speakin' gen'ral, 'do you
reckon this Off-Wheeler strikes when he goes glancin' off
into religion this a-way?'

"'Mebby,' observes Boggs, 'it's the change of licker. That
Tucson nose-paint would make a jackrabbit insult a coyote
to his face.'

"'That's not it!' says Old Monte, emphatic; 'the Off-
Wheeler's as cold sober as a fish.'

"'Wouldn't that of itse'f explain it?' asks Texas Thompson, appealin' to Peets in his role of scientist. 'Don't you
figger, Doc, that stoppin' his Old Jordan onbalances his
mind?'

"Pete snaps his fingers at sech surmises, as much too farfetched. In the end we-all settles down to wait; by what Old
Monte says, the Off-Wheeler's due to come prancin' along
poco tiempo, an' then the myst'ry envelopin' his doin's
should begin to cl'ar up."

29

Wolfville's Revival.

DURIN' the three days prior to the Off-Wheeler showin' up, the camp don't talk of nothin' else. He supplants faro-bank an' yoosurps whiskey in the public mind. Enright an' Peets allows that his holdin' services is a good scheme, as calk'lated to give 'em a splendid impression of us East.

"'Besides,' adds Enright, 'thar's a roomer that Red Dog is out to build a chapel. This'll show how, in matters churchly as in all things else, Wolfville has simply got that low-flung hamlet beat both ways from the jack.'

"'When the day arrives, Boggs hints 'round that a healthy notion would be to saddle up, an' meet the Off-Wheeler with a friendly foosilade from our guns, by way of welcome. Enright shakes his head.

"'It might give the boy a skeer,' he says, 'an' stampede him to the p'int where he abandons his idee of preachin'. It's better to let him hit camp, as though his gettin' religion's as commonplace as ground-owls.'

"Nacherally we takes our hunch from Enright, an' when the stage pulls up at the post-office, an' the Off-Wheeler eemerges tharfrom, we confines our demonstrations to sayin' 'Howdy!' He says 'Howdy!' back, an' heads for Missis Rucker's.

"Presently Rucker comes across to say the Off-Wheeler wants to see Enright. Then Jack Moore is sent for; an' a little later Jack tacks up a notice in the Red Light, settin' forth thar'll be church next day at two P.M.

"'That's the talk!' cries Black Jack, readin' the notice aloud, some enthoosiastic. 'The Off-Wheeler's no slouch! He's a wolf, an' it's his night to howl!'

"When Enright rej'ines us, he's smilin' wide an' bland. 'Nothin' could be more sincere than that yooth,' he announces. 'I asks him whatever is his little game. He explains that, after holdin' church among us this time, he's goin' chargin' back to the States to study preachin' as a reg'lar play, an' get himse'f ordained a shore-enough divine. After which he figgers on settlin' down among us, an' ridin' herd on our souls. Of course I tells him that what he plans is bound to do him proud; an' that Wolfville will be ever thar, for its bank roll, to back his game.'

"Hearin' of the comin' meetin', the controllin' inflooence of the Bird Cage Op'ry House offers that edifice. Enright, who's took to managin' for the Off-Wheeler, deeclines with thanks. He lets on that the warehouse, belongin' to the New York Store, will do better.

"'It's smaller, an' tharfore cosier,' says Enright.

"Boggs an' Black Jack now takes hold strong. They rolls in a drygoods box, an' spreads a red Navajo blanket over it—the same makin' a gorgeous pulpit. They totes cha'rs from the O. K. Restauraw ontil you can't rest. As a final break they packs over the pianny from the dance hall—Hamilton, who's gone into the racket to the saddle girths, he'pin'. After that they rests from their labors.

"Texas Thompson evinces surprise at Hamilton fomentin' this preachin', an' him wantin' t go gunnin' for the Off-Wheeler, not three weeks before.

"'You see,' says Hamilton, in explanation, 'it's me chasin' him out o' town, that a-way, which now impels me to give him a boost. I'm preyed on by the feelin' that I'm onjest to the Off-Wheeler. As makin' amends, I turns in with moosicians an' pianny an' cha'rs, an' strives to rib up these yere services, so's the same'll be a howlin' vict'ry. Even if the Off-Wheeler does tromple down my

priceless dog-house voylin, I'm no gent to b'ar malice; an'
I acts accordin'!'

"For one hour before the services begins, Black Jack an'
Hamilton shets off on the sale of snake-jooce at the Red
Light an' the dance hall bars. It's Hamilton who proposes,
temp'rarily, to thus close down these emporiyums, Jack at
the go-off hesitatin'.

"'Not from no low lust of gain,' says Jack; 'but I ain't
none certain a few fingers of Old Jordan, distributed round
in the flock, won't make it easier for the Off-Wheeler. It
might render 'em soft an' good-nachered, an' not so prone
to plant their moccasins an' hold back.'

"Hamilton possesses contrary beliefs. 'Let's send the outfit in on a cold collar,' urges Hamilton. 'Then they can protect themselves; an' afterward, if any of 'em is took relig-
ous, they can't blame no one but themselves. Moreover,
they won't be so apt to backslide. It's safer for the repyoo-
tation of the Off-Wheeler as a divine. It might be remembered ag'in him invidious, if he brings some party to his
knees, an' later that convert goes romancin' off ag'in to eat
sinful husks an' draff with the swine.'

"Jack is so carried off his feet by this, he not only coincides
yoonanimous, but declar's on the quiet to Dave Tutt that thar's
depths in Hamilton's intellects hitherto onfathomed.

"At church time Boggs app'ints himse'f corral boss, an'
shows the folks their seats. Wolfville's best element turns
out in a body. Tucson Jennie, with her infant Enright Peets
Tutt, has a front cha'r by the side of Dave; Missis Rucker,
bringin' Rucker—the latter lookin' subdooed, but sore about
bein' snatched from his refutch among the Apaches—is present; while scattered yere an' thar is Cherokee, an' Faro
Nell, an' Texas Thompson, an' the rest. Black Jack an'
Hamilton, actin' as lookouts an' case-keepers to Boggs reespective, takes seats in the r'ar.

"When everything is lined up, the Off-Wheeler, packin' a
giant Bible onder his arm, shows in the door. Followed by

Enright an' Peets, he p'rades up the middle aisle an' goes into camp, all dignified, back of the drygoods box pulpit with its Navajo blanket cover. He deeposits the scriptures in the middle of the red blanket an' then turns to Enright.

"Nacherally, while these yere various an' sundry steps is bein' took, we sizes up the Off-Wheeler. He shore does appear reegenerated a whole lot, though most likely a heap of that arises from gettin' the whiskey out o' him. All the same he wears a game, noble look, as though them draughts of troo religion has been like the milk of mountain lions to him.

"'When you all recalls what he was,' says Hamilton, leanin' over to whisper in my y'ear, 'an' then sees what he is, it jest does a sport good to look at him!'

"As the Off-Wheeler indulges in that preelim'nary glance at Enright, Wolfville's old warchief gets up. 'No one,' observes Enright, his eye rovin' mildly about the room, 'will misonderstand me bein' yere. Brother Hawkins, formerly known among us as the Off-Wheeler, has asked me to preeside, an' I gladly yields; the more cheerful, since Brother Peets consents to support my ignorance by his urbane countenance an' sagacious counsel. Should I strike a quicksand crossin', an' seem at any time in peril of boggin' down, Brother Peets will be on hand to pull me through. These services'—yere Enright consults a kyard, whereon the rootine of the proceedin's has been framed up in the nacher of a programme—'will commence by that celebrated cantatrice, Sister Sophy Silverthorne of the Bird Cage Op'ry House, leadin' us in *Rock of Ages*.'

"'As Enright resoomes his cha'r, the whole band of us— Hamilton's pianny player, seated at that instroment, beatin' out the 'companyment—onder the lead of Miss Silverthorne, lifts up our voices in the hymn. Boggs throws his heart into it to that reesoundin' extent, that Red Dog sends over a rum-soaked miscreant to ask what's wrong. No; you can go your ultimate chip this insultin' emissary don't deevelop his real

mission none. He comes projectin' 'round the door towards
the finish; but we never do know what brings him thar for
over a month. Bogg's language is sech as to kill an acre of
grass when he learns; but it's too late to get resentful action.

"On the hocks of that *Rock of Ages* hymn, the Off-
Wheeler announces he'll open the deal with pray'r. We sinks
our heads a heap deevout, for we wants to show we're wise
to the proper caper. The Off-Wheeler begins to pour forth.
He prays for Wolfville, for Arizona, an' at last incloods
mankind at large in his orisons. I never does behold a more
creditable seige of the throne, since last I sees the Cumberland.

"Also, I holds now as I holds then that if the Off-Wheeler
had stuck to glitterin' gen'ralities, the meetin' would have
gone from soda to hock without a murmur of discord. Mind
you, I don't say that even as the kyards come out o' the
box, it ain't for the best.

"After exhaustin' the sityooation, along what Peets calls
'broader lines,' the Off-Wheeler begins petitionin' for
people speshul. As a starter, he hurls himse'f loose for
Hamilton; an' the way he lays open the shortcomin's of that
onforchoonate gent is shore s'fficient to make a graven
image ketch its breath. The Off-Wheeler never misses a
trick. On he surges, t'arin' away at pore Hamilton without
reference to the weave of the cloth.

"Although it's in the middle of the pray'r, where the cur-
rent's swiftest an' the channel deepest, Hamilton struggles to
his feet.

"'I rises to a question of privilege,' says Hamilton, addressin' Enright, who's contemplatin' him mighty baleful.

"'Brother Hamilton will state his question of privilege,'
responds Enright, beatin' on the pulpit with the butt of his
six shooter, him havin' no reg'lar gavel.

"'Which I objects,' says Hamilton, 'to statements concernin' myse'f personal, as clk'lated to queer me on high. They
exceeds the limit; I asks the protection of the cha'r.'

"'The cha'r,' retorts Enright, 'passin' on Brother Hamilton's objections, over-rooles the same. Thar is no limit to pray'r. Every gent, addressin' the Infinite, does so with the bridle off.'

"'Let the cha'r b'ar with me for one further word,' returns Hamilton, turnin' sort o' ugly. 'I yields to the tyrannical dictum of the cha'r. At the same time I desires to state that, although I not only assists in promotin' this meetin', but appears yere in a lib'ral if not a contrite sperit, I shall now hold the Off-Wheeler responsible with a gun, as soon as the contreebution box is passed.'

"'The char is obleeged,' observes Enright, speakin' haughty, 'to inform Brother Hamilton that the threats jest made is neither in good nor proodent taste. Brother Hamilton must realize that Brother Hawkins, otherwise the Off-Wheeler, is oncap'ble, as a member of the clergy, of callin' his wicked bluffs. Also, I promises the brother that if he onlimbers in any smoky plays, or takes to shootin' up our pastor in sinful manner an' form as by him set forth, the male part of the congregation will deescend upon him like a tornado, me in the avengin' van. Brother Hawkins will resoome his appeals, onterrified on these menaces; leavin' Brother Hamilton to that repentance an' hoomility of heart, which I'm shore my words should prodooce.'

"It's then the onexpected happens; an' it goes a long ways toward promootin' confidence in the Off-Wheeler's ministrations. As Enright ceases, an' while Boggs an' Black Jack—snortin' challenges to Hamilton—are tryin' to cut in on the play, the Off-Wheeler demands to be heard.

"'Thankin' the cha'r,' says that amotoor clergyman, 'for its generous adherence to the good cause, I desires to submit that I freely recognizes the rights of Brother Hamilton, an' shall be pleased to make good my pulpit utterances in the carnal way he outlines. If the cha'r will pass me its gun, I not packin' sech hardware, holdin' it to be the trinketry of Loocifer, I shall hope to convince Brother Hamilton of the

error of his ways. The congregation will take a recess of ten
minutes. Meanwhile we will reepair to the street, where I
trusts to settle this controversy to the glory of Zion.'

"'But do you-all reckon it looks well, in one whose mission is peace?' asks Enright, some scandalized.

"'Thar is script'ral preecedent;' declar's the Off-Wheeler.
'Have I not the example of Joshua, of David, of Saul?—all
men of war! An' of Abner, who smote his enemy onder the
fifth rib; an' of Peter, who struck off the y'ear? Man is born
unto trouble, as the sparks fly upwards! Also, fear not for
the safety of your shepherd. Brother Hamilton is some soon
with a gun; but, behold, I rely on One that taketh the wise
in their own craftiness—even upon Him that maketh the
deep to boil like a pot!'

"'As the congregation files out, Boggs pushes up to the
Off-Wheeler. 'Mebby,' whispers Boggs, 'you'd better let me
represent. Bein' inyoored to these shindigs, I most likely
pulls off a finish more fav'rable to the cause.'

"'Nay,' returns the Off-Wheeler, who is all keyed up, 'I
shall even rebooke this son of Jeshurun, who I percive
waxeth fat an' kicks! He is like the deaf adder that stoppeth
her ear; which will not hearken to the voice of charmers,
charming never so wisely! Yea, I shall show him how man's
days are as grass!—as a flower of the field so he
flourisheth!.'

"Outside in the street, the Off-Wheeler an' Hamilton takes
their distance, the congregation makin' a rank of admiration
on the sidewalk. Enright gives the word by droppin' his
sombrero. Hamilton shoots a little wide, while the Off-
Wheeler gets Hamilton in the thick of the laig.

"'How goodly are thy tents, O Jacob, and thy tabernacle,
O Israel!' sings the Off-Wheeler, as he returns Enright his
gun.

"We-all goes back to our seats in the sanctchooary, Enright preesidin' as before, an' the Off-Wheeler takes up his
supplications where Hamilton interrupts.

"When the pray'r is done, Peets, with Boggs an' Black Jack, comes trailin' in from the O. K. House, to which hostelry they packs Hamilton, followin' the shootin'.

"'How is my injured parishoner?' asks the Off-Wheeler.

"'Speakin' as his medical adviser,' says Peets, 'I should say he'll be hobblin' about in less'n a week. Continyooin' as a fellow worker in the vineyard, I adds that I leaves him in a tem'perate an' eddifyin' frame. He asks me to say that he reckons you're right about the proper scope of pray'r.'

"'Brother Hamilton is a lib'ral soul!' says the Off-Wheeler, a heap pleased. 'Yea, I shall visit him! Peradventure, I shall show him where it is written that the liberal soul shall be made fat!' Then, turnin' to us: 'Oh, my hearers, how good an' how pleasant it is for brethren to dwell together in yoonity!'

"The pianny—the hymn bein' given out—strikes up, Miss Silverthorne puts herself in the vocal lead, an' we-all goes riotin' off on *We're Goin' Home to Die no More*, Boggs distinguishin' himse'f as prior, his tones resemblin' a wronged buffalo bull's. After the song, the Off-Wheeler reads his text: 'Is not the gleaning of the grapes of Ephraim, better than the vintage of Abi-ezer?' Which the sermon is a jo-darter, Wolfville figgerin' as 'the vintage of Abi-ezer.'

"When the contreebution box is passed by Boggs, the same bein' Peet's hat, Hamilton, to show he's with us, sends over a 20-dollar gold peice.

"'This is strength made perfect in weakness!' cries the Off-Wheeler joobilantly, as Hamilton's donation comes jinglin' in. 'I have lighted a candle of understandin' in his heart, which shall not be put out!'

"As the last note of the doxology is sung, we-all crowds for'ard to congratchoolate the Off-Wheeler.

"Enright is the first to take his hand. 'Which I talks for all,' observes Enright, speakin' so every one can hear, 'when I says that pluggin' Brother Hamilton is the most excellent element in the ceremonies. Nothin' could have happened better, nothin' gone half so far towards convincin' this commoonity of the genyooineness of your preachments. That little gun play falls in plumb right. When you return, the incident will make your callin' an' election shore. I shall yereafter think better of my six-shooter',—drawin' the weepon, an' lookin' it over approvin'ly—for its share in spreadin' gospel trooths, an' the part it plays in Brother Hamilton's conversion.'"

The Old Cattleman

30

The Popular Sourness.

"NO gent, onless locoed, would ever put a bet on the public." My old friend spoke with warmth, at the same time throwing down a newspaper from which the glaring headline, "Overthrow of a Popular Idol," started out. "Not," he continued, lapsing into his customary manner of calm not to say benign philosophy—"not that I'm likely to get caught out on any sech limb personal, me makin' it an onbreakable roole to bet on nothin' that can talk. Animals is different. A party who wagers his riches on animals, gets somethin' reesemblin' an even break for his money. Bein' onable to talk that a-way, animals is limited in their mootual commoonications. That saves 'em from given' or takin' advice, an' leaves it possible for gents of jedgment to half way figger on whatever they'll do next."

"Evidently, you don't believe deeply in the wisdom of man," said I.

"No, I don't regyard hoomanity as so plumb wise. You-all could take me into the halls of Congress, an' plant me in the legislatif foreground as a question; you might get a member to introdooce a resolootion sayin' I'm a white man without a cross. Instantly, an opp'sition will take the floor, claimin' I'm a Injun; an' I'll play in a heap of luck if a third party don't form for the purpose of showin' I'm a Mexican. All the time, too, that them statesmen is wranglin' over my tribe an' strain, thar won't be a mule between the oceans, but would know I'm white at the drop of the hat—know it in the dark.

"Shore, to my pore thinkin' animals has a heap more savey than folks. Thar's the elk. When he allows he'll go to bed some, he begins negotiations by walkin' in a half-mile circle. Then he marches into the safe center of the circle, plunks himse'f down, an' is as sound asleep as a tree in a moment—all but his nose. Bein' inside that circle, if a wolf or a man or a mountain lion is followin' his trail, no matter how the wind shifts, his nose gives him warnin'. Even a mule-eared deer, makin' a perpetyooal skirmish line of his nose, goes feedin' up the wind. Do folks? As often as otherwise they makes a speshulty of gettin' the breeze to their ignorant backs; an' go romancin' off into the teeth of trouble, talkin' about their 'reasonin' powers,' an' feelin sorry for what they calls the 'lower animals.'

"At that, you're not to go followin' off no wrong wagon track, an' assoome that animals, as eevents shift, don't shift their instincts to match 'em. When every Injun goes shootin' bows an' arrers, an' every white gent packs a squirrel rifle, bullets sixty to the pound, grizzly b'ars, as I once tells you former, treats said armaments with distain. The grizzlies knows they can't be hurt none by sech footile weepons; an', far from bein' worried by the 'Westward ho!' of the white man, they regyards emigrants an' their fam'lies with satisfaction, as additions to the vis'ble food supply. Later, when we gets to work on 'em with them high-power big-bore guns, an' knocks 'em over too dead to skin, grizzlies changes utter. To-day you-all couldn't get clost enough to a grizzle to give him a roast apple. At the sight of innocent papooses, even, he goes riotin' off through the bresh, up hill an' down dale, like his r'ar's afire.

"No; as I was observin' when I gets deeflected onto b'ars, folks ain't so plumb sagacious—not even Wolfville folks. Back in the old days, if the stage breaks down on account of rotten axles, do we-alls cuss out the company? Not at all; we burns the ground around Old Monte, when even the prairie dogs onderstands how that pore old slave of alcohol

ain't no more reesponsible for rotten axles than for the qual-
ity of Red Light nose-paint.

"Which this partic'lar victim of pop'lar wrath"—here the
old gentleman tossed a scornful thumb towards the paper,
where it lay on the floor—"is a office holder. He ain't entitled to no sympathy, for if he had owned a lick of sense he
could have seen his downfall comin'. The finish of office
holders is allers alike; it's the finish of the army mule. Each
of 'em is some day led out all onexpected, an' branded 'I.
C.' which means 'Inspected an' condemned,' an' figger-
tively speakin' your mule an' your office holder rots down
right thar."

"Did you ever have an ambition to hold office?" I asked,
more with a purpose to tease than elicit information.

"Me hold office? I'd sooner hold a baby! Not that I aims
to speak disparagin' of infants neither, deemin' 'em as
roobies above price. But nacherally you-all saveys that me
bein' a bachelor, an' tharfore onmarried a whole lot, babies
in my case is barred.

"Speakin' of office holders, I can't say I've a heap of use
for 'em. Office holders, taken in the herd, is so plumb
egreegious—doin' so little towards he'pin' the public, while
allowin' they'll do so much. At that I don't reckon it's all
their fault. A man—slam him on the scales an' weigh him—
is a mighty puny creature. The public, as ag'inst this, is
mighty big; an' for him to go talkin' of he'pin' the public
is as though he talks of he'pin' the Mississippi. The public
goes pirootin' into a 'lection, an' prodooces a gov'nor; an'
the transaction reeminds me a heap of that hill in the fables,
which goes rockin' an' weavin' all over the pampas, a-
skeerin' everybody to death, an' winds up its onseemly
ghostdancin' by bringin' forth a mouse. Gov'nor! Does
'lectin' some ornery no-'count party to be gov'nor render
him less ornery? Which you-all might as well throw a cow-
saddle onto a jack-rabbit, thinkin' to make a mustang of it!

"Take the biggest gent on the list, an' construct a gov'nor

of him: whatever can he do? The job's so gigantic, an' he's so plumb little, you'll find him as he'pless to change the eternal face to things as though you'd made him gov'nor of a mountain. The best he gets out of it will mebby be to scratch his hon'rable name on the onockepied face of some rock ledge; an' at that the moss'll overgrow it in a week an' blot it out. The next gent to climb the hill won't even be able to make out his 'nitials.

"It's my notion," went on the old gentleman, heaving a sigh—"it's my notion, foaled of years of experience, that the biggest among us might better mod'rate his se'f-esteem. He can make up his mind he's shore powerless to give his hour a lift to any great extent. An' then ag'in, it ain't needed none; it's too much like givin' Providence a lift. That gent comes nearest to gettin' his own inconsequential measure, who concloods that, when he's won out his blankets an' his three feeds a day, together with a occasional drink, he's beat this game called livin' for about all he's goin' to get.

"He'p the public? Even if you could, it wouldn't be worth while. You'd about wind up at the leetle eend of the horn, same as this office-holdin' tarrapin in the noospaper. Publics is ongrateful. He'pin' the public out of a hole, is as certain as he'pin' a b'ar out of a hole; it's bloo chips to white that the first offishul act of either'll be to chaw you up.

"As aidin' me to this concloosion, I sees somethin' of the sort come off in the c'rreer of Doc Peets. This is 'way back yonder, when Wolfville is cuttin' its milk teeth, an' prior to the dawnin' of sech evidences of progress as the Bird Cage Op'ry House, an' Colonel Sterett's *Daily Coyote*. It's before the Washwoman's War, an' antedates the nuptials of Tucson Jennie with Dave Tutt by years.

"What's the story? It don't amount to much, an' is val-yooable only as 'llustratin' what I says on the footility, not to mention the peril, of tryin' to turn a commoonal trick. Peets cuts loose to he'p the public; an' the first move he gets a stack down wrong, an' jest manages to round on the play

in time to keep himse'f from bein' swept plumb off the
board. You-all has heard me yeretofore alloode to Peets, as
the best eddicated an' deepest sharp in the territory. What
I'm to reelate is not to be took ag'inst them utterances. Peets
is young when the eepisode occurs; later, when years has
come an' gone an' thar's a pretty hefty accumyoolation of
rings at the base of Peets' horns, you-all couldn't have
coaxed him into no sech trap, not for gold an' precious
stones.

"It has its beginnin' in the comin' to town of Tacoma
Tom, an' the subsequent discovery of that kyard-expert dead
out back of the dance hall, a bullet through his back. It
shore looks like somebody's been objectin' to Tacoma with
a gun. Thar ain't so much as a whisper of suspicion p'intin'
to the partic'lar sport who thus finds fault with Tacoma, or
what for. Wolfville is baffled complete.

"This bein' left in the dark, op'rates to rub the public fur
the wrong way. Not that Wolfville feels as though it can't
keep house without deceased; at best he's but a fleetin' form
of tinhorn hold-up, of no social standin', an' it's apples to
ashes the stranglers would have had Jack Moore run him out
o' camp inside a week. Still, it's a case of a party gettin'
downed, an' the public's been eddicated to at least expect a
solootion, even if thar ain't no lynchin'. In this instance the
public don't get neither; wharfore it takes to frettin' a lttle
onder the quiet collar. Also, Red Dog goes to makin'
reemarkes; an' this last so shames the more morbid sperits,
like Boggs, they begins to talk of movin' to Tucson.

"While public feelin' is thus strained, the general eye sort
o' takes to focusin' on a Mexican, who's been hangin' out
over to the corrals for about a useless month. It grows to be
the common view that this yere Mexican may be spared
from amoung us, without upsettin' the whole Wolfville
frame-work. Troo, thar's nothin' to connect him with the
bumpin' off of Tacoma, except he's a Mexican; but in a
commoonity which favors hangin' folks not so much for

what they do as for what they are, this saddle-colored fact of a sunburned nationality goes some distance. The boys takes to murmurin' among themselves, as they slops out their Old Jordan at the Red Light counter, that to hang said Mexican to the windmill wouldn't hurt that water-drawin' contraption a little bit. Thar's even people who claims it's calk'lated for the windmill's embellishment.

"The Mexican himse'f must have been one of them mind-readers; for, while the whisper yoonitin' him to the windmill goes meanderin' up an' down, he of a sudden disappears entire. This ontoward evaporation of the Mexican, at the only time he's reely needed, is regyarded as a hoss on the camp; an' with that, public feelin' takes on a more exasperatin' edge than prior. Likewise, Red Dog is thar with the yoosual barbed bluff, to the insultin' effect that Wolfville manages its kyards so clumsy, that even a blinded greaser reads its hand.

"It's while the pop'lar temper is thus morose, that Old Man Enright an' Doc Peets comes together casyooal in the New York Store.

"'What's the matter with the camp, Sam?' asks Peets. He's payin' for a bloo shirt, with pearl buttons, he's bought. 'It looks as though the outfit's on a dead kyard.'

"Peets' tones is anxious. When it comes to settin' up all night with Wolfville, an' rockin' its cradle an' warmin' its milk, give me Peets!

"'Somethin' ought to be done,' he continyoos. 'As the play stands, the pop'lar sperit—once so proud an' high—is slowly but shorely boggin' down.'

"'It's Tacoma gettin' beefed,' says Enright, 'an' our omittin' to stretch that corral greaser. Thar's a bet we overlooks, Doc! We never should have let that felon get away.'

"'But both of us,' observes Peets, 'you-all as chief of the vig'lance committee, an' me as a member in full standin', lives well aware thar ain't the shadow of evidence that the Mexican wipes out Tacoma.'

"'None the less,' returns Enright, the 'boys sort o' lotted on a lynchin'. You saveys, Doc, that it ain't so important to hang the right gent, as to hang some gent when looked for. Besides, to let a Mexican run out from between our fingers, that a-way, is mortifyin' to the camp's se'f-love.'

"'Well,' reemarks Peets, 'somethin' to arouse public enthoosiasm is the imperatif demand. If we-all permits the boys to go gloomin' 'round in their present frame, they'll shore take to chewin' one another's mane.'

"Enright nods assent, but offers no su'gestions.

"'See yere!' exclaims Peets, after a pause—Peets is more fertile than Enright—'I've roped onto an idee. The games is dead at this hour; suppose we rounds up the camp for a talk. A pow-wow, though nothin' results, is calk'lated to prodooce a soothin' effect.'

"'Which I'm agree'ble,' remarks Enright; 'but how be we goin' to convene 'em? Back in Tennessee, in my natif village of Pineknot, we used to ring the town bell. Wolfville bein' deevoid of town bells, I takes it the next best move is for me to s'anter to the r'ar door, an' shake the loads out o' my gun. That'll excite pop'lar cur'osity; the boys'll come a-runnin' to see who gets it.'

"Enright reetires to the back door, an' bangs away some frantic three or four times with his six-shooter. The day bein' quiet, the effect is plenty vivacious; everybody comes t'arin' over all spraddled out. That is every gent but Black Jack comes t'arin'; him bein' on watch at the Red Light, he don't feel free to leave the bar.

"'Any one creased?' asks Dave Tutt, out o' breath an' pantin'.

"'None whatever,' replies Peets, easy an' suave. Then lettin' on he don't notice the disapp'intment that spreads itse'f from face to face, he proceeds: 'This yere is a bloodless foosilade, an' is resorted to as a means of convokin' the best minds of the camp. Thar's a subject of common interest to be proposed; an' to get for'ard in order my motion is that our honored leader, Mister Enright, be requested to preeside.'

"'Hold on a minute,' interjects Boggs, 'ontil I signs up to Black Jack thar ain't no corpses. He's that inquisitive, an' him bein' tied to his dooties as barkeep that a-way, he'd eat his heart out if I don't.'"

31

The Copper Head.

"**B** ACK in Tennessee," observed the old gentleman, with an air of meditative retrospection, "when in boyhood's happy hour I attends services in them sancchooaries that's scattered up an' down my ancestral 'Possum Trot, I frequent hears the preacher sharps refer to 'the cunnin' of the serpent.'

"As a child I allows that the same, with said pastors, is a mere figger of pulpit speech; the more since what serpents I scrapes pers'nal acquaintance with—an' I gen'ally scrapes it with a elm club—proves plumb doltish that a-way, an' thick. Them reptiles when tested displays about as much cunnin' as Thompson's colt, which animal is that besotted it swims a river to get a drink. Later on, however, as I b'ars interested witness to the wile an' guile of the Copper Head, as he salts the Golden Roole felonious, an' depletes Bass Drum Bowlby of forty thousand in cold dollars tharwith, I recalls that phrase of them divines as something which, if applied to the Copper Head, would shore have been plenty jestified.

"The Copper Head preceeds Bass Drum into camp by about a week. In trooth, he's adjourned to Red Dog before ever Bass Drum shows up, an' ain't livin' none in Wolfville at all. Not that he's so feeble-minded he prefers Red Dog, only Cherokee Hall alarms him so he don't dare stay.

"What rouses Cherokee is this: While not sayin' nothin', the Copper Head is guilty one evening of a deal of onnecessary starin' at Faro Nell, as that young priestess of fortune sets lookin' out Cherokee's play. Of a sudden, at the close of a deal, Cherokee turns his box up, an' briefly excooses himself—he's onflaggin'ly p'lite, that a-way—to what gents is buckin' the game. He crosses over to the Copper Head, planted by himse'f down near the end of the bar.

"'You don't gamble none?' remarks Cherokee, givin' the words a upflourish to show it's a question.

"'No,' replies the Copper Head; 'I'm averse irrev'cable to takin' chances.'

"'Then,' returns Cherokee, mighty bitter, 'don't look at that young lady none no more. Which in so doin', whether you're wise to it or no, you're takin' the chances of your life!'

"As Cherokee vouchsafes this admonition, an' by way of urgin' it home on the wanderin' fack'lties of the Copper Head, he cinches onto that serpent by the y'ear—the same bein' some wide-flung an' fan-like—an' leads him to the Red Light door. Once arrived at that egress, Cherokee desmisses him outiside by a foot in the small of the back, said Copper Head flying through the air in the shape of a hooman horse-shoe.

"'Now, don't return!' cautions Cherokee, as the Copper Head, who lands all spraddled out in the dust of the street, picks himse'f up an' goes limpin' over to the O. K. House; 'I've took a distaste ag'in you, an' the less I sees of you the longer you're likely to last.'

"'That Copper Head,' says Boggs, as Cherokee gets in back of his box ag'in, 'is ornery to the brink of bein' odious; and yet, Cherokee, I don't much reckon he's starin' at Nell in a sperit of insult. My idee is he's simply eediotic.'

"'Mebby so,' returns Cherokee, some grim; 'we-all wont argue that, Dan. Let me add, however, for the illoom'nation of all concerned, that if eediocy's to be a defense yereafter for crim'nal roodness, why then I'm some eediotic myse'f—on certain subjects. One of 'em is Nell, as that Copper Head'll shore find out a heap, should him and his red snake eyes take to transgressin' ag'in.'

"'Snappin' the deck he's rifflin' into the deal box, Cherokee addresses the circle about the lay-out:

"'Now, gents,' he says, his urbanity restored, 'when your hands is off your stacks, we'll resoome the exercises of the evenin'. 'Thar you be!—Trey lose, nine win!'

"'Which in all my born days,' wails the Copper Head, complainin' to Rucker of the voylent usage he receives— 'which in all my born days thar's never a more onprovoked assault! Cats may look at kings!'

"'That cat-an'-king bluff,' returns Rucker, mighty onsympathetic, 'may go in the far East, but it carries no weight in Arizona, none whatever! Before you-all insists round yere on lookin' at any kings, you better be shore an' have, besides a workin' knowledge of the gent who's holdin' 'em, somethin' vergin' onto a full hand yourse'f.'

"No, nothin' comes of Cherokee's rebooke, the Copper Head takin' it plumb moote an' quiescent, that a-way. Snakes may be p'isen, an' frequent is, but thar ain't a ounce of war in a wagonload. However, since early the next mornin' the Copper Head pulls his freight in favor of Red Dog, I nacherally infers said eepisode to be the cause.

"While the Copper Head done packs his blankets over to Red Dog, an' tharfore the disgrace of his citizenship belongs rightful to that collection of vulgarians, he's most every day in Wolfville confabbin' with Rucker. Not that they nourishes designs; Rucker, mental, bein' no more'n a four spot, an' totally onfit for what the actor person in the Bird Cage Op'ry House calls, 'treasons, strategems an' spoils.' But the Copper Head is so much like Misery, that he shore loves company; an', since no one except Rucker'll stand for his s'ciety, he puts in a lot of time hibernatin' round with that broken-sperited husband. As for Rucker himse'f, he's plumb willin'; for, at bein' what you-all might call a social fav'rite, said spouse of Missis Rucker's ain't got nothin' on the Copper Head. Which any contest of onpopyoolar'ty between 'em would have been a stand-off, a plain case of hoss an' hoss.

"Some darkened sport says some'ers that thar's nothin' in mere looks, in which utterances he's shootin' plenty wild. The Copper Head is instanter the least trusted an' most deespised party that ever comes rackin' into Wolfville; an' yet, if you backtracks for reasons, you finds nothin' ag'in him at the go-off but his looks.

"For that matter, thar's nothing partic'lar ag'in him at the finish, his clean-up of Bass Drum for them forty thousand, comin' onder the head of a private play, wharin' the public ain't entitled to a look-in. Mines, like roolette an' draw poker an' farobank, is a deevice to which no gent is licensed to pull his cha'r up, onless he's preepared pers'nal to protect himse'f plumb through. If he gets handed a gold brick, thar's nothing' in the sityooation which entitles him, for purposes of revenge or retrobootion, to ring the body pol'tic in on the play. This yere's Peets' doctrine; an', when it comes to a even balancin' of right an' wrong, that scientist possesses the wisdom of a tree full of owls.

"As I states, it's the looks of this Copper Head which confers on him his low ratin' in the gen'ral esteem. He's a thin, bony, scar-crow form of hoomanity, with little red eyes like a ferret, y'ears of onbecoomin' lib'rality, loose lip, wide onauthorized mouth, the whole capped by a stubble of ha'r the hue of one of them liver colored bird dogs. His hands, too is long an' knobby, an' has a cold, clammy feel when you takes hold of 'em like the belly of a fish. Rucker allows that back East the Copper Head's a sexton, an' digs graves; which may or may not be the reason a damp, moldy, tomb-like smell invests his physical bein' perpetyooal, an' wrops it round like a atmosphere.

"As a further pop'lar set-back the Copper Head lets on he's a party of exact morals. Never once askin' the way to the nearest s'loon, the same bein' the yoosual inquiry of emigrants, his first question after he hits the outfit is 'Do we-all have a church?' It's on Texas Thompson he presses his query concernin' meetin' houses, an' when Texas replies some surly; 'No, but we've got a grave yard,' meanin' Boot Hill, the Copper Head lapses into silence, savin' what's left of his stock of inquisitiveness for the y'ears of Rucker.

"Aside from him bein' reepulsive, pers'nal, the Copper

Head conducts himse'f in a sneaky, onderground way; an' he shows himse'f so he'pless intellectchooal, when put up ag'inst what few prop'sitions the camp casyooally submits to him to fix his caliber, that Boggs an' Tutt an' Texas is all of one mind that he's a eediot.

"'Not witless enough to lock up, you onderstand', explains Tutt, 'but onfit to hold commoonyon with folks whose sombreros is of normal size.'

"'Don't get your chips down wrong, Dave,' warns Peets, to whom Tutt's talkin'; 'that Copper Head's not your kind, an' you simply fails to savey him. You an' Dan an' Texas thar is one an' all the dog sort of man. This Copper Head belongs to the snake tribe. Which you couldn't count him up nor take his measure in a thousand years! You can gamble that name of "Copper Head," which Old Monte informs me he acquires in Tucson, aint no mis-cue in nomenclatchoor!'

"'The Copper Head is loafin' about, listless an' onregyarded, the same evenin' Bass Drum Bowlby blows in. This latter gent is the preecise opposite to the Copper Head, bein' so big an' broad an' thick he has to be prized out o' the stage, him measurin' wider than the door. Also he's certainly the most resoundin' sport! Which his conversation, when he's talkin', goes rollin' 'round the town like peals of thunder; an' at supper, when he's obleeged to ask for doughnuts the second time, seven ponies boils out of the corral, an' goes stampedin' off for the hills.

"'Say, pard,' he roars appealin'ly to Boggs, who settin' next, "jest please pass them fried holes!'

"An' with that, them alarmed cayouses lines out for cover in the Tres Hermanas, onder the impression Wolfville's done gone crashin' to its eternal fall.

"While I wont say we-all sets up nights declarin' our friendly admiration for Bass Drum none, still he's a mighty sight more tol'rable than the Copper Head. You-all could pass a hour in his company without feelin' the hom'cidal instinct beginnin' to move in your bosom, an' set you eetchin' to shed hooman life. For one moll'fyin' matter, without bein' partic'larly inclined crim'nal, Bass Drum possesses vices s'fficient to keep a se'f respectin' gent in countenance. He's a heap noisy an' obvious, an' owns a metallic voice like one of these yere Chinese dinner gongs; but he's sociable, an', when all's in, his voice is jest the same a good-nachered voice. Moreover, he's liable to change in a hundred dollar bill at faro-bank, or fling a ten across the Red Light counter as his subscription towards drinks for the house, in which amiable respects he proves himse'f in symp'thy with his day an' place. Also, as I observes, Bass Drum is 'ppreciative of the virchoos of vice.

"Shore! The whitest gents I ever meets up with has vices. For myse'f, so long as they keeps 'em out from onder my feet, I finds no fault. What is it Cain remarks after he bumps off Abel that time? While I don't applaud Cain none in that killin', the sentiment he fulm'nates later secoores my yoonan'mous endorsements.

"No gent ought to over-look the great social trooism that, rightly regyarded, a vice is nothin' but a virchoo multiplied. A virchoo is like a cowcumber; it's no good once it goes to seed. Which it then becomes a vice. That's the straight goods; every vice is nothin' but some virchoo over-played. Wharfore, when I crosses up with a gent who's beset of vices that-a-way, I reflects to myself thus-wise: 'Now this yere sport has virchoos; the loose screw is he's got too plumb many an' too much!' Lookin' at it from that angle, he's not only to be excoosed but loved.

"Whoever is this Bass Drum sport? All I knows is that on a first occasion of his showin' up, he rolls into the Red Light, lurches fat an' heavy up ag'in the counter, an' shouts:

"'My name's Bass Drum Bowlby, an' I invites every gent to take a drink. Them who don't drink is welcome to a dollar out of the drawer.'

"Followin' the libation, Bass Drum goin' more into details, makes himse'f heard ag'in. 'For two years,' says he, 'I've been pirootin' 'round between the Rio Colorado an' the Spanish Peaks. Which I'm shore wedded to the West!

Likewise, the reason I loves the West is it's a fraud. That's whatever; thar ain't a play comes off on the sundown side of the Missouri which you-all can p'int to as bein' on the level! Thar ain't a fact or a concloosion on the genyooinness of which you could wager a white chip.'

"'Be you plumb certain?' asks Jack Moore. 'Now it's my belief that every gent in the room has got a cartridge belt full of indespootable facts; an', if a Colt's-45 aint a concloosion, I shore don't know what is.'

"'For heaven's sake!' exclaims Bass Drum, evincin' concern, 'don't talk gun talk. My only thought is to pay the West some compliments. I only says the West's a fraud that a-way as offerin' encomiyums. Which I am somewhat of a fraud myse'f; an' I onhesitatin'ly informs mankind that, at my fact'ry back East, I a'int doin' a thing in a lowly way but makin' goose-ha'r mattrasses out o' wood pulp—not only makin' 'em gents, but sellin' 'em. Two years ago though, as I informs you-all prior, I gets wedded to the West, an' never does go back East no more. I simply stays yere, an' permits that fraudyoolent wood-pulp, goose-ha'r mattrass fact'ry to run itse'f.'

"'He talks,' growls Texas to Boggs, 'of bein' wedded to the West: an' then evolves a howl that the West's a fraud. Which he better try some reg'lar lady once!'

"'May I ask,' puts in Enright, addressin' Bass Drum plenty suave an' bland, 'whatever brings about them nuptials!'

"'It's in Vegas,' says Bass Drum; 'I'm jest in from the East, an' headed for the Vegas Hot Springs. I piles out of the kyars; a party, name unknown, throws me into a hack. "Plaza Hotel," says I. Ten minutes later we're at that car'vansary. "How much?" says I. "Twenty plunks," says he. "Shake!" says I, as I pays over the twenty bones. "This is where I stay. A country in which you can make twenty dollars in ten minutes is good enough for me!" An' so I goes romancin' along in an' registers, meanwhile singin' "This yere's the place I long have sought, an' mourned because I found it not." Gents, I've been part of the West ever since.'

"'An' prosperin' I reckons?' says Peets.

"'Not exactly prosperin',' returns Bass Drum, startin' the nose paint on a second trip; 'not altogether prosperin': but learnin' a whole lot. Bein' the other day in Silver City, I hears of this camp; an' the more I hears the better it sounds. At last I allows I'll break in, look you-all stingin' lizards overs, an' mebby make investments.'

"'Investments?' remarks Enright; 'in cattle, do you say?'

"'Not cattle,' returns Bass Drum, wipin' his lips; 'which I gets fully through with cattle over back of San Marcial towards the Black Range. You knows old Axtell of the Triangle X? Bought a thousand head of that old outlaw, thirty dollars per. He builds a chute, drives up the thousand cows, runs 'em through, claps the redhot iron on 'em, counter-brands 'em "C-in-a-box" the new mark I invents. Thar they be gents, back on the range ag'in;—a thousand head of C-in-a-box cows, an' that cimarron Axtell countin' my little old thirty thousand simoleons! Do I come forth onscathed? Gents, listen! In two months I ain't got twenty head. That C-in-a-box brand ain't nothin' but a ha'r brand; it all grows out afresh, an' them cattle returns *poco tiempo* to their old-time Triangle X form. Oh! you bet I'm learnin'! No more bovines for Bass Drum! This time I aims to break my guileless teeth on mines. If thar's any sport within hearin' of my loud bazoo, who's got a salted mine, let him prepare for the feast. Yere I stands in my ignorance, his nacheral born prey!'

"Sayin' which, Bass Drum beats his breast ontil it booms, while his eyebrows work up an' down like one of them gorillas."

32

The Salting Of
The Golden Rule.

IT looks as though Bass Drum paves the way for his own
deestruction. The Copper Head, drawn by the exyooberant an' far-reachin' tones of Bass Drum's, is hoverin' about
the portals of the Red Light at the time. He don't come inside none, Cherokee bein' back of his lay-out an' the Copper
Head ownin' a mem'ry. Presently he disappears; an', while
his comin' and goin' don't leave no profound impressions on
me at the moment, I thinks of it afterwards a whole lot.

"Bass Drum pervades the camp in an' out for sev'ral days,
an' so far as I hears gets proper action for what *dinero* he
puts in cirkyoolation. One evenin, when we're wrastlin' our
chuck at the O.K. House—Rucker attendin' on our wants as
waiter—Texas asks over his shoulder:

"'Whar's that Copper Head *compadre* of yours, Rucker? I
ain't seen him round none for four days?'

"Well,' snarls Rucker, who's testy an' spiteful on account
of him being redooced to a serville p'sition, 'you don't reckon I kills an' eats him, does you?'

"Don't wax gala, Rucker,' returns Texas, mighty high an'
cautionary, 'or the next time Doc Peets wants a skeleton to
play hoss with scientific, I'll shore preesent him yours. You-
all would furnish a fairly person'ble skeleton that a-way;
what ever do you yourse'f think, Doc?'

"'He'll do,' says Peets, runnin' Rucker over kind o' crit-
ical, like he's a hoss an' him, Peets, is goin' to buy him.
'To be shore, Rucker wouldn't afford no skeleton of highest

grade, not one of these yere top-notch corn-fed skeletons; but he'd match in plumb successful between a Mexican an' a Digger Injun, as completin' a chain.'

"'You-all asks about the Copper Head?' says Rucker to Texas, a heap subdooed; for the way Texas an' Peets goes bulgin' off about skeletons almost brings on him a fit of the treemors. 'Which he's gone to minin' over in Colorow Gulch. Thar's that prospect Chicken Bill abandons; the Copper Head re-riles on it as the "Golden Roole," an' is dee-velopin' the same.'

"'Whoever is this yere enterprisin' Copper Head?' asks Bass Drum of Cherokee.

"'Which he's a bad-mannered miscreent,' returns Cherokee, 'who if asked to set into a game of freeze-out for two dollars worth of brains a corner, couldn't even meet the ante.'

"'The more weak-witted,' says Bass Drum, 'the better; less brains, more luck. It takes a eediot to find a mine. Which I'll look this bullhead up some; if he's struck anything good I'll take it away from him.' Then, to Rucker, who's staggerin' in from the kitchen with a passel of dry-apple pies: 'How about this yere Golden Roole mine? What for a prospect is it?'

"'All I knows,' returns Rucker, 'is that the Copper Head sends what he calls a "mill run" over to Silver City for a assay, an' it shows eight hundred dollars to the ton.'

"'Whoever says sech things as that,' retorts Bass Drum, 'is conversin' through his sombrero. Thar ain't no sech ore in Arizona.'

"While I don't savey mines none, I'm plenty sapient when it comes to men, an' I sees, for all his bluff front, Bass Drum is a heap struck. The next mornin' he hires Rucker of Missis Rucker, to show him where the Golden Roole is located. It's over to'ards Red Dog in Colorow Gulch, an' Rucker an' Bass Drum finds the Copper Head idlin' about in the drift. He an' his Golden Roole mine is a heap alone that a-way, an' never another prospect within a half dozen miles.

"As Bass Drum an' Rucker draws near, they hears the Copper Head singin' a church toone, that one about 'India's Golden Sands.'

"'Is this onder-done party religious?' whispers Bass Drum.

"'Religious?' says Rucker. 'Which I only wishes I has four bits for every pray'r he's flung off! I should say he is religious! Thar's members of the clergy who ain't ace-high to the Copper Head. But see yere,' continues Rucker, detainin' Bass Drum by the arm, 'don't you go sayin, nothin' about that assay. Mebby he ain't ready to have it brooited abroad as yet.'

"'Fear not!' returns Bass Drum; 'my little game don't inclood me tellin' him things.'

"Right yere, the onconscious Copper Head pours out his soul afresh:

> "'From Greenland's icy mountains,
> To India's golden sands;
> Where Africk's sunny fountains
> Rolls down them coral strands.'

"'Which he's singin' all wrong!' whispers Bass Drum, disgusted; 'that of itse'f shows his mem'ry to be wabbly in its knees. Which if he can't think any better'n he can sing, he'll be plumb easy! Religious, too, you say? The shore mark of weakness! Look at me!' Yere Bass Drum lapses into his pastime of thumpin' his bosom. 'Look at me an' wonder!—six feet tall, an' a chest like a hoss! This Copper Head, bein' off his feet religious, shows he's of flimsy, clingin' vine-like nacher, an' no more back-bone to him than a wet lariat. A robust sport like me, who knows his way through, plays tag with sech a weaklin'.'

"Bass Drum an' Rucker deecends on the Copper Head, an' the Bass Drum says: 'How thar, pard!'

"The Copper Head gives a nervous start, an' looks 'round with his red ferretty eyes.

"'How!' says the Copper Head. Then, beholdin' Rucker: —'Whatever be you-all doin',' he asks, 'so far from your dooties? 'You ain't had time none'—glancing at the sun—'to get your noon-day dishes washed.'

"Rucker at these slights grows some heated, but says nothin', fearful with bluffs he makes gets back to Misses Rucker. Bass Drum, however, relieves him by takin' up the talk.

"'Struck somethin' rich?' he asks. 'Which if it's good I'll buy it.'

"'Friend,' returns the Copper Head, honest an' deprecatory, an' runnin' his oncertain fingers through his bird-dog ha'r, 'this yere's but a barren prospect, I fears; I'm none convinced of its valyoo. It's not for me to deloode the onwary, an' I shall avoid offers ontil I be. That's why I names it the Golden Roole.'

"Thar's a queer greenish-yellow look to the gray face of the rock, an' a sharp smell in the air that tickles the nostrils like hartshorn. Bass Drum wrinkles up his nose sympathetic, an' wipes the water from his eyes; to which man'festations the Copper Head responds like they're queries.

"'What you-all smells,' says he, 'is a prep'ration for softenin' the rock. It's somethin' like embalmin' flooid; I gets onto it when I'm in the ondertaking line. It's what gives the rock that green-yellow tinge. She shore does soften it up a whole lot, however; the drillin' and diggin' is redooced by half.'

"As the Copper Head gets off this yere explanation, he oncovers a big glass bottle, holdin' about a gallon, where it's lyin' hid beneath his coat. Thar's a rubber stopper. The Copper Head picks up the bottle, an' handles it as if it's filled with centipedes an' each clamorous for p'isenous action. Both Bass Drum an' Rucker notice how it's half full of a liquid of a greenish-yellow color, to match the pecooliar hue of the rock face.

"'It's a heap vol'tile', observes the Copper Head, 'an' I

has to keep it tight corked. I spills out what I uses as I goes along.'

"Sayin' which, the Copper Head slops out about a pint into a glazed earthern dish, with the heedfulness of b'ilin' oil. Then he sops it up with a bresh, an' paints away at the rock face same as though he's white-washin' a fence.

"'An does that soften the rock?' asks Bass Drum, sort o' held by the exhibition.

"'Leaves it like so much cheese!' returns the Copper Head, white-washin' away mighty scdyoolous.

"'What's that embalmin' mixchoor composed of?' asks Bass Drum ag'in, at the same time rubbin' his nose an' eyes, the fumes growin' doubly acrid while the Copper Head works.

"'What's it's composed of?' repeats the Copper Head. Then he shets one eye, an' grins both feeble an' deerisive. If it ain't for his liver-colored ha'r, you might think he's a sheep trying to assoome a foxy look. 'Excoose me!' he says, 'that's my little hold-out.'

"Bass Drum don't press the business of the embalmin' flooid, but la'nches out into what he calls a 'train of argyoo-ment,' calk'lated to make cl'ar how he ain't got time to wait the slow onfoldment of the Golden Roole. The best he can say is he's jest now squanderin' round on a hunt for a mine, an', if the Copper Head'll furnish him what spec'mens he wants, he'll have a assay made an' mebby buy.

"The Copper Head listens, his lant jaw ajar as if he ain't got force of char'cter s'fficient to shet his mouth. Bass Drum talks on, all sperit an' bustle an' business, while the dazed Copper Head hangs back in the breechin', like a dull mule at a quicksand crossin'.

"'I ain't ready none to deal,' the Copper Head protests final. 'Sellin' a pig in a poke is as bad as buyin' a pig in a poke. Yere I be, plumb ignorant whether I have somethin' or nothin'; an' you-all comes bushwackin' 'round an' talks of buyin' me out.'

"'Not before a assay, onderstand,' returns Bass Drum. 'Most likely this yere rock ain't got no more gold into it than grindstones.'

"'Well, I shore don't know!' returns Copper Head, crackin' the j'ints of his knobby fingers ontil they sounds like cockin' a Winchester. 'Whatever is your advice, Mister Rucker?'

"Bass Drum winks his nigh eye at Rucker as sayin' thar's somethin' in it for him, an' Rucker tharupon yoonites his voice to Bass Drum's.

"'What harm,' he says, 'to let him get a assay?'

"With both of 'em ag'inst him, the reluctant Copper Head at last consents. A blast is put in, an' fifty pounds of spec'mens knocked off the rock face.

"Bass Drum prodooces a dozen buckskin pouches from the warbags on his pony.

"'You observes,' he remarks to the Copper Head, 'I travels preepared.'

"Bass Drum fills the buckskin pouches, ties 'em up tight, an' swings 'em half an' half across the horn of his saddle, the Copper Head eyein' proceedin's with a doobious air.

"'I reckon it's all right,' he remarks, like he's tryin' to convince himse'f. 'I lets a couple of mav'ricks from Tucson have a hatful yesterday, an' tharfore why not you?'

"Bass Drum pricks up his y'ears, smellin' rivals. 'Which I'll start these bags,' he says, 'for Silver City this evenin'. Meanwhile, stand them Tucson hold-ups off. If they're the sharps I thinks they be, they'll do you out o' your eye teeth. Give 'em so much as a toe-hold anywhere, an' they'll steal everything but the back fence.'

"That evenin', about sixth drink time, Bass Drum grows confidential with Peets.

"'It's like playin' seven-up with a babe onweaned,' he says. 'Still, it ain't as if this Copper Head is otherwise safe. Which I don't mind confessin', I'd shore hesitate to lay him waste, only if I don't rob him some more hardened party will.'

"'Don't his bein' religious,' asks Peets, 'sort o' op'rate to stay your devastatin' hand? Or be you wars of commerce waged equal ag'inst both believer and onbeliever?'

"'At the game of dollar-chasin',' responds Bass Drum, mighty cocky, 'believers or onbelievers, Jews or Gentiles, it's all one to me. Whenever I gets ready to throw a stone, you bet I ain't carin' wheether it hits a grog shop or a church.'

"'To be shore, 'observes Tutt, when later he's discussin' matters with Peets an' Texas, 'I ain't no use for that Copper Head; an' yet I asks myse'f be we jestified in permittin' this over-powerin' Bass Drum to strip that feebliest of his all?'

"'Dave,' returns Peets, 'I regyards your excitement as misplaced. If you has tears to shed, reeserve 'em for that vain-glorious Bass Drum.'

"Three days, an' Bass Drum gets the returns from Silver City. The fifty pounds of ore shows forty dollars—sixteen hundred dollars to the ton! Bass Drum's ha'r assooms the perpendic'lar, he's that scared lest them Tucson coyotes gets a prior move on, an' beats him to it.

"As fast as pony can drum the ground, Bass Drum goes surgin' over to Red Dog. The Copper Head hesitates an' hangs back; he wants to hear from them Tucson parties, he says, who gets the hatful of spec'mens. Bass Drum won't hear to it, but crowds the Copper Head's irresoloote hand, namin' two thousand dollars.

"'An' at that,' observes Bass Drum when, a month later, he's roofully recountin' his financial wounds to Peets an' Enright that a-way, 'if I has a lick of sense, I ought to have remembered that, with the eight hundred dollar assay Rucker speaks of former, this Copper Head must shore possess some half-way notion of where he's at. But no; thar I go cavortin' to deestruction like a bar'l down hill! Congratchoolatin' myse'f, too, on my sooperhooman cunnin', when I evades his queries as to how that lasty assay turns out! Gents, I knows burros of inferior standin', who in intellects could give me kyards an' spades!'

"When Bass Drum says two thousand, the Copper Head falls into a brown study. The longer he studies, the sadder an' more sorrowful he gets.

"'It's all wrong!' he says at last. 'I'll never yere-after see the hour when the gnawin' tooth of conscience'll be still!' An' yet, if I must sin, let it not be for no bagatelles, which I'll shore refoose to sell my soul for a paltry two thousand. Say forty thousand, an' doubtless the temptation'll be more than I can ba'r.'

"Bass Drum sweats an' froths an' argues, but he's up ag'inst it. The eediotic Copper Head, with the pertinac'ty of weakminded folks, holds by that forty thousand like it's the rock of his last hope.

"'With forty thousand in my grasp,' says the Copper Head, 'I returns East, re-enters the ondertakin' profession, resoomes my rightful place on the front seat of a hearse, an' lifts up my diminished head as of yore. That's the figger, forty thousand; an' not a nickel less!'

"Thar's nothin' else to do; Bass Drum yields, an' him an' the Copper Head goes over to Tucson, where he endows that red-ha'red reptile with eight five-thousand dollar bills. Inside of no time, the Copper Head is thing of the Tucson-Wolf-ville past.

"It takes a fortnight for Bass Drum to convince himse'f thar ain't as much treasure to be extracted from the Golden Roole, as should belong in the bank-roll behind a ten cent game of Mexican monte. For a moment he's hotter'n a fire in a lard fact'ry. Then he simmers down.

"'Gents,' says he, 'I'm stuck! That Golden Roole's a deadfall! Between old Axtell an' his ha'r brands, an' this yere Copper Head an' his salted mines, it'll take a forest of sprooce, worked up into goose-ha'r mattrasses, to reestore my fallen fortunes.'

"Salt a mine!' exclaims Enright. 'That egreegious Copper

Head don't look like he's equal to saltin' sheep! I shore marvels how he does it!'

"Pete Bland, the Red Dog boniface at whose flapjack foundry the Copper Head's been hangin' out, brings over a gallon bottle with a rubber stopper to Peets. He finds it, he says, in the Copper Head's former room. It's filled with the same greenish-yellow liquid, wharwith the Copper Head is doctrin' the Golden Roole, when Bass Drum an' Rucker surprises him at his labors. The question is, can Peets as a scientific sharp identify the same?

"Peets oncorks the bottle, takes a sniff, an' bats a tearful eye:—

"'Chlorine!' says he.

"Then he pours about a pint into a wide glass dish. In half an hour or less, it's took to itse'f wings an' evaporated.

"Thar's enough sediment remainin' to fill two tablespoons. Peets puts it into a bowl, an' fills the bowl up with water. Then he twists an' tosses an whirls an' slops away at it, same as if he's pannin' out gold. That's what it comes to; he cleans up enough dust to make a ten-dollar gold piece.

"Bass Drum has already posted Peets how the Copper Head white-washes away at the rock face, an' Peets gets a bresh and tries a quart of the embalmin' flooid on a round hard rock, the size of a water melon, which is lyin' in front of the New York Store. The results is highly gratifyin'; the stone sucks up that embalmin' flooid like it's a sponge, thirstily gettin' away with the entire quart. Also it turns that same good old greenish-yellow color.

"When the stone has done drunk up its quart, Peets regyards it plenty thoughtful.

"'By what that pint pans out,' he says, 'thar should be twenty dollars worth of gold in this yere dornick!'

"Which the subsequent assay proves said surmise to be c'rrect.

"Thar's mebby a pint remainin' of the embalmin' flooid, an' Peets cuts loose chem'cal, an' subjects it to exper'ments.

"'An' at that, Sam,' says Peets to Enright at the wind up, 'I can't say what it wholly is! Thar's this, however: It contains, among other things, chloric acid with king's water, which last is a comb'nation of sulphooric an' nitric acids. The proportion of ox'gyn, thus secoored, is so tremenjus it makes no more of eatin' up forty dollars worth of gold to the gallon, than a colored camp meetin' would of eatin' up forty yellow-laigged chickens. Also, it's so penetratin' it'll carry the gold through eighteen inches of solid rock. Gents, we've been entertainin' a angel onawares. That Copper Head person is a genius; he has raised mine-saltin' to the plane of art.'

"It's two years before we ag'in hear of the Copper Head. A waif-word wanders up from Rincon that some deservin' party opens on him, low and satisfact'ry, with a ten gauge Greener shot gun, twenty-one buckshot to the shell, an' bombards him into the heavenly land of many mansions, where the come-ons cease from troublin' an' the mine-salter is at rest. The vig'lance committee, which considers the case, sustains the action of Cherokee that time in eejectin' the Copper Head from the Red Light; since it exculpates the accoosed shot-gun gent, on the grounds that the Copper Head is lookin' at his wife."